Norfleet

The Actual Experiences of a Texas Rancher's 30,000-mile Transcontinental Chase after Five Confidence Men

By J. Frank Norfleet

and William Franklin White

Published by Pantianos Classics

ISBN-13: 978-1-78987-289-7

First published in 1924

J. Frank Norfleet

Contents

Preface

This true story of J. Frank Norfleet, typical West Texas ranchman, in his four-year chase after a gang of international swindlers, takes the reader from the Atlantic to the Pacific; from Mexico and Cuba into Canada.

The only previous training Norfleet had had was following his pack of hounds after wild animals. In tracking human wolves, he followed the same tactics until he found other human hounds obliterating the trail.

Had Norfleet spent all his previous life preparing for his task, this would still be a wonderful story. When it is considered that prior to his contact with the gang he had been a man of peace, with kindest feeling toward all humanity and malice toward none; his success is nothing short of marvelous.

France has produced Monsieur Lecoq, England, Sherlock Holmes.

America has brought forth Norfleet, the man from the great open spaces of the boundless plains of Texas. His *true* story deserves to rank in literature with the best creations of the most *fanciful fiction-writers.*

"Verily truth is stranger than fiction!"

From a rank novice at the beginning Norfleet has become an authority — almost an institution.

In the prisons of the country are many criminals taking an enforced holiday from their regular avocation as a by-product of Nor fleet's historic man-hunt.

J. Frank Norfleet is a product of the western frontier. Born fifty-nine years ago near what is now the town of Lampasas, when that section was very sparsely settled, he has moved ever outward along the fringe of civilization, rarely living within five miles of his nearest neighbor.

From concealed vantage point he watched the proud stallions leading rival herds of wild mustangs as they battled to the death; the colonies of beavers, constructing dams with almost human engineering ability; the brown bear feasting upon luscious berries, or robbing the wild bees of their accumulated nectar; the deadly rattle-snake with sinister hypnotic spell, charming the helpless wild creatures of the forest.

These and many other lessons, young Norfleet learned at first hand in the great University of Nature, and today he is considered the best informed man in Texas on wild animal life.

More interesting than any popular novel are the stories he tells of these out-door friends of his.

From this early training a fund of patience, almost inexhaustible was developed; from the sun and wind were absorbed the sturdy hardihood of the oak.

This almost super-human health enabled him to stand the rigorous strain of the pursuit, and this patience sustained him when peace-officers gave him the "doublecross."

Tradition claims the name, "Norfleet" comes from the experience of a remote ancestor who left Scotland during the 17th century in one of the ships sailing to America by the northern route.

Months later this young man and his brother were washed ashore on the Virginia coast, the only survivors of the entire "North Fleet."

"The Nor'fleet boys," they were called by the English colonists, and "Norfleet" they both became.

, The splendid co-operation of the newspapers of the country is given due credit throughout the story. Without this wonderful help Norfleet's success would have been impossible.

The public will be astounded at the revelations in this book.

The Editor
"Norfleet"

MRS. MATTIE E. NORFLEET,
WIFE OF J. FRANK NORFLEET.

Dedicated to Mrs. Mattie Eliza Norfleet

The wife, who, when the crucial moment came, said to her husband: "Go get those miserable crooks. I will manage the ranch and keep you in expense money. Bring them in ALIVE; any man can kill, but it is the part of a brave man to capture the criminals and let the courts avenge his wrongs." Her unselfish devotion made this book possible.

Foreword

When J. Frank Norfleet related the incidents of his long man-hunt to me, I felt impelled to publish this book that the public might learn how easily these confidence-men swindle the unsuspecting victim, thus showing their "earmarks" and "trail" for the protection of the country.

Many victims out of pride do not report their losses, yet the newspapers publish daily accounts of such occurrences, thus emphasizing the magnitude of these operations.

The statement of these crooks is that they only work where PROTECTION from the local peace officers may be had. The double-crossing of Norfleet gives a color of truth to this claim.

It is interesting to note that Norfleet has borne ALL expenses of the four years campaign, totaling many thousands of dollars, with the exception of approximately three hundred dollars contributed by the states of Texas and Colorado.

I had known Norfleet for many years. We owned ranches in adjoining counties. We had broken bread together.

He was from one of the best families in the South. His grandmother was a first cousin of Robert E. Lee, Commander-in-Chief of the Confederate Army.

His father when a younger man had been a member of that famous, fearless band, known as the "Texas Rangers" and had done his part in quelling lawlessness on the frontiers of the state. His mother was one of those good women who uncomplainingly withstood the rigors of pioneering, and now at the age of 80 rejoices in the success of her dauntless son.

Frank Norfleet is the very soul of western hospitality, and many are the guests who have been entertained at his ranch-home by this big-hearted Westerner and his good wife.

Personally he has always been honorable and straight-forward. His jovial disposition has endeared him to a host of friends. His thorough knowledge of agriculture has made him an authority on cattle and land. His vast store of wild-animal lore has furnished enlightenment to many students of the fauna of Texas.

In his habits he was always clean and abstemious. No intoxicants, tobacco, or even coffee were used, and his speech was free from profanity.

He trusted his fellow-man as he himself could he trusted.

To him all law was infallible until he had seen man-made laws set aside by men as lightly as pawns in a game of chess.

We promptly entered into a contract to publish this book, and later to have a scenario written. For months we, with an amanuensis, have labored daily with Mr. Norfleet, taking notes and dictation, then writing while under the spell of his vivid memories.

All through the story the observant reader will perceive the thread of another plot— a plot as old as time.

That the second plot with its lesson may reach the public as vividly as it came to me, is my most earnest wish.

Wm Franklin White

Editor and Publisher

Chapter One - Entering the Web

Reno Miller Hamlin was the first member of the "Bunco ring" that I met and that meeting was so casual that even at this time, I cannot say positively just how it came about.

I was stopping at the St. George Hotel in Dallas, waiting for Captain Dick Slaughter to return to his office so I could make a trade with him to buy 10,000 acres of land out of the Hale County ranch owned by his family.

This was in the early part of November, 1919. I had just sold a car load of mules at Dublin, Texas, which was then on a big oil boom, and intended selling my improved stock farm in Hale County so I could pay cash for the Slaughter land.

To one of my raising, the most lonesome place in the world is a large city, especially when a fellow is almost entirely among strangers. Therefore, it was a relief to find in Reno Hamlin a man of apparently kindred tastes and experience.

Hamlin posed as a mule buyer, and looked the part. He could talk mules so well that never once did I suspect him of being other than he pretended.

He introduced himself as "R. Miller" and claimed he was from Hill County, Texas. He said he had handled many car-loads of mules and grain from West Texas but had never been there,

At his request I gave him a general description of my part of the state and told him I was trying to sell 2,050 acres of improved land out there to get money for the purchase of a larger tract.

He looked deeply interested at this, then said:

"Norfleet, I may help you out. A friend of mine is purchasing agent for the 'Green Immigration Land Company' of Minneapolis, Minnesota and is now trying to close up the purchase of 2,000 acres in Williamson County, Texas, but owing to a recent oil boom the owners have about decided not to dispose of their land, and it is just possible he might be interested in your place instead."

At this auspicious moment his "friend" walked into the lobby of the hotel and was introduced to me as "W. B. Spencer."

Spencer looked to be about 34 years of age, was well dressed in a conservative business suit and had a pleasing personality.

He did not seem especially interested in my property at first, but led me to believe he might be if the Williamson County trade failed to go through.

Next morning Hamlin returned to the hotel and told me Spencer had had a wire from the owners of the Williamson County land refusing to sell. Then Spencer drifted in and Hamlin called him over.

Spencer now seemed greatly interested in my stock farm and asked me for a detailed description. This he briefly wrote on a telegraph blank, stating he would submit my proposition to Mr. Garrett Thompson, the secretary of the company at Minneapolis.

I was led to believe the telegram was sent forward.

Spencer then said that he and a friend had engaged a double room at the Jefferson Hotel together but his friend had been called away, so he invited me to share the room with him. This would give him a chance to show me his credentials and also enable him to get better acquainted with me.

He especially wanted me to see his contract with the company and his annual report, of which he seemed very proud, almost like a schoolboy who has received unusually good "marks" from his teacher.

I accepted his invitation and checked out of the St. George Hotel.

In due time he received a telegram in reply to the one which he supposedly sent to Mr. Garrett Thompson. It was dated Oklahoma City, Oklahoma, and read:

"Your message forwarded me here. Will say that we have never dealt in lands that far west, but would suggest that you go home with this party, making personal inspection of the farm. Send us samples of soil from different parts of the land. Give detailed report of conditions and citizenship of the country. All of which will receive due consideration."

Shortly after receipt of this telegram he received another message from Garrett Thompson dated Oklahoma City, saying that he had been called to El Paso, Texas, on business and would leave on next train, going via Dallas, and would like to meet and have a personal interview with owner of the land and asked us to meet him at the Adolphus Hotel.

Just after the arrival of the train, on which Thompson was supposed to have come, Spencer and I went to the Adolphus. Spencer went to the desk and upon being advised that Thompson had not registered, came over to the chair in which I was seated. He stood back of my chair slightly to the left.

As I settled back into the seat I pressed against something which felt like a magazine. I reached behind me and drew forth a bill book. I examined it and remarked:

"Some fellow has lost his pocketbook."

Spencer moved around to my right and sat down in the chair next to me.

Upon examining the purse, I saw it contained a Masonic card which bore the name of J. B. Stetson; $240.00 in currency; copy of bond payable to McLean & Company in the sum of $100,000.00, guaranteeing faithful performance of certain things by Stetson; a cipher code letter; a card showing that J. B. Stetson was a member of United Brokers, and some other papers all bearing the name of J. B. Stetson.

Spencer asked: "What shall we do with it?"

I suggested we try to find the owner and return it to him. We found Stetson was a guest at the hotel and that he was in. We went up and knocked at his door.

Some one opened it — a crack.

I asked if this was Mr. Stetson.

He replied it was.

I then asked him if he had lost anything and he answered curtly "no," and shut the door in our faces.

Spencer and I turned to go back to the elevator when the door was reopened and Stetson called excitedly:

"Gentlemen! Gentlemen! I have just discovered that I have lost a very, very valuable pocketbook."

We went back to the door and were invited into his room.

I asked him to describe the pocketbook which he did, giving a very accurate description of all its contents.

He laid special stress on his Masonic card; the copy of his contract with his company and the code key, without which, he emphasized very forcibly, he would be unable to carry on his Company's business. He was very profuse in his thanks and stated that we had rendered him a great service indeed, for which he would deem it a favor if we would accept $100.00 reward each for the return of the purse.

I refused, stating that I was only too glad to help him recover it.

To my surprise Spencer accepted the $100.00.

Stetson then apologized for not having opened the door to us at first.

"I thought you were newspaper reporters."

He went on to explain they had been very persistent in trying to gain an interview with him and had used numerous ruses to accomplish it. He remarked that he had to be "very careful" and was doing his best to evade them. He then took a letter from the purse and handed it to me to read, remarking it was from his Company warning him against talking too freely with reporters. On one occasion, he said, too much publicity had nearly cost them a very heavy loss, so it was a hard and fast rule to avoid publicity of all kinds. He explained that this precaution was necessary due to the fact that his Company always wired him advance information on the stock market in code.

He replaced it in the bill book, took out the code key and said: "You will please excuse me, gentlemen, as I must now decipher the message which I have just received."

Whereupon he sat down at his desk and proceeded to work out the hieroglyphics.

He appeared very deep in study. His face flushed at times and the perspiration rolled from his forehead; apparently he was under a severe mental strain. After he finished the message, he arose.

"Gentlemen, if you will please pardon me, I must go over to the Stock Exchange. My Company has outlined a lot of work, and I shall be a very busy man today." As he was preparing to leave the room, Spencer said: "Mr. Stetson, if you have no objection, I would like to see that newspaper clipping you were reading a few moments ago."

13

"Certainly," said Stetson, handing him the pocketbook. "There are other papers there also that might interest you if you care to see them." Stetson then left the room.

Spencer proceeded to examine the contents of the bill fold, taking out the clipping which merely commented upon the price which a New York broker paid for a seat in the Stock Exchange. After having read the clipping Spencer handed it to me to read. He next took out Stetson's contract with his Company, then Stetson's $100,000.00 bond with McLean & Company. After looking over these papers he gave them to me, remarking that he and I were certainly very fortunate in making the acquaintance of such a big man. After Spencer had finished examining the contents of the pocketbook, Stetson re-entered the room looking elated.

Due to advance information, he announced he had just taken from the Exchange for his Company, $20,000.00. Preparatory to leaving again, he turned to me and said: "I will have to go back to the Exchange to finish the day's work. My brother, you refused to accept the $100.00 reward which I offered you for finding my pocketbook. Would you mind my placing that money on the market and would you accept what money it might earn?"

I said I would.

Spencer then asked Stetson if he would place his $100.00 on the market also, offering him the money. Stetson took it and said he would be more than willing to place it for him. He asked us to wait until he returned as he would like to have another talk with us.

In a few minutes he came back and handed me $800.00 in currency.

"That is what your $100.00 made for you!" He also gave Spencer a like sum of money for his investment.

Spencer and I made preparations to return to our hotel, but before leaving Stetson made an appointment to see me the following morning, saying he had a proposition to make. I agreed to see him at the appointed time.

After reaching our hotel, Spencer and I went to our room where he showed me his wardrobe which contained several suits of clothes, several pairs of shoes, and a large assortment of other expensive wearing apparel. He explained that as he was on the road all the time for his company, it was necessary to carry these things. He next showed me his credentials which he carried in a suitcase together with a large number of Deeds, Contracts, Releases, Abstracts and various documents, all pertaining to land deals. He showed me a compiled, typewritten and tabulated report of his year's business. He pointed out different deals on which he had made large commissions, stating that after his company had purchased my land and the deal closed, on which he confidentially told me he would make five per cent commission, his year's business would average for him a salary of about one thousand dollars per month.

"That is not so bad for a young man just out of the Army, is it?"

He laid special stress upon the large volume of business he was doing and that he was a man of action.

Upon investigation I found Capt. Dick Slaughter had returned to the City, so I went to his office to see him.

We arrived at an understanding in connection with the purchase of the ranch and drew up a contract. I made a five thousand dollar payment, the balance of $90,000.00 to be paid within forty-five days.

Next morning as agreed, Spencer and I returned to Stetson's room at the Adolphus Hotel. We found him seated at his table. As was the case in Spencer's room, I observed here two large wardrobe trunks overflowing with fashionable male attire, a number of pairs of shoes and everything that a man of his position would require.

Stetson was very busy deciphering code messages which he explained were instructions from his Company outlining his work and advance information on stocks. He suddenly turned to Spencer and asked him to go down and get the morning papers. During Spencer's absence Stetson said he was going to be a very busy man that day and expected to take a large amount of money out of the Exchange for his Company, which on certain days controlled the market on certain stocks and only upon advice from his Company to this effect and under their instruction, did he work; they advising him the condition of the market and when to buy and sell. By taking advantage of this information Stetson explained, he could make quite a sum of money on the side, not only for himself but for his helper if he could find someone in whom he could place confidence. He stated that I appeared to be everything he required in this connection, even to being a brother lodge member. He then asked my consent for him to use my name in buying and selling stock. He could not use his own on account of his connection with the Company, without endangering his bondsmen.

However, if I would allow him to use my name he would make it very profitable for both of us. He explained that he had never before, with but one exception, taken advantage of this opportunity to make money, and that was when he had taken $200,000.00 from the Exchange for a certain Chief Justice Hughes, of the Supreme Court in New York, but that his desire to do so at this time was due to the fact that there was a $100,000.00 mortgage on his three hundred thousand dollar home, which would fall due in a short time, and that he was more than anxious to make enough on the side to take care of this debt.

He stated he was confident that I was an honest, straight-forward man in whom he could place confidence and trust, and asked if I would be willing to go into the proposition.

I told him I would be willing, provided it was perfectly legitimate.

He assured me it was strictly business and being done every day. He then asked me what kind of man Spencer was and if I would vouch for him, stating that as he was a friend of mine, we might also take him into the deal.

I told Stetson I knew nothing whatever about Spencer, that he had known him as long as I and that I would not vouch for him.

Spencer appeared to be an honest, hardworking young business man, he said, and he thought we would be safe in inviting him to join us in the speculations, and he would use his name in connection with mine, providing I would consent.

Upon Spencer's return to the room, Stetson approached him in regard to the matter. Spencer said his father was a big mill and elevator man, and due to this association he was familiar with the brokerage business; that he was willing for Stetson to use his name in connection with mine in the purchase and selling of stock.

I told them both that I had no money.

Stetson said no money was required; that we could use his membership card in the United Brokers which was backed by his hundred thousand dollar bond and was good for credit to that extent. Stetson said that he would take me over to the Stock Exchange and show me the proper procedure in buying and selling; how to use the card and transact business in the Exchange.

I accompanied him and he took me all through the building, showing me the different offices, etc. We stopped at a window where he explained bids were to be submitted and money accepted.

A man walked up to us and asked me if I were a member of the Exchange. I told him I was not.

"I am very sorry to do so, but I shall be forced to invite you outside as members only are allowed here," he said.

I left the building immediately. Stetson remained.

Stetson, Spencer and I reached Stetson's room about the same time. I told Stetson I did not care to use his card or have anything else to do with the matter and would drop out.

Spencer spoke up, saying he understood the business and would do all placing of bids and selling, and I need have nothing to do with the deal except in a financial way, to which I agreed.

At this point in the conversation Stetson asked me if I would like him to invest the $800.00, which he had earned for me on the Exchange the previous day. I agreed to his proposal and Stetson wrote out a bid, my portion of which was covered by the $800.00, and Spencer returned to the Exchange.

All future bids which Stetson wrote, Spencer would take to the Exchange, always bringing back a receipt to cover.

At the close of the day's business, Spencer came to the room bringing with him sixty-eight thousand dollars in currency.

Stetson then counted out my portion of the gain which amounted to twenty-eight thousand dollars. This he handed to me just as some one knocked at the door. The secretary of the Exchange (the party who ejected me from the building and later known as E. J. Ward) came into the room and exclaimed:

"Gentlemen, your bids made in the name of Norfleet and Spencer have earned you a lot of money, but inasmuch as you are not members of the Exchange, I will have to ask if you are in a position to confirm the bids in case you had lost?"

Spencer and I both informed him that we could not.

At this Stetson arose and said: "Mr. Secretary, you know the rules of the Exchange. Settlement days are on the 1st and 15th of each month, and as a member of the Exchange I guarantee this confirmation by the 15th, which by the way is on Saturday. This will give us until Monday the 17th."

Ward stated that would be satisfactory, only he would have to return the money to the Exchange until such time as the confirmation was made. He would issue a due bill and receipt for the money, which we could present at the time the bids were confirmed and then draw the money. In the meantime we could use the due bill as credit at the exchange. He then made out a due bill for the sixty-eight thousand dollars in favor of Norfleet and Spencer. He took the money and left the room.

Stetson, Spencer and I held a conference to determine how we should raise the amount necessary to confirm the bids which we had previously made. It was finally agreed that Spencer should raise thirty-five thousand dollars, and I twenty thousand dollars; Stetson was to raise the balance.

It was necessary for me to return home in order to raise my portion of the money. Spencer supposedly wired his home in Salina, Kansas, for his part.

Accompanied by Spencer I left that day for my home in Hale County. Spencer planned to make a personal inspection of my stock farm with a view to purchase for the supposed "Green Immigration Company."

As we were leaving the Dallas Interurban Station, I noticed Ward, the Secretary of the Exchange, waiting at the depot. I saw him again on the train out of Fort Worth for Sweetwater. When Spencer and I were seated in the dining car, Ward again appeared. He came into the car with a tall young man dressed in a soldier's uniform. They sat at the same table with us. Ward was very talkative, suggesting the different things we should eat, and in a general way was very congenial.

On arriving at Hale Center, Spencer and I left the train. Ward remained going, we later learned, to Plainview. Spencer and I then went out to my ranch where he made a careful examination of the soil. He visited the different rent houses, went to adjoining farms where threshing was in progress, examined the threshed wheat and growing wheat crops. He appeared profoundly interested in the country and conditions.

We stayed on the ranch two or three days, where he seemed to enjoy the hospitality which my wife and I extended him. During his stay on the ranch, he assured Mrs. Norfleet that from what he had learned of the land, improvements, and condition of the country in general, he was certain his company would buy; in fact, he assured her that she could depend on it and that he would pay us in cash $102,600.00, which was our price, in plenty time for us to meet the Slaughter obligation.

Spencer and I started on our return to Dallas, going to Hale Center where I stopped off. Spencer and my son, Pete, went on to Plainview in an automobile. I was to follow on the afternoon train.

On his way to Plainview Spencer told my son for a certainty that he would purchase our stock farm.

Upon my reaching Plainview I went to the bank and borrowed twenty thousand dollars, picked up Spencer, and we left that night for Dallas. As we boarded the train, I again saw Ward getting into one of the coaches. He rode in the same Pullman car with us. When Dallas was reached, Spencer and I went to the Cadillac Hotel.

Early the next morning I received a long distance call from Stetson, advising me that he had been transferred to Fort Worth to operate on the Exchange there; that all of our money, business, etc., had been moved to that point. He asked that Spencer and I come to Fort Worth and meet him at the Terminal Hotel.

As agreed we went to Fort Worth and met Stetson, who explained that he could not get rooms for us at the Terminal. He then called a taxi, directing the driver to take us to the Westbrook Hotel. Due to the oil boom, we were compelled to wait almost the entire day before we could get accommodations there.

That evening Stetson took us to the Cotton Exchange.

"We will operate here tomorrow," he said.

The next morning we went to the Terminal Hotel to see Stetson. As usual he was deciphering code messages. He would often give stock quotations before they were printed in the daily papers, and without a single exception, he always quoted them right, thereby convincing me that he had advance information.

He advised us his Company had instructed him to sell "Mexican Petroleum" that day at a 2-point margin.

Spencer took the money we had raised together with the due bill for sixty-eight thousand dollars and a margin slip Stetson wrote out to sell Mexican Petroleum at 2-point margin, and left for the Stock Exchange.

A little later Spencer returned to the room, his face all aglow and apparently very well pleased with himself. He said he had had a hard time getting the business transacted as there was a terrific rush at the Exchange, and he had lost the margin slip on which Stetson had written instructions to sell, but as he knew how to write another one he had done so, the receipt covering which he showed me.

I at once noted that the receipt indicated he had purchased Mexican Petroleum instead of selling. I called his attention to the error, but he seemed very confident that he had written out the new slip exactly as Stetson had done. While Spencer and I were arguing the point, Stetson came excitedly into the room exclaiming:

"Spencer, haven't you made a mistake and bought instead of selling Mexican Petroleum? I just noticed on the board at the Exchange that some one had purchased exactly the same amount I instructed you to sell. I thought it possible you had made a mistake."

Spencer showed him the receipt which proved that he had bought instead of sold.

Stetson flew into a rage.

"Spencer, you have ruined us! You have lost every dollar we have and that we had coming to us."

Spencer fell on the bed and went into hysterics, apparently weeping and very much grieved over his mistake. He declared the thirty-five thousand dollars which he had contributed was the entire amount of an estate which his dear mother had left him; that he was sure his father would disinherit him and never speak to him again as long as he lived. He got down on the floor and rolled and tumbled. Stetson looked down at him.

"I could knock your head off, your poor miserable wretch!" He spoke as if talking to himself.

Then he added disgustedly: "But look at the ignorant fool, he is suffering!"

Suddenly reaching for his hat, Stetson said:

"I will rush back to the Exchange and try to hedge by placing an order to sell, thereby covering the loss if possible, and maybe we'll come out a little ahead in case the market does not drop off."

Later he returned to the room stating that he had just reached there before the market closed and had placed an order to sell eighty thousand dollars worth of stock at a 2-point margin.

That same evening, we had a visit from a man who claimed to be Secretary of the Fort Worth Exchange, Charles Gerber. He informed us that we had earned and had coming to us $160,000.00, but as we were not members of the Exchange we would have to exhibit eighty thousand dollars to confirm the bid.

On the 20th of November, I again started home for the purpose of raising twenty-five thousand dollars which was to be my part of the eighty thousand dollars confirmation money.

Spencer was to go to his home in Salina, Kansas, and mortgage his farm there for $30,000.00, and Stetson was to raise the balance.

After arriving home I explained to my wife the position in which I was placed, saying it would be necessary for me to raise an additional twenty-five thousand dollars in order to avoid loss of the initial amount I had invested. After some difficulty I managed to raise the money by borrowing from my brother-in-law. Then I returned to Fort Worth, stopping at the Westbrook with Spencer who had returned with his part of the money.

The three of us had raised seventy thousand dollars, leaving a balance of ten thousand, which Spencer said he could get by going to Austin and disposing of some Liberty Bonds which his aunt was keeping there for him. He was to wire the money to me in care of the Cadillac Hotel, Dallas, as Stetson said he had received instructions to transfer back to Dallas to operate on the Exchange there and that all business had already been transferred to that place.

He said he must leave at once and proposed that he take the money which we had raised and have it credited on the eighty thousand, taking a due bill

IN NATURE — The rat, under hypnotic "charm" of serpent, helplessly squealing with terror, yet powerless to escape. (from bank of Colorado River, Norfleet witnessed this scene, when a small boy.)

IN HUMAN LIFE — Well dressed, magnetic Bunco men obtain the confidence of their victim, holding him under hypnotic suggestion until they have fleeced him of his all, leaving him to die of despair. (Norfleet met the above members of the gang, was robbed, but refused to despair. instead, he became the "boomerang sucker.") top, Joe Furey, of Glendale, Calif., alias J. Harrison, of San Francisco, J. B. Stetson, of Dallas and Fort Worth, the "Master Mind"; E. J. Ward, alias Jack Thompson, of New York; W. B. Spencer, alias Chas. Harris, of Kansas; Chas. Gerber, pseudo secretary fake stock exchange; and Reno Hamlin, the mule-buyer, extreme outpost of the Bunco ring.

for the amount, then deposit the ten thousand dollars as final payment upon receipt of it from Austin.

This plan did not meet with my approval. I wanted to hang onto my money until the full amount was raised, when it could be placed with the Exchange and a full settlement made.

Early that morning I missed my overcoat from the room. I had placed a 32-caliber automatic in the coat pocket, so both were gone. However I did not mention this loss to either Stetson of Spencer, but went to the F. & M. Bank and borrowed a double action Smith & Wesson pistol from a friend there.

Stetson took the money we had raised, rolled it up in a newspaper, put it under his arm and started from the room, saying he was in a hurry to reach Dallas in order to transact his Company's business and would take the money with him to the Dallas Exchange for credit on the eighty thousand dollars.

I made it plain that I did not approve of this action and insisted we arrive at a better understanding in the matter. Upon his refusal to change his intention of departing with the money, I followed him to the elevator, and as he started to ring for the car I stuck my gun up against him.

"You are going back to the room to settle this matter, or this will be as good a place to settle it as any," I threatened.

"Don't do anything rash, for God's sake! I will go back to the room," he cried.

Upon re-entering the room he tossed the money on the bed, exclaiming: "Take the money and go to hell with it if you can't stand by the agreement we made!"

He flung himself across the bed.

Spencer became excited when he saw I had drawn a gun on Stetson. He stepped behind a chair and took hold of it with both hands. I thought he intended to strike me.

I aimed the gun at him. He dropped to his knees and grabbed a Bible from the table, placing it over his heart.

I told both of them I thought they were partners and first class crooks.

At that statement Spencer, still on his knees, raised his right hand in which he held the Bible, crying out, "Before my Angel Mother, on my bended knees, with this Bible uplifted to my God in Heaven, I swear to you that I never did, nor never will prove false to you, and that I never did see this man before I met you."

At this moment Stetson suddenly rolled across the bed and got to his feet on the other side. I turned my attention to him. He was panting with emotion and gave me the grand hailing sign of distress of a Master Mason.

I put the gun back in my pocket. Stetson smiled and walked up to me.

"You came very near having a brain storm, didn't you, Brother? Don't that satisfy you? You know I have trusted you with sixty and seventy thousand dollars at a time in your room overnight, and not once did I question your honesty, then when I started away with this money I only thought I was doing what had been agreed on."

We all sat down and talked the matter over. It was agreed that Spencer should leave for Austin to raise the ten thousand dollars and wire the amount to me in Dallas. Upon its receipt Stetson and I were to confirm the bid and collect the one hundred and sixty thousand dollars the next day and have a final settlement.

Spencer instructed Stetson to pay his portion of the amount to me in view of the fact that he was just in receipt of a wire from his home office advising him to close the deal with me for my stock farm. This amount was to be applied on the purchase price and credit given in addition to thirty thousand dollars which the Company advised was being expressed to Spencer for first payment on the land.

I went with Spencer to the express office, where he received the money. He came out of the express office carrying a small suitcase. After reaching the hotel we opened the case and counted out thirty thousand dollars in currency which he replaced in the case together with sale contract, saying he would take it to the bank and deposit it in a safety deposit box pending examination of abstract of title to the land.

Spencer left for Austin that afternoon to dispose of the Liberty Bonds, and Stetson took the seventy thousand dollars and left for Dallas, asking me to be sure to meet him at the Cadillac Hotel the following morning, Tuesday, at 10 o'clock sharp. This would give him time to confirm the bid at the Dallas Exchange and take care of his Company's business.

I went to Dallas that same day, and the following morning went to the Cadillac Hotel, arriving there about 9:30 in order not to miss Stetson in case he came before the appointed hour. Upon arriving I inquired of the clerk if Stetson had registered there and being informed that he had not, my fears of the previous day again arose.

I waited. Stetson failed to show up at the appointed time.

Fearfully, I waited another hour. I left the hotel, telling the clerk I would be back in a short time and asked him to have Stetson wait for me if he came in.

I went hurriedly from one hotel to another endeavoring to locate him. I failed. I returned to the Cadillac and was again advised that Stetson had not been there.

Conviction that I had been swindled out of my life time's savings swept over me.

I immediately went to Pinkerton's Detective Agency and explained the situation, asking their aid in locating the men connected with the affair.

They had one of their men accompany me to Fort Worth where we called on the Chief of Police and County Sheriff.

I went to the bank where Spencer said he had deposited the money which was to have been paid on my farm. Upon examination of the safety deposit box, we found it empty.

After this discovery, together with the disappearance of all the men connected with the deal, I realized to the fullest extent that I had been swindled out of $45,000,00 in cash and left $90,000.00 in debt.

Chapter Two - The World My Hunting Ground

Forty-five thousand dollars gone!

Ninety thousand dollars in debt!

Fifty-four years old!

The three facts crashed on my brain. To all else I thought or spoke, these piercing realities were an overtone

Forty-five thousand dollars gone! Ninety thousand dollars in debt! Fifty-four years old!

The knowledge paralyzed, then shook me like an earthquake, crumbling my castles into ashes about my feet.

I went down into the lobby. A surging mass of humanity swept back and forth.

It sickened me. I felt like the pivot of a huge merry-go-round.

The orchestra on the balcony blared a jazzy tune. People rushed to and fro knocking me against others. Children skipped and leaped like wild things.

I was dazed, as in a dream, when one strives with all his might to move, yet is held to the spot by unseen shackles.

I gazed dully into passing faces. I was conscious of looking for Stetson, Spencer, Hamlin, Ward or Gerber, but when I tried to recall what they looked like I could not summon recognizable likenesses in my mind. I would search the features of some one man, certain he was not one of my men. But I had the horrifying sensation of not knowing why he was not one of them.

I was terrified.

Was I going insane?

I tried first to summon Stetson before me. My senses spun like whirling tops. I could not see him! Mentally I tried to put him into the crowd. I wandered up to the desk where we had so often sat to write and converse.

I said to myself: "Now sit right down there, Stetson, I want to have a good look at you!" But I could not see him. I wondered should anyone show me a photograph of him, could I identify it?

Sickening fear choked me.

Undoubtedly my mind was going. Then my head would ring:

"Forty-five thousand dollars gone! Ninety thousand dollars in debt! Fifty-four years old!"

"My God! My God!" I cried out.

People stared at me.

A mother drew her child closer to her side.

An overpowering desire to be quiet: to be alone in stillness came over me.

I do not remember how I reached my room but somehow I got there. Perspiration beaded my body. My room, the one in which the plot had been hatched, was not large as hotel rooms go, but to me it seemed vast.

I went into the bath room and dipped a towel into ice water; wrung it out and wrapping it about my head like a Hindu turban, lay flat on the bed.

The cooling water drew the fever from my brain.

I do not know how long it was; time for me had ceased to record, but slowly normality came back; normality of pulse and mind.

The frosty band across my brow brought tranquility and presently I saw Stetson looking me straight in the eye. We looked at each other for hours it must have been.

His picture burned into the sensitive film of my brain; developed itself in the dark room of memory, never to fade.

I studied his physique from every angle. He stood six feet and weighed two hundred. His manly, swinging carriage, his chestnut hair with a line of pink scalp showing from the middle of his forehead to the crown; his round, smooth face that radiated health and vigor; his greenish blue eyes and their magnetic pull.

As a crystal gazer peers deep into the mysterious glass ball, so I peered into these eyes of Stetson.

In their fathomless depths, I saw a serpent coiled. Never since have I looked into them and not seen the poisonous fangs. Stetson's mouth sagged at the corners and from the side view looked like a cod's. He was always immaculately groomed.

I put his photograph away for the present and brought Spencer to me. As he approached I noted indelibly his splendid military carriage. Like an officer commanding his regiment, he advanced with measured tread.

Of his features, his crooked nose bent slightly to the right, was an outstanding mark of identification. His hair was medium light; eyes blue with the suggestion of an oriental slant. Keenness, alertness, a wide-awakeness and up-to-dateness characterized this young man. He was well under six feet and tipped the scale at one hundred and fifty pounds. Like his friend Stetson, he was an athlete and took pride in his fine skin and elastic muscles. Spencer was thirty-three years of age.

After turning him front and back, right side, left side, walking him, standing him and running him, I put him away, noting as the last thing, his smile. His lips parted and their edges, like thin rose petals rolled back into his mouth leaving a noncommittal expression upon his handsome face.

Next I visualized Hamlin. Reno Hamlin!

His name conjured up a romantic gambler or soldier of fortune, a Will O' the Wisp, a whimsical wanderer. But he was none of these. He was a mule buyer and ran true to form — medium stature and built like a burro, glossy black hair streaked with gray, scrutinizing brown eyes with overhanging eyelids, flaring eye-brows, a deep furrowed, weather-beaten neck and a close cropped, black mustache. He had none of the city-bred atmosphere of Stetson or Spencer. He drawled and noticeably weighed his words.

Ward's face was square, his eyes were a grayish blue. His hair grew straight up and was close-cropped. Like many of the noses in the "profes-

25

sion" his, too, inclined to one side. His eye-brows arched. A loose bag of flesh hung from his chin. From the front his mouth was strong, but from the side it slanted sharply into his weak chin. His shoulders were massive — height five feet, seven and one-half inches, weight one hundred and seventy. He appeared the most highly bred of them all. It was said he came from a prominent and respected family.

Gerber was the "killer." He was about the same size and age as Ward. His dark hair was parted and brushed high across his brow. This threw into relief two bullet eyes of black. His nose was thick at root and end; his mouth looked like a slit cut in a stretched surface and his lips, the taut turned-back edges. In his eyes I saw the reflection of six dead men.

If I were to be killed this man would be my murderer. He was the death-dealer of the organization.

After photographing them separately, I passed them before me in review. They were all there. Then I fell asleep.

When I awoke and gathered my faculties I looked into my mind to see if the pictures were still with me. They were as vivid as in life.

I picked up the telephone from the little table.

"What time is it, please?" I asked the operator.

"Ten-thirty," she answered.

"Ten-thirty?" I questioned. "Why I only came up here at 10 o'clock, surely I have been here more than a half hour!"

"I don't know what time you went to your room, sir, but it's exactly 10:30 A.M."

"Gone again!" I said to myself, and hung up the receiver. As I did so I cupped my chin thoughtfully in my hand. What was that I had hold of? It felt like a stubble field. I walked to the mirror and passed my fingers across my cheeks, peering as a woman does for her first grey hair. My beard! It was bristling! I had shaved not three hours ago.

Surely I was quite mad. Somewhere a padded cell waited. I picked up the telephone again. I might as well convince the operator of my condition.

"What day is this, please?" in the sanest voice I could command.

"Wednesday."

Wednesday? Then instead of a mere half hour I had been there twentyfour hours.

I made myself presentable and descended to the lobby.

For the first time in my experience, I was unaffected by the beauty of this masterpiece of the architect's creation; the gleaming white marble stairway, the double row of massive onyx columns with their gold-touched capitals, the royal palms softening the severe outline.

The orchestra was playing a tantalizing, popular waltz.

I had a wild desire to grab one of the pretty young women and whirl her around the balcony.

Again I searched the crowd for Stetson, Spencer, Hamlin, Ward and Gerber.

26

Not a man in the lobby resembled any one of them. Closing my eyes, I could at will call up one or all of them in startling vividness.

I knew they were mine for all time.

From that moment I began the chase, the world my hunting ground.

* * * *

During the time Spencer "visited" us at the ranch and pretended to be deeply interested in the purchase of it, some other parties came to look at it with the same purpose in view. They were from Eadonia, Texas, which is just north of Dallas. Nothing definite came of their tour of inspection but now that I found myself minus $45,000 and in debt to Slaughter $90,000, I made up my mind to go to Ladonia and reopen the deal.

It is a good thing I was born with a sense of humor, for while I was in the home of these Ladonia prospective purchasers, an account of my swindling was published in the daily paper. Fortunately for me my name was spelled incorrectly. This was once a paper was thanked for a typographical error.

The family and friends joked freely in my presence about the old fellow who had been skinned; "How easy it was to get some people," and that P. T. Barnum was right, "There's a sucker born every minute."

Silently acknowledging the compliments, I verbally joined in the fun of swatting myself. I kept the secret that this "easy mark" was in the bosom of their family as I thought if they knew it, it would complicate my deal with them.

If ever a man used all his persuasive powers, I did. I talked land, soil, crops, stock, cotton and everything advantageous about my property for days. All the time I could feel the pressure of the ninety thousand dollar debt to Slaughter. It was a case of a goat being "led to slaughter" if I could not raise the money in time to save myself from total ruin.

Another problem presented itself: If I did not sell to these people, where would I get any money to carry out my intention of going after the "bunk"? This thought and the magnitude of my debt spurred my determination to put this deal over. But to no avail. I simply could not "close" and the dotted line remained unsigned.

I was not discouraged, but my enthusiasm was a little dampened. I decided to return to Dallas at once and see if anything had turned up which would encourage me. I called Captain Gunning of the Police Force before leaving, in case he might have leads that would send me scouting in other directions. I was greeted with the news that my wife was waiting for me.

To some husbands this news might have conjured up rolling pins, competently rolled, frying pans with which to "pan" and flatirons deftly aimed, but to me it was heaven!

"Has she got that 'million dollar smile'?" I asked over long distance.

"She sure has," said Captain Gunning.

"Then tell her to wait there for me, and keep it smiling," I answered.

When I got into Dallas the Captain said she was at the station waiting. He begged to be allowed to accompany me just to see the "smile." When we met her he exclaimed, "A million is too cheap for that welcome, Norfleet."

And I want to say right here that when I caught sight of her, I knew if necessary, I could turn the world upside down. Her confidence, inspiration and faith in me were beautiful and assuring, but made me all the more ashamed now that I had permitted my ignorance to bankrupt the family fortune.

She had heard that I was in the hands of assassins and probably would never be seen alive again. With this comforting assurance, she left the ranch and started out to locate me and had just arrived at Captain Dunning's office when I called him on the phone.

At the hotel I told her everything down to the smallest detail.

"Wife," I said, my voice so husky I could scarcely speak, "I don't know how to look you in the face when I remember my vow at the altar to 'cherish and protect' you, and now to realize after all we have gone through together, I have let these crooks ruin us: have condemned you to an old age of poverty."

"Nonsense," came in comforting, reassuring tones from that wonderful woman, while her brave hand patted my arm.

"We are a long, long way from poverty, Frank! You always have found a way to handle things, and I am confident you can meet the debt when it comes due."

This helped a lot, and I began to see that a little time would work things out. But I wanted to go after those crooks.

I wanted personally the satisfaction of settling with them. But I felt too keenly the ignominy of having fallen down in this last deal, when she had taken my judgment in the matter so unquestioningly. I felt at that moment that I would never again start anything without her full knowledge and consent.

"Wife," I cried tremulously, "I want to go after those crooks myself. I want to go get them with my own wits and gun."

"Of course you do," she rejoined. "I'll take care of the ranch. You just go and get those good-for-nothing crooks. And remember, Frank, bring them in alive. Any fool can kill a man."

Up to this time it had never occurred to me just what action I expected to take when I got them. I realized undoubtedly that they had forfeited their lives to me by betraying my trust, but now I determined upon taking them alive, letting the courts decide their punishment.

Chapter Three - A "Santone" Shoplifter

From the moment I was victimized, I naturally groped for every clue, no matter how small, on which to work toward the capture of the six men. Fragments of conversations, to which I had paid little attention at the time, kept running through my mind. Bit by bit I tried to put them together, hoping in some way to fit the jig-saw pieces into place and get a logical start.

During this time the vision of a little red leather pocket address book such as most men carry in their vest pockets, kept tumbling in and out of my mental filing cabinet. One day it came to me that I had seen a book of this description lying on the bed in the room occupied by Stetson, Spencer and myself. I recalled picking it up and glancing through it to settle its ownership. It belonged, as I remember, to Stetson. It contained a long list of men's names all entered in different hand-writing.

Among these was the name of a Mr. Cathey of Corpus Christi, Texas. The reason I remembered Cathey's name, I suppose, was because I knew him. At the time I thought nothing of it; now it occurred to me that probably Cathey was merely one of the string of prospective victims. This little book was what contained the "sucker list."

The more I considered the matter the better I thought it would be to go to Corpus Christi, see Cathey and find out if he had been approached by any of the gang. If they were "negotiating" with him now, I might get them and if they had not yet "sprung," I could warn him and when they did spring, he could let me know.

My wife returned to the ranch and I left to find Cathey. On the way to Corpus Christi I stopped off at San Antonio. I knew this was a great sporting town.

My friends (?) were what the world calls "dead game sports." It was not unlikely that they might have stopped off here to spend some of my money. As there was another train to Corpus Christi that night I stayed over to have a look at the hotel registers.

All the impressions I ever had of detectives were connected with hotel registers. I thought I might just as well begin to learn how they did it.

I went to the St. Anthony Hotel, obtained the register, otherwise known as the "tattle tale," and gave it the "once-over." A "J. Harrison" had registered there a few days ago, but no Stetson. However, I saw at once that the "J" was written exactly the same as the "J" in his previous signatures of "J. B. Stetson," the name under which I first knew him.

I called to the clerk and asked to speak to Mr. J. Harrison on the telephone. "Mr. Harrison only stayed a few days and has checked out," he informed me.

"Did he leave a forwarding address?"

"No," he answered.

I then asked if Mr. Spencer or Mr. Gerber had been in lately.

No, they had not been there for some time. This showed me that they were not strangers at this hotel. I felt if I could locate Stetson I would be pretty sure to get Spencer at the same time. They worked together; Stetson, the head; Spencer, the assistant. This would make it a little easier than having them in different parts of the country.

I discussed the weather, the movies and prohibition with the clerk, then said casually:

"It just occurs to me that Mr. Harrison may not be the Harrison I think he is. I cannot just remember what the initial of the Harrison I am looking for is. What did this man look like?"

"Oh, he was about two hundred, great big fellow, good dresser, usually wore a black derby, good mixer and never drank. Funny combination!"

"Yes," I replied, "a very funny combination."

There was no doubt now about him being Stetson. The description couldn't have been better if it had been his photograph. It was a start anyway.

Evidently he had gone directly to San Antonio; to this very hotel, after finishing with me. I wondered where the rest of the crew were and why they were not with him. The reason, I found out later, was due to the "unbelievable dishonesty" of Reno Hamlin.

I left the hotel and went down to the police station to inquire if they knew anything about the bunch.

While I was waiting to see the Chief two police officers brought in a young girl. She was a nice looking little thing. Her big blue eyes and pale yellow hair gave her an innocent, harmless appearance. She was bemoaning the cruel fate that had landed her in jail.

"Believe me," she was sniffling, "I'd just like to get a line on that St. Anthony Hotel guy. I'd sure make him come through all right."

I asked her what the trouble was.

She wiped her tears on the soft fur of her long squirrel coat. "Oh, I'm the goat!" she sobbed anew. "I'm the goat!"

I said to myself, "Girlie, you and I are partners, only you do not know it."

"I got left to hold the sack while the others beat it!" she continued.

"What kind of sack were you left to hold?" I prodded.

But she didn't pay any attention to me; just continued to pour out the tragic details of her misfortune.

"I didn't swipe all of the things they found in the room. I only copped one piece of junk, a Hudson Seal coat. I swear to God! I never lifted nothin' else."

"Why do you not plead guilty and ask for mercy?"

"Ask fer mercy?" she shrieked at me. "Mercy! My God, do they actually come that green? Say Bo, whadda think this is — a helpin' hand society? By the time you been around this joint as many time as I have, you'll begin to get wised up."

I certainly felt inferior in knowledge of the functioning of the police department, but hoped for enlightenment. I was not disappointed.

"Perhaps if you returned what you took it would help some," I continued.

"Return it!" she snapped, as if amazed at my ignorance of the way things are conducted in the shoplifters' profession. "That's the reason I'll get the limit this time. The job they're hollerm' so loud about is the one I done. I can't return it!"

"Well, what did you do with it after you got it?" I asked in my best extracting tone.

"You dumb-bell, whadda you suppose I done with it, put it back on the seal? I sold it — sold it — sold it to a big stiff layin' off at the St. Anthony Hotel!"

The story was getting warm. The description warmer. I took a long breath.

"What was the — the — stiff's name?"

"That's just it. I ain't got his name. The only line I got on him is his room number. But that won't do me no good. He's checked out! The bird's gone and the coat with him an' it's sure good night for me."

"Perhaps I can find him for you," I offered.

"Well, if you're so smart in the head that you can spot a guy by his room number, I sure wish you luck! It was number 113. Go to it, old dear, you're just as happy as if you was sane."

Her attention was claimed by a uniformed escort and our interview closed.

"Room 113 — room 113," I kept repeating to myself lest I forget it. If I was observed on my return trip to the hotel, those who saw me must have remarked, "There goes what ought to be locked up," for I am sure I kept calling the number out loud. I know I nearly knocked several pedestrians down in my rush for the hotel register. But then I thought, "I am just as happy as if I were sane."

At the bottom of the page I saw it! It was there in the bold figures affected by most hotel clerks. "J. Harrison — room 113."

A wave of satisfaction swept over me. However a ripple or two of shame mixed in with it. I was certainly "green" in more ways than one. A rank amateur. I had absolutely overlooked Harrison's room number the first time.

"Well," I sighed, "we live and learn, if we live long enough!"

There was no question now about Harrison being Stetson, and also the purchaser of the stolen garment.

It had been interesting talking to the little "snitcher" and satisfying to find that it had so uniquely lined up with my mission, but I could not see how the discovery of the stolen coat and its disposal had materially affected my hunt. It is the little things in life that count, they say. This incident seemed minute in proportion to my charges against Stetson, but more than a year later after heart-breaking searches and thousands of spent dollars, I found this slender link the strongest in the long chain that reached from one end of America to the other.

I left San Antonio late that same night, going direct to Corpus Christi, and made inquiries for Mr. Cathey. I was informed that he had gone to California on a prospecting trip. This did not strike me as significant of anything unusual as he was in the habit of taking long prospecting trips in different parts of the country. I knew that following the devastating flood recently inundating Corpus Christi, it was not unlikely that Cathey had turned his holdings into cash and gone West in search of drier investments.

While I could find nothing to support my belief that in some way Cathey was to be a mark for those thieves, I could not get the idea out of my mind. The more I thought about it, the stronger grew the conviction that within the little red address book which I had found on the bed, lay some solution to my problem. I was positive that the confidence men were not ignorant of his wealth and that his name was there for no good purpose. If California was as full of "slickers" as is this part of the country, I sighed for Cathey's holdings. Perhaps he will be the prospect instead of the prospector, I thought.

The immediate need of reinforcing my funds demanded I return home by way of Plainview, where I held a conference with my bankers of the Guarantee State Bank of Plainview. I laid the entire affair before them, relating my intention of running down the fugitives and putting my own brand of capture on them.

The bankers assured me of their undivided support and whatever assistance in a financial way I needed. I was told not to worry about my financial obligations until I came back. At Hale Center, my home town, I was told virtually the same thing. The peace of mind I enjoyed during my man-hunt due to their co-operation allowed me to concentrate on the dangerous job ahead without worry of financial pressure. I am deeply grateful to these fine friends who were loyal in time of trouble.

Another thing I did before returning home was to swallow my pride and give a full account of my case to all the leading newspapers, including the Associated Press. It told the methods used by these crooks to defraud and outlined their general attack by way of the wallet. In the articles I appealed to the public to help me apprehend the scoundrels.

I received much valuable information through this appeal. Letters from every part of the country poured in for three years. Some thought they had found the gang, or one or more members of it. While they seldom sent in anything pertaining to my particular cases, their interest in the whole affair sharpened their eyes and many other crooks were discovered and are now among the "interior decorations'* of various jails and penitentiaries.

If more victims would forget their humiliation at being "hooked," many more of the bunco men would be caught.

It is a peculiar thing what an important part little things played in my adventure. I mean things that appeared little at the time they happened. Sometimes what appeared the most unimportant trifles proved the big issues. It was while engaged in a conversation of no especial import with my wife I got the idea of going to California to look for Stetson and the others.

We were discussing the different angles of the tangled problem.

Mrs. Norfleet said to me: "You know, Frank, while you were in San Antonio and Corpus Christi, I was thinking of Spencer a great deal. He did travel some, didn't he?"

I said he certainly had "kicked up the dust" in a lot of states.

"When he left our house after his visit I knew more about the geography of the United States than I ever learned in school. Sometimes I have wondered if he really had been in all the places he said he had."

"I guess so," I replied. Spencer and Stetson, as well as the others, had shown an accurate familiarity with many of the places in which I had scouted, so I saw no reason to doubt the truth of his claim.

"Yes," continued my wife in her direct way, "I counted up all the states he ever mentioned making, and California was the only one he had neglected. Strike you at all funny?"

I stopped cleaning my rifle. Being familiar with the synchronous publicity of the Los Angeleans for California and their own "home town," I could not see why the state of Golden Promise should have been sidetracked. I didn't know just what to think of her question. Either she was way ahead of me, or I was way behind her! My mind was working like the woman's, and her's worked in a circle; the number of rings she wore proving it.

"Yes, it's strange, isn't it? But I do not get much out of it," I said.

"Well, Frank, I am sure the reason they never mentioned California was because that's where they hide out! They figured by not mentioning California, it would not stick in our minds if we ever had occasion to look for them."

I bounded into the air shouting, "You've hit it! You've hit it! That's it! That's the very reason they never yipped a word about the Golden State. It all comes to me now. See! they made a getaway from here the minute they got my money. Went to San Antonio, from there I'll bet, sure as shooting, they gathered up Cathey at Corpus Christi and the whole outfit hit it straight for sunny Cal."

"It looks to me as if that's about the line up," agreed the wife.

I didn't waste another second. Together we threw a few clothes into the suitcase, hitched up the old Ford, and within two hours I was on my way to California.

Chapter Four - My Christmas Present

Having no particular place in California at which to start the search, I dropped off the train at dusk in San Bernardino. "Might as well begin the hunt from the bottom of the state and work up," said I to myself.

It was Christmas Eve.

The pretty little valley town nestling at the foot of Arrow Head Mountain, was in holiday dress. Festoons of green draped the doorways and arches of the little stucco mission homes. Wreaths pressed their wide red ribbon bows against the windows of the small shops. The town was in gala attire.

No doubt about it, Santa Claus was expected momentarily!

I walked the streets to formulate some plan of action. Where — how to make the beginning? I began to experience that feeling of panic that strikes one so often after acting on a decision made in haste. I recall thinking I must have been insane to have come way out to California simply because not one of six men had ever mentioned the place. What reasoning! I had been a fool!

Jumping at conclusions, based on what seemed now the most ridiculous idea in the world! I felt like running for home before anyone found out what a fool I had been.

Everything was quiet and peaceful but myself. I wanted some one to talk to; some contact with reality. I kept on walking and found I was in the residence section among the low, rambling Spanish houses that dot the miniature city.

Through the windows of southern bungalows, merry lights twinkled and sparkled from the branches of gift-laden Christmas trees. Lighted lamps threw on intimate family scenes, warm rosy glows. Fathers were importantly affixing small stockings to mantelpieces and mothers fluttered clouds of soft tissue paper, tinsel and colored ribbons.

Some of the younger fathers even went so far as to catch "Mrs. Mother" under the mistletoe.

I sighed. I could see through the long, undraped French windows, dolls, doll carriages and tiny doll houses. The eternal feminine! God bless them! Brignt colored horns spoke of early morning blowing. There were drums waiting to be beaten by boyish hands; rocking horses to be ridden across the "living room range," where wild animals and war-whooping Indians lurked behind chairs and under davenports. It would be a riot in the morning when the bronchos would be roped and the Red Men scalped by the stout-hearted "Freddies," "Billies" and "Jimmies."

I wondered what sort of a Christmas Day the folks at home on the ranch would have. I had left in such a rush that Christmas had not entered my mind. All I could think was how lonely and strange I felt, walking silently in the quiet of this sacred night.

Before my eyes were happy homes. Here was what men strive for and protect — wife and children.

The Nation's backbone — home!

Yet one man will destroy another man's home to preserve his own.

Strange thoughts sprung in and out of my mind. Any one of the men for whom I sought might at this moment be the center of a group such as met my gaze at each new turn. Perhaps some of them were husbands and fathers! I did not know. I tried to picture some of them distributing Christmas cheer. But my sense of humor got the better of me. All I could see was Stetson, followed by Spencer squeezing down the chimney, making a general clean-up of the presents, and departing before the man of the house could shoot them.

I did wonder what I would do if I came on one of them in the midst of his family. Would I have the nerve to carry out my resolve? Could I snatch him from his wife and children — from their candle-lit tree — their turkey and stuffing? This sentimentality will be my ruin, I thought. Perhaps the fear that I might be put to such a test brought my evening prowl to an early end.

As I went to sleep I realized that for the first time in my life, I would awaken on Christmas morning with not even one new necktie, but as a matter of fact, had Santa Claus found my socks hanging over the jail door at San Bernardino, he could not have filled them more to my liking.

In the morning I went immediately to the Sheriff's office. I had often heard of Walter A. Shay, sheriff of San Bernardino, but I was not prepared for the kind interest and co-operation he gave me.

If all members of law-enforcing institutions were one-sixteenth as considerate, conscientious and willing to co-operate in the administration of their duties as Walter A. Shay, this world would be a lot better off.

Shay was on duty. I introduced myself and stated for whom I was looking.

"I have a hunch the gang I'm after may be somewhere in this state and I thought this as good a place as any to get started," I said. "And, Sheriff, I'm depending on your help. I'm 'green'."

"Like as not I can help a little," he drawled. "The Sheriff's office doesn't make a general practice of giving every stranger in town a Christmas present, but," he added meaningly, "I may have one for you!"

I didn't get him at first. Then the truth began to dawn.

"Sheriff!" I cried. "You don't mean — you — you —" Before I could formulate the words, he cut in:

"Yes, I think I do. Come and see if I have!"

He led the way to the cells. My heart beat like a trip hammer against my ribs.

"Look in there Norfleet!"

I pressed my nose against the thick meshed cage and gazed. I turned sick at my stomach and the perspiration broke out all over me. I felt a quiver rush up and down my spine.

There in separate cells, ranged side by side, were Ward and Gerber. For a minute I couldn't speak. My first impulse was to wish them "Merry Christmas," but I stifled it.

Ward spoke first. "So you found us did you, you damned old fox?" His tone was sullen.

I just continued to gape at them. Here were the pseudo secretaries of the Dallas and Fort Worth "exchanges."

It did not seem possible. They had appeared so substantial; like secure bulwarks of legitimate finance. But here they were, trapped by their own misdeeds.

Well educated, well dressed, well mannered, but just plain, common, ordinary thieves.

How the truth of it bore into my soul. The line of demarcation between honesty and dishonesty is mighty thin in places for us all.

By the grace of God only perhaps, was I on the outside looking in.

Gerber, who had heard Ward's salutation to me, rushed from his stool to the front of the cell.

"Norfleet, for God's sake, don't identify us! Have mercy on us! Have pity for us! For God's sake, don't, don't identify us!"

I said nothing to them, but followed Sheriff Shay into another room.

35

"How did it happen?" was my first question.

"Why, a man brought me a clipping from a San Francisco newspaper the other day. It had a big account of your swindling in it and the description of some of the gang who Mid' you. The man said he had run into a bunch of 'stock brokers' right here in San Bernardino and was about to close a big deal with them when he caught sight of this item. He read it through carefully. They were the descriptions of the same crew about to 'tap' him. They had used the same methods on him that you described; even gave the same names. He wanted them pinched, so I took a chance on holding them and wired Sheriff Clark at Fort Worth for information. He wired back 'hold them.' So here they are as cozy as two bugs in a rug! Have them as a Christmas present."

"I wish I'd known this," I exclaimed, thinking of the railroad fare.

"I sent a wire to you at the ranch, but you must have just missed it. Sheriff Clark's deputy, Milton Williams, is on his way here now to take the pair of them back to Fort Worth for trial."

"Who was the man who brought you the newspaper clipping?" I asked out of curiosity.

"Oh, he's a fellow from Corpus Christi, Texas. Cathey, he said, was his name."

"Cathey!" I exploded, nearly tipping over in my chair.

"Cathey? Well, I'll be hanged."

"If it had not been for that newspaper story probably Ward and Gerber would have been this minute distributing Christmas presents bought with Cathey's money."

I looked Cathey up.

He told me he had been approached in the same manner as I had. He also had "sat" on the mysterious Mr. Stetson's wallet! Indeed, they had used the identical credentials on him that were my own downfall. Cathey fell for their line "even as I."

However just as the deal was about to be closed he saw the news story, recognized his business associates as my swindlers, and woke up with a bang! He then dashed bareheaded from the hotel into the street and inquired of the first cop he met where the Sheriff's office was.

He was seen asking directions from the policeman by one of the gang. They knew their game was up and the whole lot of them made an instant duck for freedom.

Ward and Gerber rushed for the railroad station. Stetson and Spencer left via the fire-escape.

Fortunately Cathey got to Sheriff Shay in time for him to head off Ward and Gerber just as they were in the act of boarding a train.

In a suitcase which Ward was carrying, the officers found among the contents the original papers and credentials used on both Cathey and me. The name of Stetson was signed to most of them. This at first gave the authorities the impression they had captured the master mind of the ring. I regretted this was not true. But we cannot have everything. Not all at once, anyway!

One of the most interesting finds in the contents was a check book of Stetson's, the stubs of which showed checks for large amounts had been made out in favor of "M. H. Harrison" and "Dede Winters." Who these were, of course, I did not know until much later. My original contract with them was also with the other articles.

I couldn't help wondering if Stetson had a Hudson seal coat under his arm when he went down the fireescape. He might even at this time be running around town disguised in it, waiting to catch a train.

Chapter Five - A Successful Disguise

Milton Williams, the Deputy Sheriff from Fort Worth, arrived next day. We made preparations to take Ward and Gerber back to Fort Worth for trial, but were balked by having to secure requisition papers. This meant a delay of several more days. We had to wire Sheriff Clark at Fort Worth, to get the papers by going personally to Austin for them and then to bring them on to San Bernardino.

While waiting for these details to be arranged, I let no grass grow under my cow-boots. I searched the records of both telephone and telegraph at the hotel where the bunch stopped. But there was no record of either a telephone message or telegram for or from "Mr. Peck," the name under which Stetson had registered and by which he was known to Cathey.

I also made a search of the nearby towns, going as far as Los Angeles. At the Police Headquarters there I found in the rogues' gallery a picture of Stetson which gave "Furey" as his main alias (possibly his real name).

I took the photograph and showed it to the executives in the Sheriff's office.

They readily promised to keep a sharp lookout for him and said they knew all about his operations and hoped they would have the chance to land him.

I drew tactful attention to the reward I was offering but this "trifle" was not to be considered with the importance of capturing him.

They gave out the impression that duty alone was their noble goal.

When I told them I wanted to leave my suitcase in their care until I went and perfected my disguise, I thought I caught an amused flicker in their eyes. However I set it down as a figment of my imagination and proceeded to leave for an interview with the barber.

When I left the office I was wearing a wide brim Stetson hat such as the cow-men in my part of the plains wear, an old and worn corduroy suit; the trousers tucked in the slant-heeled high cow-boots. My mustache was much as nature had directed it. When I returned, my upper lip was as clean as a whistle and my hair clipped close. I had changed my ranch clothes for a neat, inconspicuous grey business suit and in place of the big hat with the cleft in the crown, I wore a cap.

'I'll thank you to give me my suitcase and overcoat," said I to the officer in whose charge I had left them.

"You'll thank me to do what?" he returned, giving me the up-and-down.

I repeated my request for my belongings.

"Say! how do you get that way? Those things belong to a West Texas cowman. What'cha tryin' to pull off?"

I finally convinced them I was the rightful owner. Their surprise and chagrin at not recognizing me was evident in their effort to pass off the "joke on them" in a careless way.

Delays still blocked me. On returning to San Bernardino I found Sheriff Clark was there with the requisition papers.

But the authorities of that jurisdiction refused to let us budge the men on a "charge" demanding that we get a "true bill" of indictment.

Jesse M. Brown, District Attorney at Fort Worth, was forthwith wired to call a special session of the grand jury to convene on the day I arrived, which would be as soon as I could get to Fort Worth.

As I remember I left the next day.

I am a sociable soul, which is one of the marked characteristics of West Texans. When I was addressed by an elderly gentleman sitting across from my section in the Pullman, I was glad to fall into conversation with him. The newspapers had widely circulated the report of the arrest of Ward and Gerber and the probability of them being taken back to Fort Worth for trial. So it did not seem out of the way that he should speak of the pair and their capture. He folded his newspaper and looking across at me said:

"My name is Garst, Perry Garst. I have just been reading about the capture of these fellows, Ward and Gerber. It looks like they're in for it now, doesn't it?"

I told him if I had anything to do with it, I guessed they were. Of course I was suffering from the humiliating and financial sting they had given me and my blood pressure was pretty high. When I found anyone interested, I assumed that they were sympathizers, that is, with me, but now I realize I was over eager to pour out the tale of my misfortunes. Therefore I told Garst the whole thing.

He was deeply impressed and apparently sympathized with me. In fact he was so vitally interested that he declared his intention of stopping off at Fort Worth to see how the matter turned out.

"I have never been in that town and it will be an opportunity to see it."

He then leaned his head back against the seat and dozed. As he slept his head slipped into the corner against the window. A strong light played straight on his features.

Memory surged up within me. I had never seen him before. I was sure of that, still those features! They were not unfamiliar to me.

"Where, when, who?" I thought. Then I saw it.

He might have been Ward, grown older. Head, hair, the set of the eyes and general type of face, unnoticed before, now leapt into relief.

"Perry Garst!" I thought. "Well, perhaps, but not likely!"

It had never occurred to me that anyone might be trailing me; such is the egotism of the ignorant, a pleasant thing, but costly. When he awoke from his nap, I engaged him in conversation again, this time guardedly. "More or less," I mused to myself, "like shutting the jail door after the prisoners are out."

He was not loath to talk. His mind dwelt on the higher planes of life. Education and the general school problem seemed to be his pet subjects.

As the noon hour drew near he casually remarked that he believed he would not go into the diner; that a friend had insisted on his taking a light luncheon with him. He opened his suitcase and spread out on the seat opposite him a very appetizing meal. He begged me to share it with him. Indeed, he would have me devour it all. His stomach was not quite what it should be these days, and he was strong for diet.

"Oh, would I not eat something?"

"Oh, I would not," I whispered to myself. I declined the food and thanked him for his kindness.

The sandwiches were daintily made and the curly green lettuce between the evenly trimmed squares of white bread made my mouth water. There were stuffed olives — stuffed with what, the Lord only knows. These I also had to forego. There was some delicious looking cake with a thick cream filling, some fruit and two boiled eggs.

After urging me repeatedly to partake of the feast, Mr. Garst selected the eggs in their original shell wrappers and devoured them. "Ha! Ha!" I cried inwardly, and wilted the lettuce with a look.

"Do you find boiled eggs a safe diet?" I asked innocently.

"Fairly so. But I have to be very careful of my stomach."

"So do I," I declared. "I was once poisoned in Old Mexico, and since then I stick close to boiled eggs myself."

It may appear that my time on the trip was entirely taken up with Garst. But it was not, wholly. I made the acquaintance of an elderly couple. The woman said she had been a detective before her marriage. They were returning to their home in Georgia.

I decided to confide in the woman and gave her a description of the three men still at large; Furey, Spencer and Hamlin.

She said she would keep a weather eye out for them. Georgia was a state in which many of them wintered, so she might happen to see one or more of them, she said.

I gave her my address and she agreed to drop me a line if she ever found out anything.

When I stepped off the train in Fort Worth I watched my friend Garst. He at once entered a telephone booth and held a spirited conversation with someone, judging from the way his head behaved.

I had an immediate hearing before the grand jury, and when I emerged from the chambers the first person I laid eyes on was old man Garst. He jumped up and rushed toward me, gripping my arm in no feeble grasp.

"What did they do? What did they do? Did they bill those men?" he demanded excitedly.

I disengaged my arm from his clutch and shrugged my shoulders.

"Then go back! Go back! You have a perfect right to know what action they intend to take!" he cried.

"I have nothing further to do with it. It's up to them," I replied shortly.

He seemed to quiet down and affected indifference. Together we walked out of the court house.

As we reached the street and I turned to leave him he said in a hesitant tone that he had been unable to secure a room in any of the hotels or rooming houses on account of a convention going on in the city, and would I not share with him the room he had engaged in a private house. He laid stress on the fact that there were two beds and I would be more than welcome to occupy one of them. Indeed it would be a favor to him if I would! I didn't doubt it.

I declined his offer and thanking him said I thought I would have no difficulty in getting a room in a hotel. At this I left him and walked down the street.

When I reached the corner, I looked back. He was starting off in the opposite direction, walking with a surety of location impossible for a stranger within the gates.

I was practically sure he was Ward's father. The close resemblance and the vital interest in the decision of the grand jury, together with the hard-boiled eggs were pretty good evidence. I thought a little shadowing would be good practice and I was curious to see just what the game was.

Retracing my steps. I quickened my gait and was soon close behind him. He knew the town better than I did! Without the slightest hesitation he struck east off Houston Street. This path led him directly into the colored section of the town. Rather an unusual haunt for one of such immaculate appearance and such a profound uplift of mind I thought as I tagged at his heels. He stopped in front of a shabby, unkempt, tumbledown house, glanced up and down the street, then entered.

I took careful note of the ramshackle abode and hastened back to the court house where I got Frank Evans, a newspaper reporter. I wanted Evans to go back there with me and try for an interview with Garst. We planned to have him openly accuse Garst of his relationship to Ward and see what kind of a fit he would throw. Evans' nose for news went up to the wind and away we flew.

I must say that Garst found his way far more easily than I did mine. Although I had been familiar with Fort Worth for years, he was the better pilot.

Evans began to kid me about it, saying it was a fine detective who couldn't find a place he left only ten minutes ago. I was getting discouraged myself, when turning a corner, there in the middle of a row of smoky dumps, was the house of mystery. Evans remained outside. I was to go in and line Garst up for the interview and then Evans was to enter.

To my surprise, a white landlady opened the door. I inquired if a Mr. Garst was in.

She said he had just gone out.

I then inquired if he had reserved a bed in her house for me.

She said that the old gentleman had called that morning and engaged a room with two beds but as to one of them being for me, she could not vouch.

At this she pushed open the door on her right which led into what had been intended for the front parlor.

"This is the room, sir."

I stepped inside and looked it over. It was very plainly furnished but neat as a pin. The two white iron beds were draped in white spreads. Their clean-ly purity spoke strongly of heavenly regions. A small oak dresser was cor-nerwise across the angle of the wall. There were two chairs and a small table between the beds. On the table was an old fashioned coal oil lamp with a cro-cheted mat under it. "Where was Norfleet, when the lights went out?" I sang to myself.

I inquired which way Mr. Garst had gone. The "Mistress of the Manse" indi-cated, and we followed the direction in which her gnarled forefinger pointed.

We searched the district, but to no avail. This was the last I ever saw of my over-kind friend. He had said he was from Sunnyside, Maryland. Sometime later when I was in that town I made inquiries for him, but found no one who had ever heard of him, and our paths never crossed again.

Chapter Six - Mister Nee From Washington, D.C.

The grand jury indicted both Ward and Gerber. For this I was very glad. The documents were prepared and immediately forwarded to Sheriff Clark who was still in California. As soon as he received them he and his two prisoners left for Fort Worth.

When the trio arrived the papers made a big splurge about their arrest and hinted at a sensational trial.

Through this publicity, Peter J. Nee, a man of wealth from Washington, D. C, discovered they were the same pair who only a short time ago had swindled him out of a fortune.

1 shall never forget the meeting between Charles Gerber, E. J. Ward and Mr. Nee. It was one of the most dramatic I have ever seen. It had all the ele-ments of melodrama which borders on broad farce.

Nee and I went into the Sheriff's office together. Sheriff Clark, Milton Wil-liams, one or two officers and the two prisoners were already there.

Mr. Nee without hesitating walked over to Ward. He was so close he could have touched him. He looked up into the thief's face and said:

"You are my man! I positively identify you as the one who brought this weight of trouble down upon my head. You are the man!"

He kept his eyes riveted on Ward's as if to force recognition.

Ward continued to stare at him blankly with a well feigned expression of perfect disinterest.

Nee's hand shot out toward him accusingly. He gathered himself for a final bout.

"Ward! John! ...You know me, you recognize me! Why in God's name don't you say so?"

Ward continued to look as vacant as a double blank domino. Then he spoke. His voice was as metallic as steel.

"Remember you!" he uttered in a measured tone. "Remember you? I never saw you before in my life. You must be out of your head."

Nee slipped his fingers into his vest pocket. He fumbled an instant.

Ward's eyes followed his trembling fingers. A frightened look flashed across his immobile features.

Nee drew from his pocket a small object which he concealed in his closed hand.

"You are the man who betrayed my trust, my friendship and my confidence; who fed your greed upon my bounty; who broke bread with me in my home and who worshipped with me in my church!"

He opened his hand, palm upturned under the cold stare of Ward.

"Look!" he cried, his voice trembling with emotion, "look at this token of faith you gave me. Look at this Crucifix! Now, deny me!"

Ward lowered his eyes to the little emblem of life's sorrows and salvation lying in the old gentleman's hand. He uttered no word, but closed his eyes and dropped his head.

Gerber, rooted to the spot by the drama of the thing, coughed nervously and remarked with fictitious nonchalance:

"Sob stuff, sob stuff! — gets 'em every time. Why Ward wouldn't know a crucifix if he was nailed to one. He just thinks the old man double-crossed him."

An official of the U. S. Secret Service from Washington, D. C, by the name of G. C. Cornwall accompanied Mr. Nee to Fort Worth. He took a great interest in the case and gave me quite a bit of information.

"Why, Norfleet, you should not have had much trouble getting these men. They are the 'Furey gang' that used to operate out of New York. The photos of all the leaders are right here in this town. I sent them to the city detective a long time ago and asked him to be on the watch for them and to notify me if they appeared."

This almost knocked me out. All through my chase I had been handicapped by the lack of photos of the men I hunted. What could not I have accomplished if I had been in possession of these photos?

"Bu-but," I stammered, "I went through every picture here in Fort Worth looking for my men, but never one did I find."

"They are here just the same, for I sent them. It was after Joe Furey had stolen a lot of papers from a man in New York named Stetson, including Stetson's masonic membership card. Come on and we'll find them."

I hastened to follow, my mouth "watering" for the possession of these important pictures.

Cornwall paused a moment, then said:

"You stay here and I'll go hunt them up and bring you enough pictures of that gang to make a big family album."

I waited in the courtroom with all the patience I could muster.

When Cornwall returned he had lost most of his "zip." With face grave and in the manner of one who has just learned for the first time his limitations, he informed me that there must be a mistake as it was claimed the photos and descriptions had not been received.

Ward and Gerber were still in the courtroom when Cornwall returned. He seemed to forget we were not alone.

"I'll tell you one thing, Norfleet," he began, but was interrupted by Sheriff Clark who nodded to one of the officers to take the prisoners out.

"Just a minute, Cornwall. Now that they have both been satisfactorily identified, let's wait until we are alone to discuss matters."

Cornwall watched for the door to close behind the men, so eager was he to give me good advice.

"Now listen, Norfleet," he began and raised a restraining hand, "I hear that you are thinking of going out to get these other three birds — all by yourself. I admire your pluck, but man you have had no experience! Now my advice to you is to lay off! Don't go throwing your good money after bad. Keep it."

I nodded to indicate that I was keeping even with his rapid advance. He talked as fast as a race horse.

"Now!" he exclaimed in that getting-down-to-business tone. "Now we, that is my department, has just as grave a charge against some of your men as you have. We have fifteen hundred trained men — get that, trained!" — I nodded again to let him know I "got it" — "in the United States alone, and these crooks couldn't work in the lead of our operatives for six weeks!"

I explained to him that I knew I probably would have to spend a lot of good money.

"But there are other things in this world besides money." I realized nothing I could say would make any difference to him, so I let the subject drop after merely citing that while it might cost me something to get the men, still, balanced against what they probably would steal from others if left at liberty, it would not amount to very much except to me as an individual.

"Perhaps this will be my contribution to the good people of this state to rid them of these vultures. Anyway," I finished, "it's my business and I'm satisfied."

Following the trial I asked Ward and Gerber why it was after they "did" me that Furey was registered by himself at the St. Anthony Hotel in San Antonio.

Gerber was quite astonished that I knew this. He told me that all of them had gone there, but Furey was the only one who had registered. He said it was the usual practice of their "profession" after finishing with a victim to meet in an allotted place, divide the spoils, then separate, all going in different directions for a time; later to congregate and perform the ceremony, "Lifting the wad," from another prospect. He said this ritual was duly carried out in my case and that my money was split six ways over the dinner table in the grill room of the St. Anthony Hotel.

To hear that my life savings had been so informally apportioned among these vultures made my head swim and my stomach turn over like a Ford engine. It was one of the times when their windpipes between my hands would have been balm to itching palms.

A little edge was ground off the transaction by the information that following the brotherly distribution a poker game was held in which Reno Hamlin lost all of his "earnings." He got up disgustedly, according to Ward, went out and returned masked to the eyes with a handkerchief and guiding two eager looking six shooters in the direction of the bankers. He annexed enough table money to buy the White House and backed out behind his little guns.

I couldn't help laughing, and Ward himself eased out a sickly grin.

"Why did you let the dirty cur get away with it?" I chaffed.

"What did we let him get away with it for?" Ward echoed in wonder at my ignorance. "If a man has no honor, how the hell could we help it?"

When I returned to my hotel that night I found a letter forwarded to me from Hale Center. It was from my train acquaintance, Mrs. W. G. Ward, the elderly woman from Georgia. As far as I know this Mrs. Ward was in no way related to either E. J. Ward or his probable kin, Perry Garst. It was merely a coincidence.

However the letter told me that a man answering in every particular the description I had given her of Spencer boarded the train at Houston.

She said as soon as she saw him, she moved into a seat close behind him and listened to his conversation with another man sitting beside him. Spencer was telling the man, who apparently knew him well, that business in Fort Worth and Dallas was as easy as running a picture show. This, the woman thought a rather queer term for expressing the status of a legitimate business. Spencer also said that "the game" looked very good all over the country but that he was going to "play" for awhile in Miami, Florida, to which place he was now on his way.

"However," he remarked, "I think I'll stop off a few days in Jacksonville; so many of the boys are down there, and I like to keep up with the 'gang' and find out who the 'new suckers' are."

This was certainly most interesting news to me, and as I had just succeeded in selling my option on the 10,000 acres of the Slaughter ranch with the return of my $5,000, I was prepared to continue the chase.

Chapter Seven - Combing Florida for Furey

I decided to go at once to Florida. I always felt that wherever I found Furey I would also get Spencer, and vice versa.

The next night I left for the warmer clime of the eastern coast. I stopped over a few hours in New Orleans, which is quite a town for the sporting element. I went to see the Police Chief and there met Captain Glenn, Chief of the Finger Print Bureau.

We went over the records of his office, but found nothing. In the rogues' gallery we did find a most amusing picture of Furey, all gotten up in a cowboy outfit, looking as if he were roping steers instead of suckers.

In Jacksonville I introduced myself and explained my mission to the head deputy in the Sheriff's office. I had become hardened to seeing a lot of wise looks passed around whenever I mentioned I expected to catch any one of the three "buncos," but in this case they were very considerate of my childish efforts to play detective and assured me of their co-operation.

At the Police Department I met the Chief and the head of the City Detective Force, Cahoon, who in turn passed me on to the Chief Special Agent of the Florida East Coast Railway. This man was very nice and gave me the names of several prominent men throughout the state that he thought might be of use to me.

Had I been a human microscope I could not have searched Jacksonville more thoroughly for Spencer and the others, but if they were there I could not train my discovering lenses on them.

I left for St. Augustine, then worked all the principal towns as far as Tampa. In these gay winter resorts with their flood of grown up children playing madly at the game of forgetting, I thought I might see familiar faces. I watched the theaters, the cabarets and the Atlantic "swimmin' hole."

For hours and hours I walked the broad board walks, swept along in the same tide that floated the millionaire; the husband who has left his wife at home, the husband who couldn't leave his at home; the society queen, the vamp, the little stenographer whose year's savings will go for one week's pleasure; and the amateur detective. With these, I was carried up and down the great stretch of beach upon whose satiny sands, a sapphire sea spreads a flounce of scalloped ermine.

From Tampa I drifted with the tide of gayety and hope down to St. Petersburg. This little watering place was not as lively as Miami, Palm Beach and Jacksonville, but I could not afford to overlook any bets.

I spent a good deal of time at the boat landing, watching the newcomers as they came ashore. Faces! faces! faces!

At the end of the day my brain reeled with the memory of them. Seldom did I see one I had seen before. It was tiresome work.

There is a strain, physical as well as mental, watching for a certain face among the thousands. Mentally one rapidly compares each new face with the one indelibly photographed upon his brain. One selects, compares and rejects, all in the flash of an eye.

I was well prepared for this conscious and subconscious cataloguing of types, after developing the pictures of my men in the dark room of memory, immediately after I had been fleeced. To date, I had had no opportunity to test the finished picture.

One early afternoon, I decided to call it "a day" and go back to the hotel. I left the boat landing where one of the lovely white liners had just emptied her human cargo for St. Petersburg and inland points.

On the way I took a turn through the home section of the town. I had gone only a short way when my attention was attracted to an old couple in the front yard of a modest cottage.

The little lawn was enclosed by a low picket fence. In the middle of the plot of green grass sat the old lady. She was very fat and short and had on a dark dress. Great sobs shook her frame until she resembled a huge black umbrella opened out on the ground to dry. At her side stood an old gentleman. He was trying to stay the overflow. He patted her shoulder soothingly with one hand; with the other he wiped the tears that slid down her broad, slippery cheeks, using the leg of a union suit which he stretched from a taut-clothes-line to meet her face. The old man seemed to be utterly helpless in the gush of tears which rained to the ground like a snapped string of crystal beads.

I leaned over the gate.

"What is the trouble?" I asked.

The man turned toward me, the leg of the union suit still clutched in his hand. In a vague, stunned way he replied:

"There isn't anything much the matter."

"Not much the matter?" wailed the old lady, bursting out in a fresh saline solution.

The old gentleman again brought the underwear into play, straining the line to a dangerous angle. He proceeded to blot her face. I fancy tears were not a novelty to him. She paid little attention to his ministrations but continued to talk through her optic flood which poured forth as if she had forgotten to turn off the faucets.

"Not much the matter? Well, we've lost every cent we have in the world. If that's not much matter, I'd like to know what is." She nodded to her husband. "He always takes things so calm. I don't know what would happen if we were both that way."

I stepped inside, asking if I could do anything to help matters.

I felt inclined to tip the old lady over the rain barrel; let nature take its course, and permit the old man to tell me what was wrong. Things began to dry up and presently they told me their story.

They had come to St. Petersburg to bask in its winter warmth. While living in this little cottage they made the casual acquaintance of three men. During

46

a conversation with them one day, the husband said he and his wife liked Florida so well that they figured on buying a little home in the center of an orange grove. One of the men spoke up and declared himself a "realtor" as the real estate men now term themselves. He said if they were interested in St. Petersburg property he had the exact place they wanted.

"I am the agent for the property," and indicating one of the other two men with him, "this gentleman owns it."

The old couple, whose name was Bockerman, went the next day to view the new estate. It consisted of several acres under cultivation and a charming bungalow. The orange grove appealed to them as its fragrant blossoms would renew in the autumn of life, a honeymoon in springs gone by.

They were very happy.

The price was set at ten thousand dollars. This was a sum far less than it would have commanded in the hands of genuine real estate operators.

The old people did not know this, and no doubt considered themselves fortunate at securing such a perfect home. The deal was agreed upon.

The property owner, so the "agent" said, required the money in cash over the board.

This met with the approval of the Bockermans. It was decided to transfer the money and close the deal in a bank in Clearwater, the county seat.

In line with this arrangement, the Bockermans had instructed their bank in Pittsburg, Pennsylvania, to transfer their savings account to the Clearwater institution. In order that the sale and transfer might be done right, and in order to protect themselves, the couple employed as their legal counsel a combination attorney and official of the Clearwater Bank.

At the appointed time the property owner, his "agent" and the third man, together with the Bockermans and their attorney met in the directors' room of the bank.

The attorney called the Bockermans' attention to a slight typographical error in the deed. He was so cautious that he ordered a new one made out.

They congratulated themselves upon their choice of such a careful adviser. At the mention of a new deed the third man spoke up.

"Quite accidentally," said he, "I have a portable typewriter with me. I would be glad to type a new deed for you. It will save you time, and possibly money!"

The Bockermans thanked him. Everyone was so kind. Perhaps it was because they were elderly, Mrs. Bockerman had thought. At any rate their attorney had told them the abstract and title had come up in perfect shape.

They waited.

The young typist made a mistake in the first copy he prepared. Almost at the end of a flawless second attempt he made a grievous error. He was very particular about his work. It would not take long; to make out another one. He would hurry, yet be careful. The third was ruined. Something was the matter with the typewriter. But he would surely have a perfect copy now!

While in the midst of this perfection of art in deed making Mr. Bockerman noticed the clock. He nudged Mrs. Bockerman.

"It's almost 4 o'clock," he said.

"Yes, I hope he gets through soon, I hate to keep all this money over night."

She wound the strap of her brown wrist bag once again around her arm. She said to her husband behind the shelter of her hand: "If the bank closes before he finishes we will not be able to put it in the safe deposit. I do wish he would hurry!"

The keys of the typewriter clicked sharply in the silence. No one seemed inclined to talk. The owner of the property had been reading a newspaper. Now he apparently dozed, while the flies made merry in his stiff beard which stuck off his heavy chin like a whisk broom over the edge of a dresser.

The other occupants of the room were engrossed with their thoughts. The sinister finger of the clock crept nearer to the hour of four. The Bockermans twisted uneasily in their seats.

"I am going to ask our lawyer to see that there is a safe deposit box left open for this money if that fellow doesn't get through in time," Mrs. Bockerman whispered to her husband.

Mr. Bockerman nodded acquiescence. They both turned to their attorney. His chair was vacant. They looked questioningly at the other men. Their gaze brought no hint of information from the trio.

He had been there only a few minutes before. Now, he was gone. Swallowed up in thin air. Not a trace of him. They looked at each other. Neither had seen him leave.

He had sat on a straight line with Mrs. Bockerman. There was a door leading somewhere just at his elbow.

"When I leaned over to speak to you, I turned my back slightly to him," she exclaimed in an undertone. "He must have gone then." Mrs. Bockerman became nervous. "What shall we do?" she cried in a low voice, gripping the little brown leather bag tighter.

One! Two! Three! Four! — whanged out the clock.

The Bockermans rose as one.

"The bank is closed for the day. See, they have closed the front doors," said Mr. Bockerman. "We cannot close the deal until tomorrow. It is too bad, but the bank is shut!"

At this the agent came suddenly awake. All three men sprang to their feet.

"It may be shut for you," the owner of the property cried, "but it's never closed for us!"

With this exclamation he snatched at the bag on the relaxed wrist of Mrs. Bockerman. She flung her hand in the air when one of the men behind her caught it above her head and tore the bag from her, peeling ribbons of tender flesh from the old lady's arm.

Before they could think, let alone speak, the three thieves had dashed through an open door, bounded into a waiting automobile and in another minute were nothing but a cloud of dust down the highway.

This is the story, they told me.

It resembled that of many others I had heard since my own. But someway it seemed more dastardly to rob these two gentle old folks. I came to learn that the weak and unprotected are the choice prey of these serpents.

Of course they went to see the Police and the Sheriff. At both places they were told to go home and what could be done to apprehend the outlaws would be done and they be notified.

So, with home gone, savings gone, hope gone, they spent their few remaining silver dollars, each inscribed "In God We Trust," for carfare back to the rented cottage in St. Petersburg.

When I met them on the lawn they had just received a letter from the Sheriff's office, saying nothing could be found of the absconders.

I knew how these poor people felt. That gone, hopeless feeling as if one had stepped off the top stair in the dark or the universe had been pulled out from under his feet.

As my own affairs were not prospering in the way of capturing my own men, I decided to see if I could do anything toward getting any of the Bockerman offenders. "Birds of a feather flock together." Perhaps if I found any of the bank bunch I might run into my own buncos. At least it would not be wasted time and both the Bockermans and I might benefit.

I announced my intention of going to Clearwater and trying to see what I could do for them.

They were very grateful. The old lady's tears had entirely gone behind her sunny smile. They thanked me and said their prayers would follow me. I was glad of this as I believe in the power of prayer and had a feeling that I might need it.

It was still light when I set out for the little town with a clear name but a cloudy history.

Chapter Eight - A Long Night's Vigil

At Clearwater I went immediately to the Sheriff's office. Although several days had elapsed between the robbery and my meeting with the Bockermans, I thought perhaps since the letter from the Sheriff's office had been received, some clue might have developed.

The officer on duty was seated on a high stool in a caged off portion of the room which separated the general waiting room from the executive part. At his side was a large oak desk and in front of him was a counter, across which the townspeople seemed to be shoving their taxes. A high latticed partition reached from the counter half way to the ceiling. In front of him the wicket was open and his sour countenance was framed in the oval.

He scratched a "paid" on a tired looking woman's receipt, flipped it back at her, snapped his pen behind his ear and lifting his half -chewed cigar on his tongue set it in the opposite corner of his mouth. He squinted at me and uttered some sound which I took to be "next!"

As enthusiastically as possible in the face of such gloom, I explained that I had just come from Brother and Sister Bockerman.

He knew about their being robbed?

Yes he knew all about it!

"Well!" said I, tapping a little friendly tattoo on the counter. "I suppose you do. The papers spoke quite freely on the subject."

His upper lip lifted off his stained teeth. I thought he was going to snap at me.

I continued my explanation. "I have a little time on my hands and came over to offer my services in the search for those infamous hounds who got their money. I hate to see them lose it!"

"Well," he sneered, "all I hate about the thing is that the thieves didn't get every damned cent they had and make 'em walk back to St. Petersburg!"

This nearly toppled me over. For a minute I looked him in the eye. It was so venomous it didn't seem I had heard right.

To clear my senses, I asked: "How was that?"

"I said," he repeated viciously, "that people who let men swindle them out of their money that way are worse than the swindlers and ought to lose every cent they ever had! That's what I said!"

This got under my own hide. I lit up like a pan of powder.

"You dirty scoundrel," I yelled in his face, "I'll crack you for that!"

I pulled my gun and made for the opening around the counter.

He saw what I was going to do and hopped off his stool like a toad from a rock.

We met at the corner of his desk. I had the drop on him. He had reached for his six shooter, but not quick enough.

"Drop your gun!" I cried. "You great big, dirty, good-for-nothing hyena! If you aren't satisfied with the deal, I can satisfy you and that quick."

I had placed myself directly in line with an open door which led down a hall to the outside entrance of the building. My back was to the open door and left it unprotected from behind. At the same time I realized this awkward position, I heard footsteps. They were certainly coming up the passageway. I was in an elegant position to get popped in the back. I could not turn to see whose feet they were, being too busy, so called out:

"Don't get excited! I'm not a hijacker, trying to rob your sheriff. He insulted a good old lady and I'm making him eat his words."

He evidently could see who was coming. "You — you — misunderstood what I said," he mumbled, looking mighty uncomfortable.

"Well, you didn't misunderstand me, did you?"

"No! — I — I gotchu," he said nervously.

I could see from the drift that there was no hope for the Bockermans from this source and that my efforts were useless. I backed up against the side wall to see who was at my back and to save a piece of my spine for future use.

My surprise was no greater than my delight.

"That's all right, stranger. We've seen and heard it all."

There stood four men all grinning from ear to ear and giving my ex-prisoner the Ha! Ha! I distinctly felt four silent messages of congratulation.

Thankfully, I replaced my gun and left the office.

One of the first things I learned on the range as a boy was, when you go after an animal, stay with it until you get it. If you're aiming to rope a wolf, rope him or kill him in the effort.

So although the trail of the three Bockerman wolves had been obscured in the dust of flight for a time, I decided to scout around and see if I couldn't find the trail. Of one thing I was reasonably sure. They probably knew the police and sheriff's office would not look very far for them, so they would not use undue caution in their movements.

I hailed a passing automobile and impressed upon the driver the necessity for a lift into St. Petersburg.

As soon as I reached town I went to see the old people. They were over-joyed and trembled with anxiety to know the result of my visit to town. When I saw the desolate future of those two old people what couldn't I have done to those bestial fiends!

Both had recovered their mental equilibrium to some extent. But most of the time they just sat and waited patiently for the return of their money.

It was beautiful to see the faith these people had in the efficacy of prayer to restore their fortune. They certainly placed much more confidence in the Almighty's ability to recover the little brown bag than they did in the police department's. In this they showed rare good judgment.

They never failed to include the thieves who had robbed them in their prayers.

I hadn't the heart to tell them of my fruitless efforts at the Sheriff's or of the apparently slim chance of ever getting the criminals. I said simply that I had investigated the matter and that so far nothing was known of the miscreants. I assured them I would not give up the search and when I heard anything I would let them know.

They again armored me with prayers and I left them as I had found them, except that Mrs. Bockerman was considerably drier.

On the way to the hotel I stopped in front of a garage to watch a young red-headed mechanic change a tire on a big touring car stalled within a few feet of the garage entrance. Silently, I admired the efficient and methodical man-ner in which he handled the unruly rubber ring. He struck me as being a mas-ter of his trade. When he finished the job I saw the driver of the car slip a five dollar bill into his grimy hand. The boy gave it a careless look and stuffed it into his overalls. Five dollars is not much in his life I thought to myself.

I watched the powerful motor speed away and remarked to the boy, "That's some car, isn't it?"

"She's a pretty classy bus all right," was his rejoinder.

I remarked to the boy that tips grew to quite a size in this warm climate.

"Yas," he said as he picked up his tools, "we get lots of big tips." He wiped the sweat from his forehead on his black sleeve. "You know, mister, there's an ole savin' — 'Many an honest heart beats under a ragged coat,' but it looks to me more like it's never an honest heart ticks under a swell suit of clothes!"

The lad has had some experience besides automobile repairing, said I to myself.

"What do you mean?" I asked him.

"Well there's a lot of funny things goes on these days," he drawled. "It sure seems the crookeder you are, the more jack you gets!"

I took a long chance: "You mean perhaps such crookedness as the robbing of the Bockermans?" I counted on his having read the report in the paper.

"Yes," he laughed in a superior, sarcastic way. "But they'll be safe from the police, that's one thing. Believe me, if I was ever on the force I'd know where to catch them high-flyin' purse snatchers or any other of that gang of crooks. Believe me, I ain't worked in St. Augustine for nothin'."

I fell into a long conversation with him. He confided to me that he knew the haunts of many of the members of the bunco ring. He told me, among other things, that lots of them stopped at the St. Augustine garage for gas, oil and air.

I asked him how he knew these patrons were outlaws and he said because their tires were punctured with bullets instead of glass and nails.

He explained the garage was located on the west side of the river close to a little bridge which all motorists must cross to reach the country club that nestled cautiously among a cloistered forest of tropical growth, a short distance from the bridge and just off the main highway.

Every car making this secluded spot passed over the bridge, he said. He also had been told that the virtuous looking club house was headquarters for a gang of internationally known confidence men and wire tappers. He added that many persons were supposed to have gone across the bridge and never returned.

Evidently then this was a place worth watching. I got from him full directions as how best to get there, though I do not suppose he thought I was any more than idly curious.

I decided it might pay me to station myself in some vantage point and spend a night or two watching the various bunco men who steered their expensive four wheeled get-aways up to the exclusive headquarters.

Acting on the tip I went to St. Augustine the next day. I soon located the garage. The bridge was close by and the general topography exactly as he had described it. Directly opposite the garage and jutting the roadway was a dilapidated, weather-beaten, corrugated iron, cold-drink stand. The colorful posters of cooling liquids clung in torn ribbons to its rusted sides. It was shedlike and tottering with age. It looked as if the slightest breath of wind would send it to the ground. Its fluted canopy was still intact in places, and would conceal me within the deep shadows it cast behind the wobbly counter.

Back there in the darkness I could watch the midnight revue in the spotlight of the street lamp that sputtered in the heavy moist air. Here I could watch with safety from inquiring eyes.

All through the night I waited. Wrapped in the cloak of darkness, I watched. An endless procession of cars passed over the little bridge and up under the shelter of the trees that nodded slightly in the gentle warm breeze...nodded like one who is very wise to what is going on.

One after another, they swept past the little stand that had cooled many a parched throat. Cars of all sizes, colors, makes, and occupants...men and women, young men, middle-aged men and men upon whom Father Time was resting a heavy hand. In the searching rays of the arc light the faces of the women came into momentary relief...young women, middle-aged women and women upon whom Father Time was resting his other hand. Most of the faces were painted. But paint will not cover the spirit within.

Some of the faces were drawn and grey looking, but cunning and shrewd like the silver fox, the trappers' prize. Others were just rouged blanks. The younger women had already begun to blot out the lines of dissipation with heavy powders and coats of red; smooth polished skins, like winter apples hardened in the frost. Beautiful evening wraps fell from white naked shoulders. Brazen bosoms lifted and fell. Flashing jewels gleamed and glinted from facile fingers that found a natural rest in other people's pockets.

I saw none that I knew. I waited in my billet until the first rosy show of dawn. Then the inner man spoke; the vision of a golden omelet, a stack of "wheats" with rich amber syrup spilling down rounded sides; crisp bacon or sizzling ham. Who could withstand that urge?

I crawled out of my lookout and, like my Airedale, "Ranger," put my nose to the wind and sped off in the direction of an inviting little cafe and an early morning breakfast.

Chapter Nine - Just My Gun and Me

I was the only diner in the cheerful little eating house. My eyes closed and I was indulging in a momentary drowse when the harsh, rude voice of a crabbing male broke in upon my reverie.

Said the voice: "What's the idea you can't get a hustle on when you see you've got customers?"

I looked in the direction of the tirade. It came from one of three men who were seating themselves at a table in line with the door. The largest of the three, a big burly, blonde brute, was doing the shouting.

The little waitress hurried nervously to their table and stood with order book and pencil poised for instructions.

While the men were going through the category of stewed fruits and breakfast dishes, I was busy connecting this disagreeable voice with something Mrs. Bockerman had told me. She had described the overbearing, ugly, blonde real estate agent.

He was, she said, more than six feet tall, blonde, with a Vandyke. His chin was massive, and he . had a way of sticking it out when he talked, like a plow that shoves aside all in its path. I took stock of the other two men.

Mrs. Bockerman had given me a description of one of the other two who had assisted in the bank. This was of the owner of the property. He was a rather slender fellow with an appearance of strength. His complexion was dark and though close shaven, his beard showed through the olive skin and his red cheeks gave his face a brilliant coloring.

Undoubtedly this description coincided with that of one of the other two eaters. The third man I could not match with anything I had seen or heard.

By the time I had catalogued the trio and made up my mind I was making no mistake in the two men, the waitress returned bearing a heavy tray of food. Had there remained the slightest doubt about the identity of the blonde it would have been dispelled.

When the girl set his eggs before him, he turned on her with a ferocious scowl and thundered, "What the hell ails you that you can't get it through your head that when I say scrambled eggs soft, I mean soft, not hard? My God! are you dead from the neck up?"

This, I thought was a perfect example of how the "agent" would act. "He is the kind of man who is naturally so ugly and overbearing that he would insult you for nothing when he'd get cash for courtesy!" were Mama Bockerman's words.

There was no longer need to wait. Action was what was needed.

I rose from the table, paid my check and passed quietly into the street.

It was still early morning, but luck was with me I thought.

It just happened that the Chief of Police was in his office. He was as fine, clean, stalwart and honorable appearing a fellow as I had ever set eyes on in a police department. But then up to this time I had not set eyes on many. Quickly I told him the story, from the robbing down to the scrambled eggs.

"Without the shadow of a doubt, Chief," I exclaimed, "I have two of the thieves spotted. They are this minute swallowing their breakfast down in the little coffee shop. If we hurry we can easily get them before they finish."

The Chief looked surprised, but swapped his hat for his official cap and said, "All right, Boss! We'll certainly grab them!"

He hesitated, adjusting some papers on his desk in an absent-minded manner. For an instant I felt he had forgotten I was there or that such things as crooks existed.

However, he came to, and said, "Well, let's be going."

I was thinking how kind fate had been and how happy the Bockermans would be to get the men. Perhaps there would be a chance of getting a portion of the money back.

As we left the office the Chief slipped an automatic into his pocket. I thought it odd he did not enlist the help of any of the patrolmen lounging around the office, but I supposed he hated to break in on their sleep so early in the morning. Most of them were sitting in chairs tipped back against the wall, eyes closed and lower jaws sagging. I flattered myself that he thought the two of us equal to the roundup.

We walked in silence toward the restaurant. My heart was thumping with excitement and the nearness of success. When we had almost reached the entrance, I turned and said:

"Chief, what do you want me to do? Or, if you don't want to tell me, shall I do just whatever I see is necessary?"

I rested my hand on my six shooter and waited for him to instruct me. He stopped short. Then he turned to me, I thought, to give me final instructions, but instead, he pulled out his watch and looked at it in the same way he had adjusted the papers on his desk. Then he seemed to force a surprised expression and exclaimed:

"Why! I almost forgot! I have a very important engagement down here on the corner. I have only seven minutes left. If I wait any longer I will be late. It's a shame but we'll have to get those fellows some other time!"

With this parting speech he stalked off toward the corner.

I walked the remaining few feet to the door of the coffee shop and peered through the plate glass window.

The three gentlemen of "big game" were just getting up from the table. They paid their checks, gathered a tooth-pick apiece, and walked out down the street in the same direction the Chief had taken.

I could not help wondering if they too had an engagement on the corner that they could not afford to miss.

A sudden fit of weariness seized me. Up to the present I had not felt the reaction of the night vigil in the drink stand. Now I seemed very tired. A knowledge of the world, the thieving, conniving, and dishonesty of it; my ignorance of the administration of law and order, began slowly to break through my preconceived ideals.

The shrines of truth, loyalty and honor began to sway in my mind. Would they be set firm again or would they topple over and crash about my feet?

I tried to feel that this was just an unfortunate experience, quite out of the ordinary. Still there was that toad in the Sheriff's office at St. Petersburg! But then these were only instances...I must be wrong, it could not be the usual thing.

I thought about my own affairs for a while. It would be a good plan to see Sheriff Boyce while here, and learn if he had any report of activities on the part of Furey or Spencer. He might have some news of them.

I went to his office. He lived in the prison grounds some distance beyond the historic gates of St. Augustine and seldom put in an appearance until much later in the morning, so a deputy informed me. I waited. Finally he came in.

I went to the bat with him and told him the story of my near capture of the Bockerman holdups. I made no mention of the pressing engagement of the Police Chief, not wanting to start any trouble.

Boyce appeared interested in the case and at once set into motion executive machinery to bring the outlaws within the grasp of the law.

I showed him my deputy sheriff's credentials from Hale County, Texas, and papers for J. B. Stetson, alias Joe Furey, W. B. Spencer and Reno Hamlin. I felt I could confide in Boyce. He seemed a sincere, trustworthy man.

He willingly wrote on the back of my warrants the authority for me to execute them in his county. This was a great help as it gave me as much power as if I were an officer of the State of Florida.

After leaving the Sheriff's office I walked down to the railroad station to see who was getting into town.

Crowds drew me like steel to a magnet. In them, I might see my men.

At the station I walked up and down, mixing freely with the crush of people. All at once I sighted, some distance down the long, broad walk, the dark slender man who was the "property owner" in the deal, and who not two hours ago had breakfasted so securely under the official eye of the Chief of Police. The fellow was standing near the revolving gates through which arriving passengers gained the street.

I went up to a patrolman and engaged him in conversation. Meanwhile I kept my eyes on the figure by the gates.

The officer said his name was Ward. (Would I never get rid of the Ward family, I thought to myself!) Officer Ward said he was one of the town's "old timers." He was candidate for Sheriff, running against Sheriff Boyce, the signer of my warrants.

This news gave me a degree of confidence. What better opportunity would a candidate for public office want than to have the honor of capturing one of the Bockerman robbers?

Surely, this was a gift from the gods. If the Lord had served Mr. Ward to me on a silver platter, I could not have been more grateful. This was a chance to prove Ward's trust and worth as a public servant. "The right man for the right office" would be his rightful slogan.

I hastily sketched the morning episode, again omitting the Chief's name.

"Now!" I exclaimed. "What would you do if you saw one of those buncos?"

He got quite excited and started up from the running board of an automobile parked along the curb.

"Say!" he cried, with a tone of conviction. "Say, if I ever got my eagle eye on one of those birds, believe me, he'd never get away!"

"Well," said I, "it won't take you long to get your eagle eye on one of them!"

"Well I'll be damned!" he ejaculated. "What do you mean?"

"I mean that one of them is standing just over yonder behind that electric light pole beside the exit gate right now! This minute!" I whispered, pointing to the leaning figure. "Now if you follow your eagle eye we'll have him in another second!"

We walked toward the man. As we got almost to him, Ward stopped short. He leaned his big body to one side and peered at the form of the miscreant. He trained his eagle eye on him. Then he turned to me and said in a low tone:

"I'll never forget that guy as long as I live. I'd know him anywhere on earth. But I think we'd better lay low and get him sometime when his whole gang is together. That's the best way!"

With this parting speech he also turned and strode away, to duty or some "important engagement."

In a way I regretted the loss of time from my own affairs. Failure to get the men, when I had them all but in jail, discouraged me.

I began to see how things were run in St. Augustine. The sooner I got out of this part of the State, the better luck I should have, I thought.

My two experiences made me sure, that had I caught both Furey and Spencer, I could not have counted on anyone but Sheriff Boyce, and sometimes an organization is too strong for one man on the square.

Having a naturally hopeful disposition my gloom did not stick long, and I determined to look upon these two episodes as mere accidents.

How far I was from graduation in the school of experience, I little knew. At least I was beginning to see who could be depended on and who could not!

There seemed to be just two of us, myself and my gun. One thing I knew, when it was on my hip, my gun was on my side!

Chapter Ten - Almost a Celery Grower

The next day while searching the morning paper for possible clues or reports of arrested fancy-financiers, I came upon an article which briefly stated that three confidence men had been arrested in Tampa. Three of them!

It might be my own trio, Furey, Spencer and Hamlin!

One lead being as good as another, I left for Tampa.

When I got there I lost no time heading for the police department. I inquired if the three bunco men who had been arrested the day before were still there and what were their names and could I see them.

I got a cold reply that informed me very distinctly they were "Not there!"

They had furnished bond and were out!

I asked if their pictures had been taken and was told just as coldly that they had not! It certainly was a refrigerative atmosphere.

I tried to wring some other information from the dry-cell in the brass buttons, but he evidently had a short circuit for speech came hard with him. Sometime later I found out that the three men were not mine. They had put up bonds, how good, I do not know. Anyway they never showed up again to claim them.

I had conceived a little scheme of my own which enabled me to start a conversation with any one, regarding the operations of the con-man. I carefully cut out and preserved every item published in the daily papers which bore on the subject of suspected or arrested confidence men. Then I would take a current issue of the daily paper and neatly paste my item over some unimportant news article in an inside page of the paper.

This method made it possible for me carelessly to open the newspaper at the proper moment and apparently read directly from the news columns this important happening in bunco circles.

A simple homemade recipe, but it worked like a "graveyard rabbit's foot" in a darky's pocket.

This little "home edition" of my editing I called my "Extra," and throughout the three years and ten months spent in trailing the fugitives I was seldom without a copy of it in my pocket. I must have used a gallon of paste and worn out several brushes, keeping my "edition" up to date. No matter how old the notice was, I pasted it in a current edition of the paper.

I usually read these accounts of criminal activity to police officers, as I knew they would have more general information than the average person regarding the movements of the crooks.

As usual I was again haunting the train tracks.

At the entrance to the waiting room I braced an important looking blue coat. Perhaps it would be possible to get some information out of him regarding the three who had put up bonds and left for parts unknown.

Once at a vaudeville show I heard a comedian say: "All the world loves a hick!"

As the police apparently owned a great portion of the globe, I thought perhaps I would get on better with them if I appeared a little "hickier" than I really was.

I took out my "extra" and went toward this member of the fraternity. I grinned a grin as wide as the prairie and looked up in his face with an "Oh, Sir-could-you-please-tell-me" expression. I said in a high cracked voice as nearly like the comedian's as I could command:

"Can you please tell me what is meant by this here b-u-n-c-o men, and this here c-o-n man?"

I spelled the words out slowly, looking into the depths of the paper.

"I see as how some of them was arrested here. Three of them! I seen it in this mornin's paper."

I rattled the edition to confirm my statement.

He looked at me with surprise and struck the tone some people take when explaining something to the childish mind:

"Why don't you know what that means?"

"No," said I, round-eyed with curiosity. "No, I don't. I thought mebbe as how you'd learn me?"

This brought results.

He told me of the different units of swindlers in this country. How they had "done" many men of shrewd business ability. Their victims included bankers, merchants, doctors and lawyers and others of high financial standing, not omitting ministers of the gospel. The game they played was no childish sport, he said.

While he was dramatically impregnating my absorbent mind with these thrilling details of daring operation of the "b-u-n-c-o man," he was joined by two other uniformed brothers of the law. Not wanting to stop his voluminous flow of information lest I miss some definite tip on my gang, I at once included the newcomers in the family party and exclaimed:

"Howdy, officers! Cap, here has jest been a tellin' me about these here c-o-n men and their mates the b-u-n-c-o kids. By Heck!" I cackled in such a way my own rooster wouldn't have owned me, and jabbed the inside page with my finger.

"I never heered the like of it. Gol dern their hides, if they ain't got more nerve'n a pack of coyotes! I never heered none of 'em howl!"

My crass ignorance evidently stamped me as a character of no importance, for they ignored me and fell to talking among themselves.

I still clung to the outside of the group. I gazed up at them in apparent admiration and respectful awe for their super-intellect.

"Say, fellows," remarked Cap, like one who casually imparts a startling piece of news with bored calm. "I just got a tip, personally, that one of the links in the big con-chain has opened headquarters in the Montezuma Hotel, in Sanford."

The others smirked knowingly. They separated, going different ways and left me standing there.

The train thundered in. I watched the passengers alight, and meet the loved ones who waited to greet them. I thought what a happy reception I could give Furey or Spencer had I the opportunity.

That night I followed the proverbial arrow to Sanford. All I prayed was that the "Cap" had not given me a fake lead.

However they all had seemed so totally unaware of my existence, I felt it was probably a real inside tip.

I leaned back against the Pullman seat. The country swung past me in straight rows of cultivation. Orchards and truck farms passed before me in review like the even ranks of a marching regiment.

I have never seen such a great spread of vegetables and fruit as lay across the rolling hills. It was the finest that nature's banquet table afforded. The dark pungent soil in rich furrows rose between each length of vegetation.

It was a sight to make you think. A veritable paradise!

As we drew near Sanford I noticed the celery. The landscape was a picture in tender green and white rooted into black earth. Such celery!

It was a garden of Eden. I had heard that the Sanford celery farms eclipsed any on earth. I believed it.

And what better mission for me than the pretended purchase of a celery farm?

From a man seated across the aisle, I learned the name of the owner of the last farm we passed before getting into Sanford.

He believed the price of the property was forty thousand dollars.

Dusk was falling as I alighted from the train.

I walked leisurely in the direction of the celery field. The air was a little sharp and moist. Deliberately I let my good leather shoes sink deeply into the oozy black earth. I hated to do this and bade a fond farewell to their faithful soles. Down, down, down they sank. The cool wetness of the mud sucked in around my ankles and crept stealthily up, up, up!

Ugh! I shuddered, and thought of the pull of quicksand. Higher and higher up, until my trouser legs joined hands (or cuffs) with the landscape.

So firmly was I rooted into the general scheme of nature that I expected any moment to blossom or be pulled up with other bunches and served for dinner.

I pulled out one foot after the other and with difficulty trekked my way to the hotel, walking on two big balls of mud. Certainly I was taking with me as perfect evidence of an intended investment as Florida mud would ever provide.

I registered at the Montezuma Hotel under an assumed name. I was assigned to a good room on the second floor in a faraway corner of the long, low, rambling structure.

After washing my hands and promising my shoes a later restoration I descended into the lobby. It was a long room and had a fire place at each end. Bright fires burned on both hearths. The flames leapt and licked with a great cracking and snapping, the oak logs piled high in the openings.

It was a cheerful sight. At one end of the lobby was the office and at the other end, the guests usually congregated.

I seated myself close to the fire, my back slightly to the room, but not enough to cut off my view of those who passed up or down stairs. I reached and tore off several flat splinters from the wood heaped beside the fire place.

I crossed one leg over the other and began elaborately and thoroughly to peel off the half dried mud from my ankles and trouser legs, meanwhile taking note of all who came within my vision.

Several impressive male guests paced back and forth the length of the lobby; a favorite posture being head and shoulders humped forward at a belligerent angle; arms clasped behind backs while darting furtive glances that swept the room and occupants in one look.

Sitting across from me on the opposite side of the cheering blaze was an elderly couple. They watched my operations with interest and curiosity.

"You must have taken a bad tumble," ventured the bid lady.

I explained that I had not exactly taken a tumble in the mud, then raising my voice so anyone passing could easily catch my every word, I continued to inform them that I was a stockman and farmer from Blackwell, Oklahoma.

I followed this announcement by broadcasting that I had come down to Sanford to look over some celery farms and intended to purchase one. I added that I didn't like to ruin good shoes, still it was necessary, when one expected to invest a large sum of money, to make personal investigations. Hence the terra firma!

I threw the last strip of evidence into the fire and indicated with my improvised scraper the general direction of the particular celery farm I favored.

We chatted about irrelevant things a little while, then I got up and went in to dinner.

When I returned I again directed my remarks about my intended purchase of the celery farm to the same old couple, but in a tone loud enough to register in the acute ears of the gentlemen making mileage on the lobby floor as they puffed fragrant after-dinner cigars.

There was little I didn't expound regarding the buying, raising and selling of the little crisp white stalks.

I retired early. As I went up stairs I had the satisfaction of seeing several pairs of eyes follow my ascent. I felt pretty certain in the morning I would have some mighty interesting "get-rich-quick" proposition put to me.

As I fell asleep I laughed at some of the signs I had seen in the shop windows on my way to the celery beds. They read "Beware of Confidence Men!" Well, I thought there was little danger of encountering any of them in the shops tonight, as they were all downstairs in the lobby outlining tomorrow's campaign for the "sucker" upstairs.

Chapter Eleven - Spinning another Web

My surmise was correct. The next morning when I went down to breakfast I was approached in the lobby by a sleek, prosperous appearing man. He was of medium height, blonde and had "gander" eyes. He was quick-mannered and dapper.

"Fine morning!" said he.

"Fine indeed!" I replied.

"Little bit cool, but brisk weather always invigorates I think," he continued approvingly.

"Yes it's cool, and I dare say it'll be cooler before it gets warm again!"

"Yes, yes, no doubt," he said, throwing his cigarette into the open fire.

"I believe I heard you mention a celery farm. I happened to be passing through the lobby last evening, and I thought I understood you to say you intended purchasing one. My name is Johnson." He offered me a well manicured, smooth, taper-fingered hand.

"My name's Parkinson. I'm from Blackwell, Oklahoma. Glad to meet you, Mr. Johnson!" I said, wringing his hand and wishing it were his neck.

"Oh, yes," I continued casually, "I believe I did tell that old gentleman and his wife about the celery farm I hope to purchase. I went out to look at one last night and got mud up to my ears, almost. It's dirty work, this personal inspection, but a man cannot afford to sink forty or fifty thousand dollars into the mud, unless he's sure it's rich mud, can he?" I smiled disarmingly.

To hear me mention a mere fifty thousand dollars, one would have thought I might expect to use the mud for mud pies.

"Do you expect to sink that amount in a celery farm?" he asked in well feigned amazement.

"Oh!" said I apologetically, "it's not a great deal of money to be sure, but still it's enough to buy a nice little garden and more than I want to lose!"

"Of course — of course. Naturally you would not want to lose it. That is just the point. I think I can be of help to you, Mr. — Mr. —."

"Parkinson!" I supplied.

"Mr. Parkinson, I beg your pardon. I am not quick to remember names, but faces! I never miss those."

I felt like telling him I didn't either; that was why I was looking at him so hard.

"Can't we find a comfortable seat?" he asked, looking for a chair. He found one and dragged it up beside another, well within the sunny window which looked out on the not far distant celery beds.

We talked for sometime. He told me that he hated to see anyone put a lot of money in celery unless he was an experienced celery raiser. He informed me the overhead expense would eat up all the profits and I would find only too late that I had made a poor investment. Besides after I had had the place awhile I would not be able to sell to an advantage, as the farm would exhibit proof of my inability as an agriculturist and therefore discourage a purchaser. He really knew more about what I was going to do with the farm than I did.

He was a good, convincing talker and had I been in earnest about buying the property I feel sure he would have talked me out of it. However I did not let him think that what he said against it was making the least difference to me.

I invited him to go with me to inspect some other farm property which I planned to look over in the afternoon. He declined, saying that he thought he would take in the races at Daytona Beach.

"That's some fine country for you!" he exclaimed. "If I were going to invest in farm lands, I would certainly consider Daytona, or property near there. Really, Parkinson," laying an advisory hand on my arm, "you ought to have a look at it before deciding definitely on this acreage out there."

He indicated with a deprecating jerk of his head, the adjacent property.

"There are going to be some automobile races this afternoon down at the Beach, and I would like to have you go along as my guest. We could spend a pleasant day and it would give you an opportunity to give that location the 'once over.' How does that strike you?"

I thought he was a trifle too eager. "It's very kind of you," I said, but I still held out for Sanford celery.

"Well," he compromised, "tell you what let's do. I'll go with you to look at the new prospect if you'll go this morning, then this afternoon you come to the races with me, as I said before, as my guest! It will not take long to get to Daytona Beach and we'll have a good time. That's fair, isn't it?"

He certainly was heavy on the "guest." I considered. There was no question but that Johnson was a plant. I knew that the "big link" in the confidence chain was quartered in this hotel. The other slickers, who were pacing up and down the lobby the evening before were now nowhere to be seen. They were under cover until the right time.

Johnson had some game he wanted to pull off in Daytona Beach. If I went with him I might get out alive. If I did escape from his trap, I might gain some knowledge of the whereabouts of Furey and Spencer. They might even be there! It was a chance.

"Yes, that sounds fair," I replied, "and I'll accept on your very kind terms."

I was determined that he shouldn't get the better of me with his politeness. It always amused me to note how well these crooks played their roles. No character actors surpass them.

Johnson began to fit into the groove. He had a certain patronizing manner which they all have.

"Fine!" he exclaimed and rose from his chair, "Then that's settled."

We went to another celery estate and looked it over. On this occasion I thought it not necessary to get my feet so muddy.

When we returned I appeared favorably impressed with the land and again Johnson launched into a "knocking" campaign. As soon as we entered the hotel he got in a great hurry and began to fire directions to the hotel clerk about sending the bell boy up for his luggage and getting his bill made out.

"Are you going to stay down at the Beach?" I asked.

"Yes I may for a day or two," he replied. Then as if it were an afterthought, he suggested I take my bag along as we might want to remain over night.

"Not want to," I thought, "probably have to!"

I did not act very enthusiastic over the prospect of the trip, as I did not want to spoil matters.

He seemed to sense my indifference and tried to hustle me along before I changed my mind. All of this play on his part indicated to me that there was a trap ahead ready for me to step into.

Before leaving I examined my guns and put two in my bag and two on myself.

We got started about three in the afternoon.

"Won't we be pretty late for the races?" I asked.

"Well, I am afraid we will," he said regretfully. "But there is a County Fair going on this week so we can make the races tomorrow."

Ah! a county fair, I mused. The best stamping ground in the world for the light-fingered gentry.

My reverie was interrupted by Johnson springing to his feet. He bounded across the aisle and looked out of the car window in the opposite seat. He motioned me to follow him.

I arose. From his excitement I thought perhaps an alligator was swallowing the Florida coast.

But it was something far more important — at least to Johnson!

"Did you see that man passing in his automobile?" he cried, forcing me in front of him and nearly shoving my face through the window. "Say, I would give one thousand dollars to see that man for ten minutes. He is a man I met in Judge Hughes' office in New York City. Did you get a look at him?"

"I saw him, but he looked about the same as many other men. Was he peculiarly marked?" I inquired with inward fun.

I could not resist the temptation to kid him a little, he was taking himself so seriously.

"Why, he is known as the mysterious man who took one hundred and twenty-five thousand dollars out of the Stock Exchange in one day. He is a marvel of finance; a tower of intellect when it comes to stock manipulations."

Stocks! Here we met again! The same old badger game, played in the same old way, by the same old crowd.

I did not want to disappoint Johnson, especially after all his trouble bringing me down to the dragon's den for the others to eat up. So, like the good little sucker I seemed, I piped up:

"I wish we could see that fellow. Maybe he could make us both some money."

"I'm afraid we cannot," he replied in just the correct tone of regret. "He is a power in the world of wealth and we are small fry."

However, I was not at all convinced that the "mighty one" would not sooner or later "accidentally" run into us. The handwriting was on the wall.

We got into Daytona at 5:30 that afternoon. I suggested we walk to the hotel. This met with Johnson's approval. He hurried on ahead.

When he was some hundred feet in advance of me I stopped to speak to a woman standing on the front porch of her little cottage. There was a sign in the window which advertised a room to rent. I quickly engaged a room from her and whistled to Johnson. I suppose he and his kind are whistle trained. Anyway, he turned like a hawk in the road and came swiftly back to me.

"What's the idea of that whistle?" he exclaimed nervously.

"Did it frighten you?" I asked in a tranquil tone. "I just wanted to tell you my rheumatism is so bad I can't walk any further. I have engaged a room here until tomorrow." I was a bit lame as he must have noticed, for he said he guessed my damp mud bath last night hadn't helped me any from the way I limped.

I told him I was tired and would go to bed, then see him at eight o'clock in the morning. This suited him. We said good night and I went into my room.

Chapter Twelve - Riding Into New Perils

The next morning at seven I arose. As I closed my window and raised the shade to let in the bright sun, I gave the little rustic bench a quick look.

Johnson was there! Whether he had remained on duty all night, I do not know. Perhaps he worked in "shifts" with some of his confederates.

At eight o'clock, as chipper as a bird he rang the doorbell of my domicile and inquired of the landlady for Mr. Parkinson.

I was ready to start the day and met him on the front porch. We breakfasted together. I asked him if he had had a good night.

He replied, "Very satisfactory indeed!"

"That is good," I responded, thinking that as I had not escaped him, he probably considered it more than satisfactory.

After breakfast my companion suggested we take a walk along the beach. We started out. Neither of us seemed inclined for conversation.

In the distance I noticed a man coming toward us. As he neared us I saw that he was absorbed in some yellow papers he held in his hands; he looked neither to the right nor to the left. As he stopped alongside of me, I saw the yellow sheets were telegrams. His eyes were riveted on their contents.

He brushed against us, though there was plenty of room on the beach, but did not seem aware of our existence, so deeply engrossed did he appear in his telegraphic communications.

I turned a little as he passed so I could watch him and yet do so unobserved by Johnson, then commented on the fine beach, the freshly painted craft, the bright new flags and the beauty of the entire scene.

"I told you you'd like it down here," Johnson exclaimed, slowing up his gait.

The stranger stopped a little distance beyond us and sat down on a fallen log. He yawned and lazily stretched his long form. He was watching us. Almost at once he got up and beginning again to peruse the messages, he started back toward us. As he came close, Johnson for the first time apparently, noticed him and whispering under his breath to me said:

"By the way, what do you know about that? He is my friend, the 'mysterious man.' The one I met in Judge Hughes' office in New York and who shot past the train in the automobile. I think I'll speak to him and see if he remembers me."

"By all means, do!" I urged.

Just as he came opposite Johnson, my escort said, "Hello! Atlantic City!"

The mysterious one evidently did not hear or appeared not to, for he kept on walking, though more slowly.

"Hello, Atlantic City!" repeated Johnson. This time with more assurance.

"Did you speak to me, sir?" asked the stranger, looking up from his work.

"I did, sir!" declared Johnson.

"Well, why address me as Atlantic City, please?" retorted the unknown one in an indignant manner.

"Why, many people call a man by the name of the town with which they associate him, or where they have met him. I assure you I meant no offense. If I have taken too great a liberty I humbly beg your pardon."

More of this polite stuff, I thought.

Johnson's explanation seemed to satisfy the man, for he smiled almost humanly and said he believed he DID recall meeting Johnson in Hughes' office. "Was it not Hughes' office?" he faltered questioningly.

"It was," said Johnson, "but in Atlantic City, first."

Then in a burst of inspiration it seemed all to come back to the man of the telegrams and he and Johnson knew each other better than brothers in no time.

The stranger gave me an apprehensive look and said in a low tone, though one I could not help hearing, "Who is your friend?"

Johnson introduced me, calling him "Steel." He said I was an acquaintance of his and he would vouch for me.

Steel relaxed his tense look and apologetically explained to me that he hoped I was not insulted, but he was always a little skeptical of strangers. He asserted that so many times his best deals had been spoiled by newspaper reporters.

"They are so damned clever you know about getting things out of you that you don't suspect you are giving away, that I have to be very cautious with whom I talk. We manipulators, you understand, must protect the secrets of our business. Publicity has ruined many a good man!"

I wanted to say, "You bet it has! Look where Ward and Gerber are!" but I put the desire behind me.

Steel seemed more interested in his telegrams than in either of us. He kept muttering snatches of sentences regarding how busy he was; what a heavy day he had ahead of him; what terrific responsibilities he labored under and thrusting the sheaf of telegrams in our faces, declared loudly that it was a shame to work a man as he was being worked!

"Just imagine, I have to carry out all of these wired instructions! It's work enough for six men!"

Johnson asked him if he were still in the same business.

He said he was.

Then in a laughing way Johnson asked him if he would mind placing twenty dollars for him, saying he wanted to buy his friend a good dinner.

Steel looked amused, but said he would be very glad to accommodate him.

Johnson pulled a roll of bills out of his pocket. He peeled off a few tens, then took a twenty and handed it to Steel, saying in a jocular manner, "Don't lose it for me, now!"

Steel looked at him archly, accepted the bill and strode hurriedly in the direction of the town. It was not more than a few blocks.

While he was gone Johnson and I took his seat on the log, and I was let into some of the wonders of the stock game.

Within a half hour, Steel came back. He handed Johnson eighty dollars as if it were a mere penny.

Johnson offered me half. I refused. But he insisted, so in order not to block whatever their game was, I accepted it.

Johnson then handed his forty dollars back to Steel begging him to reinvest it for him. He stated to me that he believed he would stick around Steel for a few days and let him make some investments for him. Steel smiled at the remark made to me and intended for him.

"I do not mind taking the money away from the 'bookies' for my friends — and their friends," he bowed significantly to me, "only I am too busy to keep running into town to place the bets and running back here with the profits to you two boys!" He smirked patronizingly, and got out his wires as if it were his cue to enter the stage.

"Now the best thing for you both to do if you want to make a little wad, is to come with me up to the club!"

The club! Ah, now the plot thickened!

"We have rented the country club up on the hill and use it as an exchange. We have a splendid equipment. Come up there with me and we'll do the work from there. The betting today is practically all on the horse races in Cuba."

"That sounds good and it's mighty kind of you, Steel!" agreed Johnson, getting up from the log and dusting his clothes off.

Steel was getting co-operation, if nothing else.

"What do you say, Parkinson?"

"Oh, it sounds fine to me!" I echoed. "Only I haven't a great many thousands on me. Besides," I commented thoughtfully, "I must be careful not to let the horses run away with my celery farm!"

A fraternal look shot from one to the other of the men.

"No danger of that," threw in Steel, and fishing from his leather wallet a newspaper clipping he handed it to me, telling me to read it if I thought there was any danger of his not knowing his business.

As we walked back to town to get an automobile, I read the item. It told how he had broken a bucket-shop, in one day taking out over one hundred and twenty-five thousand dollars. At the top of the story was a photograph of Steel. It certainly looked like him from the eyes down. The top of the head was torn off. This Steel explained he had done in order that the ever present newspaper reporters couldn't identify him.

He dreaded publicity!

The drive from a scenic standpoint was beautiful. The air was warmer than in Sanford and the morning still early enough to have that sweet smell. Some way or other I could not relax and let my spirit rise to the beauty and quiet of the forest on each side. My mood was as heavy as the dense undergrowth which screened the intimacies of the jungles. The stillness of nature became oppressive. The even purr of the motor sounded like the thunder of great machines. Every sound was magnified in the stillness of nature.

Although close to the Gulf waters, which send inland a warm gentle breeze to stir the stately palmettos and delicate ferns, not a leaf moved. Not a blade of grass swayed. A petrified forest could not have been more silent. I felt like letting out a long "Hallo" just to see if I could get an echo. Sweet pungent odors of swampy growth carried to my nostrils. I thought how peaceful all the palmy glade appeared; to the eye, beautiful, to the senses, dangerous! Beneath mossy carpets and entwining creepers poisonous fangs awaited. Death, I knew lurked in the stagnant pools below the surface of this serenity.

The car was making about twenty-five miles an hour.

I had no idea how far the country club was. Steel nodded his head in the direction of a hill back from the beach. I took it that it was not a great distance.

Both men were silent. Not one of us spoke. I stirred uneasily in my seat.

This was the first time I had had a chance to consider just what might happen to me. It seemed we were speeding from safety into certain danger. The silence was worse than the spoken lies of the men.

Suspense! There is nothing so horrible. I had rather be in the middle of a good active gun fight than sit and wait for it to begin. My breath seemed to grow thick in my mouth and came with difficulty, as if something closed round my heart with a squeezing pressure. In all my life I have never had this sensation before or since. The road spun from under us like a narrow thread. As I looked down the slope we were climbing, I thought of my mother's work-basket.

It is odd that in great moments the most trivial and unremembered things flash into our minds. Why my mother's work-basket came to me I do not know, but I recalled how, when I was little and worrisome, she used to place in my hand the end of a tangled mass of threads, telling me I must follow the slender lead through all its twists and turns, undoing the knots one by one until I came to the other end.

This memory faded into what lay directly ahead of me; the heights in the distance; the remaining bits of road to be covered, brief stretches of which flashed into view at one turn and disappeared into the unknown at the next.

The now sighted club house! Its tall chimneys like feudal towers! The steep cliffs, dropping straight into the churning sea! All these must be followed; the twists and turns and knots undone, one by one.

What fate I was approaching I did not know. That I was rapidly driving into a death trap, was a certainty.

Having lived close to nature I noticed many things on the way. The road had been little traveled. The grass in the path of the wheels stood erect much of the way.

A rut in the road suddenly threw me against my companions. For the instant we rocked against one another.

I seized this opportunity to clutch my hosts about the waist. I bounced like a rubber ball from one side of the seat to the other. I felt carefully to see how many guns were planted on my neighbors' hips.

My hands told me there were none.

We all laughed with a good imitation of genuine fun and bromidic remarks were made about every "bump" being a "boost."

After what seemed a thousand years but in reality was not more than a half hour, we came to the bottom of the last hill. The club house was now easily seen. Slowly we made the steep grade.

I glanced behind me down into the little town, now a speck in the distance. I thought perhaps I was giving my eyes their last look.

A jumble of things mixed in my mind. Every move I made I felt might be the last of that particular type I would ever make.

An atmosphere of impending disaster wrapped me as in a cloak.

Chapter Thirteen - Mountains of Money

"We're here!" exclaimed Steel.

He and Johnson each opened a side door. We all stepped into the road. They banged the doors shut.

I jumped as if a cannon had gone off. My nerves certainly were on edge. The club was at the summit of a steep hill. Not exactly a mountain but quite an elevation, the top was not spacious but dropped away to the base with unexpected suddenness. North, south, east and west, spread before the eye. It was a sight to arouse if not dazzle the imagination...the sea on one side and valleys on the others.

The country club was not a large structure but a rambling one-story building such as might house a good-sized family of comfortable means. It was anchored on the edge of the cliffs. Their smooth sides shot straight down into a bed of jagged rocks whose pointed reefs rose from a churning sea like huge, sharp teeth in a frothing mouth, upturned to catch its prey. Far out the water was a reflected sapphire; inland it was serpent green. Its breaking waves crashed against the cliffs with the roar of battle. The fury would die away, and then it seemed the ocean took another deep breath and its towering swells beat themselves against the coast.

This booming suited my mood. The same mighty struggle went on within me. I was the cliff, my two companions the sea. Would they succeed in breaking over me and washing away my foundation as the water had the land from the reefs, or, when the tide turned and the coming storm spent, would the angry waves lap peacefully about my base? All of this I thought as I stood there on top of the world.

A boat landing ran some distance out from the shore. Fastened to this was a little white motor boat which pulled and tugged at its mooring like some animal struggling for freedom from an ugly master.

Perhaps I was to pay a high price for my desire to know if Furey or Spencer were connected with this outfit or if by some twist of fate they were in the club house. I had chosen to run the risk for even a clue. There was nothing for me to do but gird myself with caution, advance and take the enemy if there.

"Take the car back to town!" This remark of Steel's put a stop to my wool gathering.

I turned and saw that he had spoken to the chauffeur.

"Get gas and oil. We won't want it again for four or five hours. Possibly not until late afternoon. I'll let you know when to come back," he added.

This struck me as peculiar. I saw no reason why Johnson and I should be forced to remain here until Steel wished to return to town. With the driver gone, and the car gone, all means of rapid escape would be cut off. Simultaneously the chauffeur and I looked at the oil gauge. It was nearly full!

The negro started to oppose the unnecessary refilling when Steel glowered at him, shouting:

"I said get oil and gas!"

The boy recoiled and blubbered, "Yas, boss! Ah gets yoh, Ah gets yoh!"

I got him too, but I didn't tell him so — not then. I stepped close to the trembling darkey and increased his comfort by telling him in a whisper that he had brought me here and he was to wait and take me back.

I said: "If you stir from this car as far as that nearest tree, I'll blow a hole through you!"

Then I remarked in a loud casual tone, "Your carburetor is leaking, better fix it!"

The kid got me, and began to tinker with the mechanism of the car, rolling his eyes toward heaven and jabbering, "Dat carburetor sure am on de bum, boss, it sure am!"

I joined the two men who had started up the front steps. Together we three entered the house.

There was no hall. The door from the porch opened directly into what was intended for a big living room. It must have been thirty by forty feet. The ceilings were high raftered affairs and the general interior finish rustic. The plate glass windows were so large on the sea side of the room it seemed the entire side wall had been left out. The view was gorgeous.

Opposite the front door and against the back wall of the room was a table at which two men were seated. One on each side. At first I thought my eyes were deceiving me. I felt them grow big in their sockets. I unconsciously rubbed the back of my hand across them, and blinked as if to clear them of cobwebs. I went nearer the table.

No, it was not an hallucination!

There in plain sight piled high on the table, was a mountain of money! It was heaped up as if some one had carelessly dumped a clothes basket of bills on the table and gathered up those that fell from it and flung them back on top of the mound. It staggered me. The greenbacks were stacked according to denomination and banded with regulation bank markers.

But the money was not guarding itself. Each of the men seated at the table held a carbine rifle across his knees. Buckled to the belt of each was a scabbard into which was meaningly tucked a six shooter.

To the left of the money table against the side wall opposite the windows, was a large blackboard checked off in small squares. Before this bulletin board stood a perspiring youth in his shirtsleeves: hair rumpled and tie awry, after the manner of most approved stock markers. He was frantically making little chalk notations in the lined off spaces. He did not turn or give us a glance.

In the center of the room was a long table with telegraphic equipment. The telegrapher was the usual type, quiet appearing and rather dark and pale. He ran true to form and wore the indigenous green eyeshade. He paid us no attention but kept his orbs riveted on his instruments and appeared to be conscientiously ticking a contact with Cuba. Click! Click! Click! Click! Click! went the little keys with that metallic tick which is Greek to most of us.

Shoved in front of the window against the casement was a long bench. This faced the bulletin board. Two prosperous looking men sat on it. They wore light weight overcoats over their business suits. There was nothing unusual about them except the expression on their faces. It was drawn and strained. Their eyes were glued to the board, the movements of the stock marker they followed as if their lives depended on them.

This was the scene that met my vision. You know how in a flash one may see much and think more.

All the hazards and potentialities festering in this room I sensed immediately.

My circular gaze came back to the money on the table. As if drawn by its magic I crossed to it. I was not at all sure it was not stage money. No one seemed to inhibit my inspection so I laid the backs of my hands on the table and shoved them under the mass of wealth. I brought them up through the packeted bills. As I did this the top one slipped off my palms and tumbled back on the pile of fortune.

I rubbed the edges of some of the one thousand dollar green leaves between thumb and finger. They were genuine! Some of the bills were dirty and ragged; others clean and crisp; the balance merely limp from occasional transfer.

My senses reeled with the sight of so much "root of all evil."

It magnified a million times the loss of my savings wrung from the earth by toil and sweat. Here before me was all and more than I had lost. Probably the combined misfortune of three or four of us "suckers" was represented.

Fate was rubbing it in! Where she left off, those steely mouthed carbines would begin.

Steel had come to my side. I asked him if he had ever seen so much money before in his life.

He laughed in a hollow way and replied that it was quite a tidy little sum, but that it was necessary to have a large amount on hand to carry on the day's business.

"We pay out this amount, and more on heavy days," he explained.

"About how much filthy lucre do you reckon is in this junk heap?"

"Well," puckering his sloping brow reflectively, "today's capital stock I should say is about one hundred and seventy-five thousand dollars!"

I caught my breath.

"You've got to spend money if you expect to make it," he vouchsafed casually and asked me to excuse him a moment as he wanted to look over the incoming wires.

I took this opportunity to examine the place a little more closely. Leaving the Midas Mine, I went over to the two men sitting on the bench. They were still anxiously watching the bookkeeper who kept jotting down small figures on the board. They looked just as wild-eyed as ever. When I was directly in front of them, I said:

"I have never seen so much money in my life, gentlemen."

They leaned around me to continue their optic riveting and ignored my remark.

However I thought I would make another attempt at conversation. I was letting their faces print themselves deep into my mental film and could hardly stand in front of them without some stall at speech.

"Just think of it, gentlemen, on that table is one hundred and seventy-five thousand dollars! Can you realize how much that is? What it would do; what it would buy?"

They turned their attention to me in unison. They relaxed their tense facial muscles and nodded with a wooden manner, then dropped back into their characters. A couple of marionette actors, I thought.

I moved a few feet to one side of them and looked out on the sea. I could hear the breakers pounding against the rock shore. Boom! Boom! Boom! Boom! they crashed.

I thought a cry for help from this pinnacle of the earth would be as a sigh in the roar of thunder.

A little to one side of the blackboard was a door slightly ajar. I sauntered over there and pushed it open a little further. Opposite the door was another large window which framed the valley below.

"What a wonderful view!" I exclaimed.

Johnson looked toward me. He was in executive session with Steel across the room.

"Yes, isn't it grand? Just look around and amuse yourself. It's a little early Mr. Steel says for things to start."

This speech struck me as about the most truthful one he had uttered. How long, how long, I thought, must I endure this suspense? When would the real game commence?

I drank in the beauty of the fertile valley and swiftly examined my guns to see that they were ready to talk. As I turned to come out of the room, I was facing the window looking out across the water.

Only a short distance from the boat landing was a little white speed boat racing for the shore. It was like the one already riding at the landing. I could hear the quick heartbeat of the motor. Its little white nose was lifted clear of the water and spat the spray aside as it slit the waves. There was a man in it.

I stood still an instant. The room was silent. Something charged the atmosphere with a stifling quiet.

The put! put! put! of the motor boat engine filled the room. Activity inside slowed down.

Johnson announced that he had looked over the horses and believed he would place a few bets.

"I would rather take my chances with a live animal than a bunch of green celery!" he chided.

Whether or not the "greens" were intended for me, I did not know but felt convinced before the day was far gone some of us would need flowers.

Evidently the six of us were alone in the house. The other rooms in the dwelling seemed to be permanently shut off and some of the doors boarded up. I figured perhaps these two or three rooms were all that the gang rented. Anyway, I could see no trace of Spencer or Furey, and decided to leave. Probably the attempt would open up the fireworks: for my part, the sooner the better.

From the remarks of Johnson based on those I had thrown out regarding my money, I was sure he and Steel thought I had a lot on me.

I crossed slowly toward the front door. When I got in line with it I saw that the chauffeur was sitting in the car, his black hand on the steering wheel.

Steel blocked my path half way to the door. Over his shoulder I saw a man running up the hill from the boat landing below. Some steps had been hacked into the steep cliffs. He bounded up these three at a time and made the turn on the top which headed him for the club house.

He was undoubtedly the man I had seen in the motor boat.

"We have an ideal location for work, haven't we?" Steel asked.

I answered that as far as I could see it suited his purposes perfectly.

In that minute of fill-in conversation, Steel and I knew that we were wise to each other. I could feel that he knew I knew he was ready to use desperate methods. Of course he knew the stranger was approaching; they had all known the meaning of that engine out on the sea.

At this moment the man entered. He looked swiftly from one to another in the room. Steel stepped a little away from me and the man instantly went close to him. He pressed a crumpled scrap of paper into Steel's hand. His fingers closed over it and dropped to his side.

I pretended not to observe the transfer. The bearer of the missive went over to Johnson. They spoke in low tones and walked together into the little side room.

Steel smoothed the paper out with the fingers of his hand in which he held the message. Guardedly, he glanced down at it. Evidently the writing was illegible for he raised his hand and pressed the wrinkles from the little sheet with the thumbs and forefingers of both hands. He attempted a casual perusal of the contents as if they could not be of much importance.

Suddenly his face changed. He clutched the paper in one hand again and tremblingly lowered it to his side. His face blanched and became death pallored.

It seemed as if a silent signal of distress went from one to another around the room. Steel's hand shook as if palsied. I had never noticed the great paw before, but now I saw it. The back of it was horrible to look upon. Heavy scarred seams of flesh marked it. On three of the fingers the hair grew the wrong way. It made me shiver. However he was doing enough of that for both of us. He trembled from head to foot.

His self-control was off duty, for when he tried to speak, the words stuck in his dry throat.

Whatever the information in the note was, it meant business, so the sooner I attempted to get away, the quicker I would know my fate.

Chapter Fourteen - A Scrap of Paper

I took another step toward the front door.

Steel, who was recovering his poise to some extent, deliberately kept in front of me, matching his backward steps to my forward ones.

Johnson called across the room to me to get in on the game and do a little betting on some of the fast horses.

From Steel's attitude and his measured distance from me I knew he was working to get me in the right position and then let me have it. I did not believe him armed. This somewhat relieved my mind.

As far as I knew not one of the men in this outfit knew my real identity. I had never seen or heard of any one of them. Evidently their game was to "roll" men for the money they had on them. They probably thought I had at least a substantial amount. I had intended they should.

Steel echoed Johnson's invitation for me to play the horses. As he repeated the request for me to gamble, he stepped slightly to one side of me and back a little. Keeping my eye on him, I asked of anyone who cared to answer:

"What day of the week is this?"

One of the wooden images sitting on the bench replied that it was Sunday.

"Sunday!" I exclaimed in a tone of regret. "Well, that's too bad. Gentlemen, when I was a young man I promised my mother that I would never bet a dollar on the Sabbath! I have always kept my promise. This lets me out. However, I'll see you all again!"

I evened my distance with Steel so that he was on a line with me, not in front nor behind, but exactly even at my side. He instantly edged toward my back.

This movement flashed a warning across my mind. A warning my wife had given me before I left to tackle the hunt was: "Don't let them get at your back, Frank!" she had said. "Don't, don't let them get at your back!"

This mental admonition was followed by another which darted into my mind. It was an old saying of my father's. "Be quick! Act, always act! my son, before the other fellow organizes!"

So I acted!

Suiting the action to the advice, I backed closer to the wall, as I did so turning slightly out from Steel. He edged around and tried to slide in behind me. As I cut him off I said:

"Well, I must be leaving!"

To indicate a fond farewell, I made a sweeping gesture of adieu with my left hand. My words and motion brought the room to tense silence. The clerk at the bulletin board turned toward me, chalk poised in mid-air. The two bench-warmers glued their "stock" expressions on me. The telegraph instrument stopped clicking.

As my hand dropped in leave-taking it was caught in the vice-like grip of Steel's powerful hand. As he bent me over with the strength of a lion I closed my right hand on my six shooter.

"You won't leave here until we get ready for you to go!" he cried and swung me down and in toward him. But instead of going to the floor I swung myself up on his brawny arm as if it were a gymnasium bar. Our bodies crashed together.

On the impact I struck him a wallop in his solar plexus with the barrel of my revolver.

"Stick up your hands! Hold 'em high!" I yelled.

The jab in his vitals sent him sick. He rolled his eyes and shoved his hands up above his head.

I reached for my other automatic with my free hand just as Johnson lunged at me with a rope, held taut from hand to hand on a level with my neck. The second gun caught him. His position was now squarely between me and the money guards. Steel was still reaching for the ceiling just to my left.

"Now you two young fellows just walk out of this front door straight to that automobile. When you get there you stand close beside it and if either of you turns to look back at me, I'll shoot your eyes out! I hope that's plain!"

They about faced and walked out of the door and down to the waiting car without turning their top pieces the fraction of an inch. I knew they were unarmed and would not dare to look behind them.

This gave me the drop on the money guards as when Johnson passed out from between us, it left me in control of them.

"If you fellows start anything with me!" I said, "I'll finish it for you. I hope that's plain to you!"

Still keeping them and their carbine rifles covered I sidled out of the door, down the steps and over to the waiting automobile.

I came directly up behind Johnson and Steel and ordered them to step into the car.

They got in and sat down, both facing directly ahead of them. I stepped on-to the running board, buckled my arm about the bow of the car and placed the muzzle of my guns at their broad backs.

"Now you'll find the scenery on the left side of the road will look a lot prettier to you than on my side. You better plan on taking it all in."

The driver clasped the wheel in his shaking black fingers and we swept down the slope.

It is a funny thing what a couple of automatics in the right place will do for a man. The scenery on the way back to town surely looked a lot prettier to me than it had on the way up. The road seemed wider and the turns fewer.

As we rounded the curve at the foot of the hill I got a last glimpse of the ocean. It no longer writhed among the crags, but billowed in gently rising swells as it rubbed its blue sides against the cliffs.

The next problem was what to do with my prisoners. Having no charges against them, I knew it would be useless to take them to jail. But I made up my mind to one thing; I would have some real fun out of these birds to repay me for all I had undergone at their hands.

No word was spoken on the descent. The negro attended to his business, Johnson and Steel to theirs, and I to mine. Presently we came in sight of the bridge separating Daytona from Daytona Beach. As we approached it, the driver slowed down.

"Go on across!" I told him.

But he said he could not as he had no license to operate a car on the other side of the line.

"All right!" I answered, "the walking is good and it's turned out to be a fine day after all."

I ordered the two men out of the machine and suggested they proceed across the bridge ahead of me.

They walked side by side as meek as two pussy cats until they passed the bridge-keeper's station which was one of those miniature lighthouse looking affairs at one side of the bridge. After getting past this structure they began looking back at me.

While they were two to my one, I had the bulge on them on my hip. Possibly they thought I was in a good mood and might be talkative. They started a conversation at the same time spreading slightly apart from each other.

"Look here!" I called, "you get back together and walk like a yoke of oxen. I'd rather put you in this river than put you in jail! Step close together and stay there! Make it snappy!"

The far end of the bridge connected with one of the most beautiful small parks I have ever seen. The trees were live oaks of immense size. From their bending limbs swung long garlands of delicate moss. It was marvelous to watch the great ropes of this growth reaching from the top limbs of the trees nearly to the ground sway in the river breeze. The earth was carpeted with soft fallen leaves and tender new grass and sloped down to the water's edge. Here and there were rustic benches inviting a pause.

As our weird procession passed one of the benches placed close to the road side, Steel and Johnson dropped dejectedly on its log seat.

They both began to wail and bemoan their fate. This I knew to be the usual order of things. Steel said he had an aged mother eighty-four years of age.

"It would break the dear old lady's heart to find out that her only son was in jail!"

Johnson followed suit by crying out that he also had home ties to protect.

"My God!" he moaned, clasping his hands and wringing them at me, "What shall I do? Just think of my beloved invalid wife with her four precious little baby girls! God knows, I have had trouble enough without having to go through anything like this!"

Now far be it from me to bring suffering upon aged mothers and invalid wives or their precious little "she babies," but I was in no hurry to alleviate their fears and deal out their freedom with a lavish hand. My silence must have impressed them as unfavorable, for they both dropped on their knees to the ground in supplication. Steel on his knees looked like a big squatty toad and Johnson more like a nervous grasshopper. The air was filled with snatches of pleas and prayers.

"Oh! For God's sake! For God's sake! Don't turn us in! If you do, it will be the means of killing our dear ones at home," continued to pour from them like unstayed streams from the gargoyle mouths on public drinking fountains.

"I would rather die a thousand, yes ten thousand deaths than to have my baby girls know their father had been in jail!" shrieked the "grasshopper," clawing the road in simulated agony.

Then they began all over again the chorus of "Oh God's!" and started to turn their pockets inside out on the ground before them, crying:

"We'll give you all of our money. All of it! Oh, if you will only let us go. All we want is our liberty!"

Gold, silver, bills and checks tumbled from their pockets into small mounds on the road. As Steel shook his last pocket over his pile of loot, the worn crumpled note the stranger in the club house had pressed into his ugly hand toppled out and lit on top of the heap.

Steel reached for it but a fortunate gust of wind raised it high in the air and deposited it at my feet.

"It's an ill wind that blows nobody good," I thought to myself as I tucked it into my pocket.

"What's all the noise about?" came a voice from under the park trees.

I looked in the direction from which it came and saw a man walking toward us. He had a little girl of about eleven years by the hand.

"There is no trouble on my part, stranger," I answered, "but these men seem to be in some difficulty."

I asked him if he lived in this town and if the child was his daughter.

He replied that he was a resident of this community and that the child was his daughter.

"I am the county surveyor," he informed me.

"Well then, suppose you just survey these two prayin' fools."

He looked surprised and I said I thought it would be a good idea if he would excuse his little girl as I had some important matters to discuss with him.

He got the drift and told the child to run home to her mother.

The little one started out looking back first over one shoulder then over the other until she had gone about fifteen feet, when she darted off like a jackrabbit.

I took in a long breath. "Here are two of the worst swindling scoundrels that ever knelt in the dirt to pray," I exploded. Then I felt better.

The man said his name was Hughes.

I explained to him that I had just escaped from a den of thieves and murderers! I told him of the club house on the distant hill and its type of inmates. How I had gone there at the invitation of these two gangsters, now at my mercy.

I related the methods used to lure victims there and what probably happened to most of them who had no money on their persons or who could not escape.

I described to Hughes in lurid terms what cutthroats, swindlers and tigercats infested the dive and how they tried to rob me of my money and when they could not do that had endeavored to take my life.

"Now!" I said kicking up a cloud of dirt in their faces, "I think I ought to turn them over to the police. But this big meat head," indicating Steel, "says he has an aged mother of eighty-four whose dear old heart will be broken if he goes to jail! And this good-for-nothing, black-hearted panther says he has an invalid wife and four valuable little daughters at home who will feel something terrible if I send him to the pen. Now what I want to ask you, Mr. Hughes, is, what shall I do with them?"

"What will you do with 'em?" he yelled. "Kill 'em! Kill 'em! And I'll get you out of it! It's just dirty dogs like these who are ruining our town and state!"

"So you think I better kill 'em, do you?" I echoed giving him the wink.

"Yes!" he thundered in a rage, "Kill 'em!"

"All right! I will!" I cried.

At this last statement both waved their arms heavenward and broke into wild cries for mercy. "Don't take a brainstorm, man! Oh, for the love of suffering humanity! Don't take a brainstorm and do a rash act. For God's sake! Wait! Think! Don't!"

"Well, I'm afraid they've nearly out-talked me." I weakened.

"If you will just let us go we will show you how fast we can run," pleaded Johnson, for himself and companion.

"We'll leave this town in fifteen minutes and the state in two days and never come back!"

"Well, go! And be sure you do go," I said.

By the time the words were out they were ten feet on their way leaving the contents of their pockets behind them.

"Hold on!" I called after their retreating figures, "come back here and get your spoils!"

They looked back as if I were playing a practical joke on them. They wanted distance more than money. They hesitated.

"Make it snappy because I've something to teach you the quick-step with if you don't!"

"What do you give those low-lived crooks that money for?" Hughes asked disgustedly.

I explained all I wanted out of the "kitty" was satisfaction.

They scooped the money into their pockets at about seventy-five miles an hour, and turning their faces once more toward freedom, they started on a mad dash for liberty — one tall, the other short, running side by side like two pistons. We watched them fade into the distance.

It was a "Mutt and Jeff" race.

I bade goodbye to my friend, the surveyor, and followed in the footsteps of Mutt and Jeff until I reached the bungalow in which I had spent the previous night. I got my suitcase and as I came out of the house, hailed a passing automobile.

"Noble!" I exclaimed holding up a detaining hand as the car slackened speed, "I would like a lift into town if you could manage it."

He looked down at me and nodded at two elegantly attired women in the tonneau.

"We haven't much room today," he replied. "You see there are two beautifully dressed ladies sitting in the rear."

I glanced at the cold beauties in the back seat. Instant action was needed. I might not look as stylish as they did but I certainly had come mighty near being beautifully dressed and trimmed myself a few hours ago.

"I've positively got to get into town!" I said.

With that I dived in between the two pretty ladies and sat down on the seat. It was a "rash" act as Steel would have said, but necessary. The machine started and the dolled up ones haughtily drew to the extreme ends of the seat. This gave me ample room for which I was grateful to them.

I asked to be allowed to get out at the railroad station when we reached town. The sixty miles of uninterrupted travel passed in stony silence.

When we reached the station I said to the driver of the car, "If you have never played the good Samaritan before, you have on this trip. I cannot explain but you have been very kind to me."

He said it was all right, he was glad if he had helped me.

The train came in and we had no further words.

When I was comfortably settled in my Pullman, I took out the little crumpled note.

"That is Norfleet, himself. Don't get him started. If you do, he'll kill every dam one of you. Don't let him get away, boys. Don't let him get away! — Joe."

So Joe knew I was there. I wondered how he knew and where he was, and resolved to keep the note and the first time I met him again, ask him. There was one thing sure, he was miles away from the place by the time I got the note.

Chapter Fifteen - On to Cuba

I got off the train at Palm Beach.

To Sheriff Baker, of this town, I confided my mission.

He was responsive and took my warrants, writing on the back of them authority to execute them anywhere in his jurisdiction. Before I left he suggested I get in touch with some people he knew who perhaps could give me a line on my men.

Two of his friends were Peg Umble and Mrs. Umble, registered at the Salt Air Hotel. Mr. Umble was interested in my case, said he knew Furey and gave me many side-lights on his history I had never known.

It was while in Umble's company, I saw in the New York World the item of the five million dollar bond steal in New York City by Nicholas Arnstein, alias "Nicky Arnstein," husband of the noted actress and Broadway favorite, Fannie Brice.

Connected with this deal in the story were E. J. or "Big Bill" Furey, Irving Gluck and Joseph Gluck. The picture of "Furey" published with the sensational story so closely resembled "Joe Furey," that I immediately wired the New York Police Department, who gave me prompt information that the "Furey" they were holding was Joe's brother. They said my "Furey" was well known to them, but was not the man they had in the Tombs.

Finding nothing of further importance there I went across the river to West Palm Beach and registered at the Royal Ponciana Hotel. In this hostelry I made the acquaintance of the house detective, John Casey, formerly of New York City.

He showed me a number of photographs of Joe Furey and said he knew him well. From him I learned that Furey had not been at West Palm Beach for many a day. This information made it advisable to move on to other towns to continue the search.

In Miami, I met Charles Racken, mayor of the Canadian town, Ontario. The very day I met him he had been swindled out of a large sum of money by three men. I showed him the pictures of Reno Hamlin and Joe Furey. When he saw Furey's photograph he exclaimed:

"That's the man who did the job! He's the one who got my money!"

He gave me the address where Furey had stayed while engineering the hold-up. I went to the place as fast as a taxi could get me there. It was a little inconspicuous bungalow in the middle of a pine forest. An ideally situated place for Furey to hide out! The landlady's deafness added to its advantage. She identified Furey's picture as that of the roomer who had left, "just yesterday."

I had gone to Miami looking for Spencer as well as Furey, but now that Joe had left I felt sure if Spencer had been with him, he, too, would be in other parts of the country. However I remained for a few days to do a little digging.

I became friendly with some of the Federal authorities and from them found out about another "job" the gang had put over.

A farmer from Illinois had been swindled at Key West, Florida, by some of the confidence ring. It was the same old story of the fake stock exchange. The farmer had started home to obtain more money with which to operate. On the way, he did some thinking. Suspicion rose in his mind, so he got off the train at Miami and notified the Federal authorities. They wired the farmer's son in Illinois to wire to the crooks in the father's name, asking for advice as to sending the money to them instead of bringing it back himself,

Upon the crooks' reply it was hoped to establish grounds on which to place a Federal charge. The "wise Willies" however, did not answer the wire and the Federal authorities had to drop the matter.

I armed myself with the farmer's name and his Key West address, then left for there on the first train.

I arrived in the nick of time as he was about to leave for home. He had returned to Key West to collect his belongings. When alighting from the train at the station on the return trip he was seized by the band of scoundrels, taken out of the town limits in a car and there beaten and kicked, then warned to get out of town and stay.

I asked him where the "stock exchange" was located. He showed me, then said a hasty good-bye. This fake exchange was a long building of three stories, a combination of business offices and studios.

I shadowed it for twenty-four hours. The day was one of wind and storm. I wondered where I would conceal myself for the night watch provided I saw nothing during the day. Darkness lends mystery to a standing figure and I was anxious to station myself where I would not be told to move on.

Nature came to my rescue. The wind felled a tall, thickly foliaged fir tree cornerwise across a fence directly opposite the entrance to the building. In this three cornered pen I would be safe from searching eyes.

At dusk I saw a man enter the building whom I took to be Furey. I was at some distance, but that athletic figure and swinging stride could not deceive me. I figured that as long as the outfit had wreaked vengeance on the farmer, they probably would look about for another victim and ply the same crooked tactics without interruption. Undoubtedly Joe was on his way into the "exchange" to rib up the scene for tomorrow's business.

I decided to wait for him until he came out. Then I would simply walk up to him and holler: "Hands up! an' stick 'em high."

It all seemed simple. Watching for his reappearance was the difficult part.

All night long the heavens dripped.

I waited. The wind howled. The arc light across the street sputtered. Umbrellas passed in obstructing masses like piled up black clouds. I was drenched to the skin and my hands torn and bleeding from parting the rough fir boughs to sight the enemy. As the pedestrian parade grew thin, I realized the hour was late. I dared not strike a light to see the time. I could feel that loud silence which settles over a city near the midnight hour. One by one the lights in the building went out. I counted and for every light extinguished a man soon left the building. Finally it was totally dark and Furey had not come out.

At dawn, stiff from enforced bending and rigid with cold, I crept out of the wet bower. I was afraid to leave my look-out, still I could not continue to watch indefinitely.

I sought out the Sheriff, explained the situation to him and asked his assistance in searching the building.

He was very sorry he could not personally serve in this capacity as he was temporarily lame from running a rusty nail into his foot, but he would send a substitute or two. He said they would be the best men on the island for the purpose and I could depend on their help.

I arranged to meet the men at the building. In the interim I hurried back to take up my lighthouse work and await their arrival.

After two hours they put in an appearance. Both were dressed in police uniforms which they wore awkwardly. The larger man struck me as being about two sizes too big for his suit. He was evidently uncomfortable in it and kept trying to adjust his huge bulk to its juvenile lines. He was the spokesman of the team.

"Now you guard the two avenues of escape!" he instructed me in a deep official voice.

The two entrances referred to were both in front of the building.

"Let your assistant take care of these," I argued, "and I'll go through the building with you."

"No, he's got to watch the side!" he replied curtly. "You take care of the front, he'll watch the side, and I'll go through the place an' if I don't catch him I'll scare him out to one of you!" He smiled knowingly.

There was nothing to do but obey his directions. The other fellow ambled to the side of the building and the "general" went inside.

I glued my eyes to the front for several minutes. Suddenly I heard a commotion at the rear of the building. I left my post and hurried around to see what it was all about.

Before I could reach the back I heard the chug — chug — chug — of a motor boat.

The rear of the building backed up to a sea wall and as I raced to its edge I saw Furey and my two police officers leap from the narrow planked landing into a launch and put out to sea. Before I could realize what had happened they were beyond pistol range.

It was a hard hand to receive so early in the morning but I was so determined to catch Furey that I lost no time in grieving. I set to thinking where the trio would land and how I could nab them when they did.

I knew Cuba was a logical connecting point from Key West and that if I was to be there to greet them when they arrived, I would have to make it snappy.

I returned to town and secured passports, chartered a hydroplane and slid off with the pilot for Cuba. We swept the gulf with binoculars as well as our own eyes, but could see nothing of the little craft.

We dropped down on Miami in hopes of finding them there. We circled all the little islands on the way to Cuba and gave each one's dockage the once over for sign of the little seafarer, but there was not a trace of the "three men in the boat" who had put off from shore only a few minutes before. Cuba itself refused to yield any indication of their presence.

For the present, the sea had washed out the trail of Joe Furey.

The next day I went back to Miami and conferred with Mayor Racken. While talking with him I bought a paper and glanced at the headlines.

I saw an item stating the magnificent estate of Colonel William Jennings Bryan would that afternoon be thrown open to the public. It went on to tell what rare shrubs and exotic blooms were in the gardens and that once each year the Bryans kindly gave the world an opportunity to feast its eyes upon their fenced-in beauties.

"Thousands of persons usually thronged the winding paths and wandered among the fragrant flower beds on this day of days," the paper reported.

Crowds of this sort are ideal places to start casual acquaintances that frequently ripen into "business deals." Knowing this, I decided to go early, stay late and see who was there.

At one end of the huge estate were heavy bronze gates.

These were thrown open and I suppose were intended to remain so, but in order to get a good look at all who passed into the grounds I assumed the job of "gate keeper" in the employ of the Bryan family.

It was one of the most interesting "jobs" I have ever had.

The only person known to me out of the thousands who filed in and out was Whitey Arlington's wife. She had distinguished herself sometime before by leaping unhurt from a window of the courthouse at Fort Worth, Texas. At the time she made her "Steve Brody," she had seventy thousand dollars "swindle money" on her. Her other half known as "Whitey Arlington" was then in jail on a swindle charge. He must have escaped or had been released, for when Mrs. Arlington recognized me at the gate, she instantly exchanged hat and coat with a woman accompanying her and together they plunged

83

into the crowd where they were met by Whitey. They evidently thought I was onto some deal they were framing, for they hastened on their iniquitous way at sight of me.

That night I received a wire from my son, Pete, telling me I was needed at home to adjust some pressing business matters. I knew I should go home, but I hated to let up on the search just as things were crystalizing.

The old "saw" about "duties never conflicting ,, has had its teeth worn off. My duties conflicted at every turn.

In this instance I decided on a "home run" with a stop-over in Daytona Beach. I had no desire to see the place again but felt as long as I would be so near, it might pay me to hop off the train and see if anything had happened in bunco circles since I had started "Mutt and Jeff" on their Marathon.

I had no idea how to start my information quest in the little beach town as I knew no one but my previous landlady and Hughes, the County Surveyor. I walked the main street and racked my brain for inspiration.

A portable sign on the sidewalk reading "Triple City Land Company" attracted my attention and reminded me that Spencer's favorite pose was as a landman. My mental processes carried to the point where I wondered if Spencer had ever tried to do business — his kind, with this Triple City affair.

I thought it would be rather comical to go up and calmly inquire at the information desk if they had ever been swindled by Messrs. "Spencer and Furey."

The firm name I had just given them pleased my imagination and I decided to take a flyer to see what would happen.

The Triple City Company was doing business on the second floor. Up I went. There was the information desk, the pretty little blonde informant and all. My courage failed as I looked at her piquant face with its sad expression. She could never understand and would probably have me arrested, I thought.

"Is the manager in?"

"No!" she replied, with a wave of her hand toward his empty chair.

"Will he return soon?"

"Perhaps!" she retorted and looked at me suspiciously.

"I'll wait!" I replied and looked back at her suspiciously.

I showed myself to a chair, took out my "special edition" and pretended to read. In a few minutes I turned to her and said, "What is the meaning of this thing, 'con men'?"

"Well if you knew as much about them as we do you wouldn't have to ask foolish questions!"

The child has a grudge against them I told myself.

I asked her more on the subject and found that she and her father, the manager, had just lost a fortune through their operations on the "gentlemen's stock exchange" — located on the high hill, overlooking the sea.

I asked her what the main operator looked like.

From her description I could see Spencer looking at us.

"Did this man ever give you anything with his name on it?" I asked.

84

"Yes! A check. A cold one!" she replied, drawing a package of them from a desk drawer.

I took from my pocket a specimen of his handwriting and his signature. My paper was signed "W. B. Spencer" and hers "W. B. Spear."

"Look at them," I said.

They were identical.

"They swindled two other parties in this town, then before the police could get them they escaped in a car," she explained.

Evidently after I had removed Johnson and Steel, Spencer and others had remained to close other deals. I saw now that the town was cleaned of them and felt better satisfied to return to the ranch for a brief time.

When I reached there I found a wire from Sheriff Clark of Fort Worth stating that Reno Hamlin had been arrested and was in jail there.

Hamlin was the first of the swindlers I met and the one who picked me for a prospect.

I congratulated myself that the third one of the five was now eliminated from my search, but I was to learn that arrest, conviction and sentencing do not always mean what we think.

Chapter Sixteen - 2,000 Miles after a Fur Coat

After getting things at the ranch in shape I was restless to hit the trail again.

From the time I started the man hunt, every clue connected with the affair had been cleared except one; the episode in the San Antonio Police Station, where I had encountered the wailing shoplifter, who had sold the stolen fur coat to the "big man" in room 113 at the St. Anthony Hotel.

After turning inside out every pocket in my mind I could think of no other clue which had not been accounted for. The more I thought about the coat, the more important it grew in my mind.

It seemed so small in comparison with the magnitude of my discoveries at the hotel, that at the time I had dismissed it without even a casual look into it, but now that all other leads had come to an end, I grasped at this as a drowning man at a straw.

While it had happened a year ago and the trail was probably "cold," still age often brings unlooked for things to light.

I turned my attention to trailing a fur coat instead of a live man.

I felt so certain of success on this issue that I obtained the legal services as well as the pleasurable company of Jesse Brown for the trip. Many times technical advice on the spot would have saved me time and money and on this latest venture I decided to leave no loopholes of the law to thwart my progress.

We went to San Antonio and took up the old line from there.

We sought out Chief of Police Al Mussey, and the three of us went to the St. Anthony to confirm my findings regarding the registration of "J. Harrison." This was satisfactorily accomplished and from there we went to the Express Office and searched the records for the three days of Furey's stay in San Antonio, to see if he had shipped out any packages.

Our reason for this was that at the time of the finding of Furey's suitcase and belongings when Cathey had spoiled the deal — there was no fur coat.

When Furey departed from the Stewart Hotel via the fire escape it was not likely he was wearing or carrying a lady's coat. Therefore it seemed logical to think he must have shipped it out of San Antonio in some way before leaving for San Bernardino.

We found out nothing through the Express records. There was no trace of anything having been shipped anywhere by Furey.

The next move was to get the Parcel Post records. This was not as easily accomplished. When the facts were made known to the Federal Executives, their files were opened wide to us.

After thumbing dusty records for hours we came on a peculiar thing, a package shipped to no one, from no one; that is, as far as names were concerned.

During the three days of Furey's known stay in town, a package was shipped through the mail to No. 506 Stanford Court Apartments, San Francisco, Calif. It was addressed to no one in particular and bore the name of no sender. Neither did it have a return address and was not insured. Had it been insured the sender's name would have been required. From the weight of the package which appeared on the record it might easily have been a fur coat. At any rate it was an object of several pounds.

While there was nothing tangible to connect the package with Furey, still the Post Office inspector said it was a little unusual to ship a package in this vague manner. Considering that it was mailed within Furey's "three days limit," its destination California; and shortly after it was shipped, Furey had gone in the same direction; there might be something in it.

A consultation was held.

It was unanimously adopted by Brown and myself to follow the package to California. We left that night.

When we reached San Bernardino I suggested we drop off and give a "hello" to my old friend, Sheriff Shay, and see if anything had turned up since he gave me my last year's "Christmas present."

Shay was glad to see us. He said nothing had come to light regarding any of my men since Sheriff Clark had taken Ward and Gerber back to Fort Worth for trial.

We decided to leave for San Francisco the next morning. In the meantime I thought I would make another search for possible telephone messages from Furey while he was at the Stewart Hotel.

Life with me was just one search after another.

The telephone files of the hotel disclosed the information that a long distance message had been sent to "684 J. Glendale," and charged to the occupant of room 202. This checked with the one occupied by "Mr. Peck," at that time one of Furey's aliases.

It was unfortunate that at the time I searched the phone calls on my previous trip I overlooked the possibility of telephone or telegraph messages being charged to a room number instead of a specified party. Had we thought of this a year ago this story might have ended very differently.

I was so ever joyed at what looked like a direct lead I could not wait until morning to be off. I knew Brown would not return until late at night, as he was being entertained by Shay. Therefore I left him a hurried note stating I had caught the train for Los Angeles and for him to join me there the next day. I was so excited I believe I even forgot to mention to Brown why I was leaving in such a rush.

As soon as I reached Los Angeles I registered at the Alhambra Hotel. The first thing I did was to pick up the telephone.

"684 J. Glendale," I said to the operator.

Although it was late in the evening, I could not wait until the next day to find out what luck awaited me at the other end of the line.

"Hello," said a pleasant feminine voice in my ear. My heart thudded against my ribs.

"Who is this speaking?" I asked.

"This is Mrs. Furey," answered the even voice. "Whom did you wish to speak to?" it continued.

"Pardon!" I exclaimed as I hung up the receiver, "I believe I have the wrong number."

My jubilance knew no bounds!

'At last! At last! Thank God, at last!" I cried.

In my ecstasy I slapped my own knees and reached to pat my own back. No cowboy ever rooted louder for his favorite "bronco buster" or threw his hat higher at a rodeo. I felt like "setting them up" and telling the world it was on me. I do not think if I live to be one thousand years old that I will ever again feel the same wild thrill of triumph.

My wife and I had often discussed the fact that some of these men must have families. It was not too much to suppose they had more than one apiece. Such things have been heard of. We used to remark that if we only knew where they kept their households, the track could be picked up there.

However it was a long time after the hunt began before any of the domestic relations of the gentlemen came to light. I believe the locating of Mrs. Furey (she pronounced it "Fu-ray") was the first I knew of any of the women folks of the confidence gang.

At the crack of dawn I was on my way to Glendale. It is a lovely little town about one hour out from Eos Angeles. Wide, even streets, velvety green lawns spread beneath modern bungalows give it an air of spick and span.

Before leaving the hotel I looked up the address in the telephone directory. It was No. 412, Piedmont Park, Glendale.

This proved to be a very aristocratic residence section. The homes were either immense, rambling bungalows or imposing mansions. Presently I came to No. 412.

As I looked at the handsome home with its massive stone pillars, shade trees, blooming gardens, I thought with a wry smile:

It is quite natural that Joe should have this residential luxury. He has so many "suckers" working for him.

It was still early morning. The faint, sweet haze that hung over the little village was beginning to lift. The purple hills in the distance were drawing it toward them. I drank deep of that soft liquid air which hovers over cities, big and small, just before they awake.

I gazed at the upstairs windows. They were open. The shades were drawn half way, and back and forth in the sway of the gently moving air, delicate meshed curtains of white swam in and out, brushing their ruffled edges across the sill.

Probably Mrs. "Fu-ray" was still asleep. Perhaps dreaming? I wondered if she ever had nightmares. Perhaps Mr. "Fu-ray" was also sleeping. Everything about the house spoke of money. Some way I knew this was to be a future battle field.

Would I, like Samson, place my hands upon the stone pillars and bring this temple of hypocrisy down on their heads, as well as my own?

I looked across the street from the palm-lined strip which ran like a green carpet through the center of the wide avenue. I noted with satisfaction that they were building a big hospital.

"New Research Hospital," the sign said. They must have known I was coming. Certainly I was searching, and no doubt before long either Joe Furey or I would need its first aid department.

I made a complete survey of the house. I observed carefully its sides and back, looking with particular attention to all avenues of escape.

After studying the rear of the structure I saw that there were three separate and distinct means of get-away. One passed through the orange grove, another through the vineyard, both of which were at the back of the house, and the last through the garden, joining the vineyard at the north side.

I made up my mind to watch the house until I saw something of what was going on. I could not hold my unprotected position any longer without arousing suspicion, so I picked up a torn piece of blue print which scuttled in the breeze alongside a pile of lumber and pretended to consult it.

The workmen on the hospital building were beginning to arrive. It gave me the idea of posing as a landscape gardener. In this way I could keep the house in sight and pretend to be immersed in "laying out" the land instead of Furey.

For two days I hung around, keeping the house constantly under watch. I spoke to no one and no one spoke to me. While I attracted several glances from the builders and different neighbors, their looks seemed simply a recognition that I belonged in some unknown way to the general scheme of construction going on in the community.

Directly across from the Furey home was a large open park. Trees, flowers, the usual wooded shade and curving paths made up its topography. From almost every point in the park I could get a clear view of the house. This was fortunate as it enabled me to keep continuously on the go and thereby evade the eye of the Police.

I knew little indeed about the functions of landscape gardening, but I did my best to come up to what I believed the requirements might be.

I gazed up into the trees and looked in among the branches. I shaded my eyes with my hand and peered across the lawns endeavoring to give the impression that I was about to recommend the palms be pulled up and replanted in groups of twos and threes. I paced off the distance from bench to bench, measuring the footage and looking garden-wise.

Then I would lie down on the ground, spread the blue prints of the hospital laboratory out on the grass and carefully plan out how best to slope the new lawns, locate the sunken gardens and bury the ammunition.

My mind was apparently on everything but telling the new grass the way up. I picked up small pieces of wood and whittled them into prospecting stakes. These I drove into the soft earth so that my gardening assistants might be guided as to the shapes of the beds. In this manner I laid out diamonds, hearts, clubs and spades.

I might still have been playing solitaire had not my attention been claimed the third day by a little boy who came bounding down the front steps of the Furey domicile.

The first two days of vigil I had seen nothing out of the ordinary or to suggest that Furey was at home. On the first day in the afternoon a woman had come out of the house and had gone off in a sedan. She was out only a brief time and drove the car herself. She was attractive looking, about thirty years of age and smartly dressed. I was certain she was Mrs. Fu-ray.

The child was playing with a large rubber ball which he bounced up and down on the sidewalk and when it did not roll into the gutter, caught it with chubby hands.

I walked toward the curb, and just as I crossed to talk to him he ran laughing into the street kicking the ball nearly into my face. I sent it flying with the end of my foot back to him. He dashed back to the sidewalk in time to throw his little body over it and pin it to the ground.

I wondered if it was to be through an innocent child that I would find what I sought. I am not overly religious but it kept running through my head — that Bible phrase — "And a little child shall lead them."

It wasn't a pleasant thought. But as I stood watching him springing up and down in play, I thought of the countless other children, hungry, destitute and orphaned, that this little fellow might have his pretty ball and smooth green lawn to play upon.

"Well," I said, "that's a fine ball you have there."

"Yes," he replied.

I saw that he was friendly and it would not be hard to draw him into conversation. After tossing the ball to him again, I said:

"You ought to have a nice little puppy to play with. They are great playfellows for little boys."

Wreathed in smiles, he said proudly: "I am going to have a puppy. I'm going to have one soon!"

"You ought to get him for a Christmas present," I urged.

He stopped his play a moment and burst out that he was going to have the puppy before Christmas, even.

"I'm goin' to have my doggy soon as my papa comes home. And he's coming in a few days, too."

I felt warm all over. Everything quickened inside of me. I thought a minute. Events had happened so thick and fast I had lost all track of time and dates. Yes, that was true; only a few days until Christmas.

Furey was expected home soon. And little Furey, Junior, would have his dog.

Then I would have his father! That is, if all went well.

"That will be fine to have the little dog!" I said, coming out of my dream. "I hope you will be able to get a nice little Airedale. They are good friends for boys."

Oh! I'll get a good one all right," he exclaimed confidently. "My papa will give me the money to buy him."

He stood legs apart, hands stuffed into his little blue linen trousers; boyish chest stuck out like a pouter pigeon.

"When my papa gets home my pockets will just stick out with money," he boasted, doubling up his fists and ramming them nearly through the pockets to show me just how full of money they would be.

I went immediately back to Los Angeles to the Sheriff's office. Saw Under Sheriff Al Manning, whom I had met on the previous trip. I told him everything. How I had for days laid in wait for Furey to return home. How I had watched the house and finally become acquainted with the little Furey child and from him learned that Furey was expected home within the next few days.

I asked him for his help, telling him I believed this was going to be my chance to get "Joe."

All the assistance in the world was promised me. He at once detailed two deputies to carry out the capture. They were Walter Lips and Andy Anderson, two of the best known enforcers of the law in that vicinity.

Together we three went out to Glendale. I showed Lips and Anderson the Furey home; pointed out the three avenues of escape I had noted on my first visit. We drove around the place but did not stop.

On the way back to town they discussed the best plan of getting into the Furey home. It was decided they should disguise themselves as telephone line-men. They would supposedly inspect the telephones and get the "low-down" on the inside of the house.

That evening they carried out their plan, returned to Glendale as line-men and inspected the Furey telephones. I was waiting in the Sheriff's office for them to report.

Only one of them returned. This was Lips as I recall it.

"What luck?" I cried, eager for news.

"Oh! we got in the house all right," he said, as if it were an every day occurrence. "I left Andy out there on duty. He's going to keep a sharp lookout," he added, beginning to strip off his disguise. "And believe me, Norfleet, don't you ever think if Joe Furey shows up there that he'll ever get away. We're no suckers!"

With this he started for the next room, saying he must hurry and get his clothes changed, grab a bite to eat and get back to relieve Anderson.

For a few days one man at a time reported. They kept saying they were watching, but that so far Furey had not put in an appearance.

I began to get uneasy. They warned me to keep entirely away from the place.

"Furey would know you on sight and if he was home could shoot you or us from the window," they declared.

However under the disguise of night I went out there and gave it the once over. This action of mine I reported to the Sheriff's office and told them I had been unable to see either of the officers on duty.

This brought a loud laugh from Manning. He roared with such volume I feared he would split his tonsils.

"Didn't see 'em! Didn't see 'em!" he choked. "Why if you could see 'em, so could everybody else! My God, man! They're working under cover."

I felt well set down after this outburst of super intellect.

In the meantime Brown had joined me. We went to see Thomas Lee Woolwine, district attorney of Los Angeles.

Mr. Woolwine took a great interest in my case. He declared he would assist me in every way within his power. To "leave no stone unturned," was his promise.

He started at once to make good his word by putting the well-known Malcolm McLaren on the job.

Chapter Seventeen - A Frisco "Coal Mine."

Thinking I had clone all I could personally in regard to capturing Furey and believing I had left the house in the hands of patient trustworthy watchers, Brown and I decided we would go to San Francisco and see what No. 506 Stanford Court Apartments looked like and if we could trace the mysterious package.

Sheriff Shay was a "Native Son" as they say in the Golden State. He knew every nook and corner of its mountains, valleys and deserts. He was also well acquainted with many people in San Francisco as well as in the South.

I asked Brown what he thought of having Shay come along to San Francisco with us as my guest.

Brown said he thought it not a bad idea as we both would be almost total strangers in the city and might need substantial backing. Through Shay we could get this. Calling him on long distance, I invited him to go along, saying that I would like to get acquainted in San Francisco and didn't know anyone better able to introduce me to the right people.

He accepted and the three of us left on the morning train.

On arriving we registered at an obscure hotel. I registered under the name of E. H. Shaw of Orin Junction, Wyoming.

Shaw was a wealthy cattleman of that place. I borrowed his name so if I was questioned about that part of the country I could answer intelligently.

Our first call was at the Hall of Justice on Kearney Street where we met Opie Warner, a newspaper representative of the San Francisco Call. We told our story to him and asked advice, service and secrecy.

The idea of telling a newspaper man a live story and in the next breath asking him to keep it a secret, might sound like the raving of a lunatic, but from Opie Warner we got all this and extra consideration besides.

Through him we were ushered into the private office of Chief of Police White. Chief White was confined to his home with a serious illness from which he died that night. In his absence we saw acting Chief of Police Dan O'Brien, who listened to our story and said, "Count on me for aid." He was familiar with my swindling experiences and knew the records of most of my fleecers.

The Chief called in Messrs. Gallivan, Frank McConnell and another tall, slender blonde fellow. They were all city detectives. We were introduced and our needs briefly outlined for the information of the trio.

I shall never forget McConnell. He is a husky, fine-looking personage.

I say "is" because I understand he is still with the Police Department.

Anyway, we had no sooner stated that we believed Furey to be somewhere in the city than McConnell pulled a five dollar bill from his pocket and waved it under my nose.

"I'll give you that five dollar note if you can show Joe Furey to me."

He continued to rattle the cash at me and declared he had a personal matter to settle with him. It was the way he did it that got me. Right then I saw that any assistance we would get from him, we could put in our pipes and draw on them indefinitely.

"You'll never see that Furey bird lightin' in this town as long as I'm here," he said with modest dignity. "But," he spoke as one inspired, "Oakland is a wonderful place for those guys."

Under the personal direction of Gallivan and the blonde young fellow, whose name I cannot recall, but who seemed the cleverest of the three, I went across the beautiful San Francisco Bay to Oakland. We hung around Hotel Oakland. My escorts said a great many thieves and bunco men made this their headquarters when working their spurious stock games around San Francisco and the Bay cities.

We stuck around for a long time but nothing happened. Everyone we saw looked unusually honest.

I left the crowd and went down to see Ezra De Soto, the district attorney of Oakland. De Soto was in the midst of a mess, himself. One of the prominent Oakland banks had been robbed and his brother-in-law had been shot and seriously wounded. De Soto was preoccupied with this affair and not overly eager to take on mine. He was very busy but I stayed with it and finally he said:

"I'm about cuckoo with worry, but come upstairs into the office and I'll see what I can do for you."

We went up and had a long talk. He arranged it so I could go around with the detectives working out of his office.

This did not prove of any especial value except I became well acquainted with the Bay District and the dives and meeting places of many criminals.

I did not get track of any of the men I wanted. The more I searched for them, the more I realized they probably would not come out of anywhere; that I would have to spend years perhaps searching the earth for them. This thought was not comforting.

In my mind's eye I saw a fast dwindling bank account. It was money! money! money! every time I turned around. How long my cash would last all depended upon where my hunt would lead me. I fervently prayed that San Francisco or its environs would yield me at least one of the three men.

The next day I took the little cable car that so nimbly climbs Powell Street and passes the Stanford Court Apartments. I clung on for my life while it lifted itself over the top of the hill and plunged down the other side to destruction, it seemed.

"California Street," yelled the conductor.

I got off. The Stanford Court Apartments were at the corner of Powell Street and California. They occupied nearly a solid block. A buttress of rough, grey stone blocks, fort-like in appearance, it was built up about ten feet from the sidewalk at the top of the hill, and must have been nearly thirty feet at the lower corner.

From this support rose the white granite apartment house. The plate glass windows were draped in rich velours and expensive lace curtains. White-capped maids now and then bobbed into view at small pantry windows.

I walked up the steep hill on California Street for half the block.

The entrance to the community dwellings was a high arch of granite with imposing portals of marble through which pedestrians entered as well as the motors that constantly swept in and out of the beautiful circular court, landscaped after the order of a Pompeian garden. Flowering shrubs shielded marble benches and a fountain whirred water from the mouths of water

93

nymphs. Within the court were four separate entrances to the cliff of homes. Each exterior entrance had several separate interior entrances with its own elevators. As far as I could find out there was no open connection between the different entrances and their sets of apartments. Everywhere were liveried flunkies asking you who you wanted, why you wanted them, and daring you to get them.

I was told I could not see any of the occupants without an order. Just who was supposed to sign my order I did not know. Belligerent looking individuals requested my immediate departure.

I withdrew slowly as if their insults had been unnoticed; explained that I had heard an old cowboy built the structure and I only wanted to see what kind of a "bunk-house" a cowman would put up on a "city range." I dared not ask who lived in No. 506.

With a sinking heart I thought the persons for whom the package was addressed had moved long ago, perhaps. Finding it impossible to pass the stationed gargoyles, I took a long look at an old white haired, broken nosed, but genial looking Irishman running one of the elevators. Then I went down town and took in some of the sights.

About the time I thought the Irishman would be off duty I returned and waited outside for him. Presently he passed close by me.

"Howdy, stranger,'" I said.

"Howdy yersilf," he returned.

"Say," said I, putting my words into his ear at close range, "do you know where a Scotchman could get a little smile?"

"Well," he answered promptly locking his arm in mine and pulling me gently toward the towering stone wall, "I know where an Irishman and a Scotchman could get a smile — if the Scotchman had the money."

I told him I had it. Together we went in search of the laughing water.

He led me to "Mike's," where I saw a lot of smart looking young fellows whom I guessed were reporters. For this reason I talked in as low a voice as I could, considering the number of my smiles.

Again I dared not ask directly who occupied Apartment No. 506. Direct questions are more often remembered by the questioned than statements made by one's own volition. At any rate we laughed a good deal and late in the night we parted to go our separate ways.

All I found out was the license number of the car owned by the people living in the apartment, and that a mother, her daughter and two sons lived there. This was progress, but slow.

The next day I went again and made another try at getting by the guards and up into the apartment house. I got into the elevator.

Again I was asked by the pop-eyed elevator driver if I had permission to go upstairs.

I felt like telling him "No, teacher didn't give me any" — but merely said I had no permission, that I had no idea it was necessary.

94

At this he blew shrilly on a little police whistle. "Well, we'll show you this time that you need one."

"We put you out yesterday and you came back! This time we'll make a good job of it!" said the two house ejectors who grabbed me by the arm.

Firmly pinned between the two men I was started down the hill in the direction of the city and county jail. We crossed the street at Powell and California. As we passed the Powell Street exit of the Fairmont Hotel I noticed the ivy-covered, cave-like entrance dug into the steep terrace. I judged it led underground for some distance to elevators which lifted to the upper regions of the hotel high up on top of the hill.

It occurred to me that this subterranean channel looked like the entrance to a coal mine. I dragged on my convoy. They stopped to see what was the matter with me.

"Well, I'll be dinged!" I cried, acting like a country hick. "What d'ye know about that? I always heered as how Frisco was a great minin' town, but I never expected to see a coal mine dug right off the sidewalk." I strained my body from them and peered into the opening, simulating great astonishment at such a civic phenomenon.

They seemed highly amused at my ignorance and eased up on me so that we three walked close to the mouth of the tunnel. I craned my neck and twisted my arms from their grips a bit.

"Well," I cried in a cracked voice, "I suttenly wish the home folks could see this...a real coal shute right in a city street. But say, boys, if this is a genwine coal mine, she don't look much like the old ones uster, do she?"

They laughed and mocked me saying, "Do she? No, she don't she!"

Gradually they let me lead them into the long narrow white walled passage that winds far into the hill and ends at the top of a gentle slope where elevators do the rest of the work.

By its right name it is known as "The Fairway" and now boasts of beautiful shops and a lovely art gallery to lure the guest up into the beautiful hotel, which like a proud king's coronet crowns "Nob Hill."

I looked up at the smooth walls of the passageway. "They sure keep this mine clen'er 'n a whistle! I wouldn't mind being a worker in this dump."

One said to the other in a low voice, "Let's see what the damn old fool will do."

"He's ready for the bug-house," said the other. But they let me get farther and farther into the opening.

A bell boy came running down its length and dashed out the door.

"Why they even got brass buttons on the miners!" I cried. "And boys, look!" I pointed to a rising elevator. "Ain't them the swell cages? Minin' coal ain't what it uster be."

In their laughter they let go of me.

I raised my hands high above my head and rubbed the glossy walls.

"An' then we hears about coal strikes and dissatisfied workmen! Why them strikin' coal miners must be plum loco! This here coal shaft is better'n my own parlor to home."

I turned my back against the wall. The next instant they were laughing into the muzzle of my six-shooter.

Their grins froze. Up went their hands as if they were used to facing guns.

"Now you better get back to your Stanford Court, and attend to your business there if you have any," I snapped.

They looked dazed.

"Aw, come on, Bill," one of them said condescendingly, "let's let the old fool go. He ain't got no sense nohow!"

With this they both backed out of the entrance and as far as I know returned to the confines of the Grecian garden across the street.

I returned home myself.

All night I figured on some way to get into the apartment house. There was some way it could be done. Many different ideas came to me. Several seemed easy and logical but I was afraid to trust just anyone I might employ. I knew no one on whom I could absolutely rely. I could not afford the risk of again attempting to force myself into the place.

Now I have found when you want a secret kept a woman is every bit as good a guardian as a man. That statement is not a challenge to the male sex but is merely based on my own experience. Therefore I decided to get a woman to do the job. Where to get her was the next question. I could not go out on the street and commandeer the first young lady I saw, or the second or even the third; no matter how capable they looked. It might have been possible to make the acquaintance in a casual way of some young woman and later seek her services, but San Francisco at this time was going through a phase of "Gangster" outrages and seven or more young girls had been lured from the straight and narrow paths of the city; others had been kidnapped, and all subjected to the most infamous brutality. Thus any method I might employ "to meet up," as they say, with an unknown member of the feminine squad would, no doubt, be misunderstood.

No matter how I racked my brain or what plausible plan I formulated the jail doors yawned at me. I yawned to myself. What use to plan any longer? Dawn was creeping above my window sill and I had not closed my eyes. I turned my face to the wall and gave it all up for the present.

It was noon when I awoke. The telephone bell called me from oblivion.

Was Mr. Shaw in?

We were, or else how could we answer our phone?

Some newspaper men would like to interview me.

Very well, I would be down soon.

I saw at once they thought I was the Orin Junction Shaw. I had no idea I had selected the name of such a celebrity. At least from a press viewpoint he was a prominent figure. I thought rapidly. It would not do to undeceive them as to my identity. That would only bring more publicity down on my head. I saw that Shaw I was, and Shaw I must remain!

They asked me questions about cattle conditions in Wyoming, Texas, and other ranching States. As I remember they asked me nearly everything from who my favorite movie vamp was, to whether or not I thought women's clubs were an advantage in the modern home.

Chapter Eighteen - Pepper Sprinkled On My Trail

Among other things I was invited to attend a banquet given that night in honor of the visiting "Wool Growers" at the Wool Growers Convention in session in San Francisco.

I declined, pleading a previous engagement.

The "newsboys" persisted and refused to take "no" for an answer from "Mr. Shaw." They were sure I wouldn't "go back on my ranching fraternity."

What could I do? I accepted.

It was a large dinner and everyone was feeling keyed up for a good time.

The waiter asked me what I would have to drink. I was on the water wagon as usual.

I tapped my goblet of water and bravely said, "This is good enough for me!"

At my modest choice the stalwart Australian seated next me held up two of his fingers and said: "Waiter! Make it two coffees — black!"

In the twinkling of an eye, thick white coffee mugs, such as you would expect to find coffee in, were set before us.

I thought it was coffee — until I got a whiff of it.

Well I stepped off the water wagon for about two cups, and as I let go of it entirely, the toastmaster called on Mr. Shaw for a speech.

I was then sorry I had accepted the invitation. I had not counted on the speech. But what could I do? Besides I gathered from the applause which met the toastmaster's request that I speak, that my friend Shaw was an after dinner talker of no mean ability.

I was a wool grower myself, and now also a "coffee drinker," and I wasn't at all sure I was not Mr. Shaw. Things were not perfectly clear anyway. I stood on my feet, at least that's where my friends told me I stood, and began:

"Gentlemen, I have only one thing to say and this is that there is something wrong with the wool business! Sometime ago I priced yarn in the stores — yarn to knit garments and found we had to sell fifty-one pounds of raw wool to pay for one pound of finished retail wool yarn! It seems to me there is too much difference between the producer and the consumer. This is a criticism and I realize that no criticism is worth much unless accompanied by some suggestion for improvement and the only way I can think of to improve the grade of wool that we fellows sell, and which goes out to the housewife with a 'pure wool' guarantee, is to keep our sheep from grazing in our cotton fields!"

This speech was printed in all the papers next morning under the heading: "Wool grower pulls some wool off the eyes of his brother growers."

I have often wondered if some friends sent Shaw a copy of "his" speech. I have not run across him since this episode, but when I do I intend to let him know how popular he was and how they can make black coffee in San Francisco.

After I returned to the hotel and was thinking over what a good time I had had and how grateful to me my friend Shaw would be for the few words I had spoken; words that had saved him coming all the way from Wyoming, the great idea dawned.

I had seen little of Brown since reaching here. As I had not needed legal advice, he had been amusing himself by getting acquainted with those whom we were likely to need. But now I recalled hearing him speak of some friends of his; a woman and her daughter. They were the only friends he had in San Francisco that he knew before coming. He had said that I should meet them. Perhaps one of them could get into No. 506.

I asked him how about it.

He said he would arrange a meeting and did so the day before he and Shay returned home.

We met in a little Italian restaurant where the spaghetti swung in succulent rhythm with the animated eaters. Hot French bread with paprika, crisp green lettuce with a red wine-vinegar dressing went down easily with the other "red." I had a good time. Everybody knew everybody else. If they didn't when they came in, they did by the time they left. I found a few old acquaintances myself.

At least they said: "Why 'scourse ole scout 'member you fum years'h an' years'h ago."

Perhaps they did. I didn't deny it. I was even glad for it. However I was studying the two women, Mrs. Jesse Carson and her daughter Lucille. Mrs. Carson was an attractive woman with soothing voice and magnificent hair. It was like burnished silver. Lucille was small and slender, apparently about eighteen. She had a certain dainty manner and appealing blue eyes. Eyes that could draw out secrets.

That night I said nothing to them of my proposition.

We met again the next day. In the meantime Brown had told them something of my story and in a general way why we were in San Francisco.

I decided to broach the subject to the young lady. I asked her if she would like to play detective. Her round, blue eyes grew rounder.

"I think it would be lots of fun!" she exclaimed.

I explained to her and Mrs. Carson my ineffectual efforts to find out who was living in No. 506 Stanford Court.

Both women caught on readily and soon we were busy discussing what sort of disguise would be the best for Lucille to wear. I had already made up my mind if she would attempt the job, what I would have her do.

I asked her mother if she had any of the clothes Lucille used to wear three or four years before. She had.

We chose from among them a little red frock and tarn o'shanter. When she got them on she did not look a day more than fourteen years old. The next day she was to meet me on the terrace of the Fairmount Hotel, directly opposite the Stanford Court. I was then to give her instructions.

The next afternoon I waited. Soon from the distance a little girl came toward me. I could scarcely believe it was the child. She tripped along like my own little girl of twelve.

"I'm here!" she said, scrambling up over the edge of the stone coping and sat down beside me on the terrace grass.

I complimented her on her school-girl appearance and she said she was glad I approved and felt sure she would not disappoint me or get thrown out as I had. I promised to protect her if the police got her and we both had a good laugh, then she begged me to tell her what she was to do to be a detective.

"You see," said I, "the idea is this. I want to find out if Furey lives there. If he does not, then I want to know who does! Look for him, his picture or a Hudson seal coat! Find out all and everything you can." Lucille listened intently.

"You are to pretend you have a little 'Airedale' puppy to sell. Whoever comes to the door, say that you have the little dog they bought from your mother and if they are ready to have it delivered, you will bring it to them. In this way you may have a chance to talk long enough to get a line on things."

I gave her two little slips of paper. One of them had written on it No. 506 — but the numeral "6" looked very much like "1." The loop was all but omitted. It could have been taken for either one or six. The other paper had a pin stuck through it and Lucille's telephone number in plain figures.

I told her to get into the elevator driven by the big pop-eyed elevator boy. I pointed out to her where this elevator was located. She sat as still as a mouse and I knew she was following me accurately.

"What are these papers for?" she asked.

I told her the one with No. 506 on it was to show to the person who opened the door, in proof that she was on a legitimate call. Then naturally they will say, "This must be intended for apartment 501 — see! though it does look like a six at the first glance." I told her they would probably then pat her little head or else stoop down and kiss her.

She blushed again and said she did not look for anything like that.

"If possible, when they discover you have the wrong address, ask if you may use the phone to call your mother and get the correct address. In this way you may be able to get right into the bosom of the family. Anyway before the elevator man asks where you are going, or who you want, tell him that you are going to apartment No. 506 where you expect to sell a little dog. Act very pleased about it.

"Can you flirt?" I asked.

She lowered her eyes and admitted that if it was absolutely necessary, she could — a little.

"Very well then, I think I would flirt a little with that elevator boy. It may make things easier. If you have no success at the apartment, when you come down in the elevator tell the elevator boy that when the father comes home, they are going to take the little dog. Tell him you are afraid they will forget their promise, and then pin this other slip of paper in his cap, and say that if he will let you know when the father gets home, you will give him half the money they give you for the dog."

I asked her if she thought she could remember all this long rigamarole.

She said she could perfectly. So she dropped down over the wall to the sidewalk and skipped across the street to the big entrance.

From where I sat I could look directly into the court. I saw her enter the building. She passed several employees, but they took no notice of a "child."

I waited. It seemed hours. The longer she is gone, the better it looks for our little scheme I thought. In the meantime I counted passing Hudson seal coats and hoped for luck.

Lucille came back all smiles. I knew to some extent we had triumphed.

"Well," she gasped, "it worked fine. What do you think?"

Then she told me how she had flirted...a little, with the "pop-eyes," and how he had flirted back — a little more. That when she rang the doorbell a little boy had answered.

She spoke of delivering the ordered dog.

The child called to some one within the apartment regarding it.

A young lady appeared and informed her that she was quite sure there was some mistake; that her mother had not ordered any dog!

"Why, yes!" Lucille exclaimed, "I am sure your mother wants it because my mother told me to find out if you were ready for it. It was to be a Christmas present for the little boy."

At this she handed the slip on which was written "No. 506 Stanford Court Apartments."

The young lady looked surprised and stepped inside the room to ask her mother about it.

Lucille followed her in looking anxious about the miscarriage of the sale.

The mother, a mature woman with a harassed expression, declared she "knew nothing at all about any dog!" She spoke quickly and jerked out her remarks irritably.

"Why mother you surely know something about it!" the young thing had declared. "Here is the address as plain as your face." They bent their heads over the scrap of paper.

"It's a mistake," snapped the mother. "It must be intended for Apartment No. 501. It does look like No. 506 though."

Lucille all the while had been eye-gathering. On a hat tree in the little reception hall hung a black derby hat. Of course this did not convey anything to Lucille. Thrown across the back of a small mahogany chair in the artistic living room was a long Hudson seal coat. This did convey something to Lucille.

There was no photograph in sight of the corpulent Furey.

The mother said she did not want any dog. She had had one but it died and she wished not to become attached to any more animals.

At this my little agent exclaimed, "Did he die of the flu?"

The woman said he had.

Lucille was sudden sympathy for her bereavement and said she had a flu remedy for dogs and would be very glad to send it to her. "To whom shall I address it?" she inquired.

"Mrs. Mabel H. Harrison is my name."

Lucille knew that this was one of Furey's aliases. She remarked she must be getting home or her mother would be worried.

The woman did not even bid her good-bye. She paced the room — her hair disheveled and face distraught. She kept pressing her hand to her forehead in a despairing gesture. She took in deep breaths and let them out wearily. She clasped and unclasped her hands and trod back and forth, back and forth, the length of the living room. A dumb dread shone from her feverish eyes. Perspiration studded her forehead.

Going down in the elevator, Lucille told the boy that she had not sold her dog and she was so disappointed! He was sorry too. She explained in tearful tones that the little boy had said, perhaps, they would buy her puppy when the father came home.

"Did the nice elevator man know what the papa looked like?"

I should say he did. He was a big, husky, rich stock-broker man from New York. He came home about every six months. They were expecting him now, Christmas time.

Lucille asked if he would let her pin her telephone number into his cap.

He would.

Then when the father returned would he telephone her and if she sold her little "Airedale doggie," the elevator man should have half the money.

"I'll sure do it!" he said.

We knew now that Mrs. Mabel H. Harrison was one of Furey's women; that undoubtedly the fur coat flung across the chair was the one sent from San Antonio and for the stealing of which the little shoplifter was probably doing time; that the checks indicated by the stubs in Furey's check book had been made out in favor of this woman.

From her agitation I knew she had received some sort of news from Furey. Was he on the way home? Had he been caught? Had he been killed?

I wondered what was passing through the mind of that woman. What does pass through the minds of women who live off the money filched from others? How do they feel at the touch of stolen gold? Does it never turn their hands cold with dread? In its brightness, do they never see the darkness? In the rich garments that wrap their calloused bodies, do they never feel the cling of others' rags?

That evening we celebrated with a nice little dinner, Mrs. Carson, Lucille and I.

At midnight I returned to my hotel and found a message for me from _____ _____ asking me to get in touch with him immediately. I did not get him that night, but the first thing in the morning found me at his office in the Hall of Justice. I thought it best to say nothing about the Stanford Court Apartments.

He looked very glad to see me; I couldn't imagine why. However he said he had received a wire from certain Los Angeles parties saying that Furey was registered right now at the U.S. Grant Hotel in San Diego. He advised me to get down there as quickly as possible. He told me the best way and the quickest route.

It seemed strange that he should be so kind to me now as his manner had been so unbearable the first time I met him. I thought it would be advisable to go to San Diego, but didn't like the rush act from him, even under the guise of sincerity. He continued urging and pressing me, declaring he knew the exact train I should take. He put my own hat on my head for me, took my arm and started to lead the way out.

Just before we left, I said to _____ in the presence of others: "Well, if you hear anything of Furey or my other men while I am away, let me know."

He dropped his suave oily manner and looked at me like some snarling animal and answered: "Let you know if I hear anything? I do not recognize you in the matter at all. If I get any news I'll let Jesse Brown know."

With this he plunged his hands in his pants pockets and tipped back and forth from toes to heels in an attitude of "Now what are you going to do about it?"

I was, of course, unprepared for this unwarranted turn of affairs. While, of course, Brown was my attorney — still I saw no reason why I should not be allowed to collect news for myself.

"I am the only party interested in this particular case, Mr. _____," I said. "I am also an officer of the law and am paying all the bills. Therefore, I can see no reason why I should not know the progress of my own affairs, regardless of Jesse Brown."

"Well," he jerked out like a snapping turtle, "I'm not going to recognize you in the matter at all. So there you are! Now, let's get going!"

We had little time to spare and I barely got aboard the train before it left. _____ waited until he saw me depart and then returned I supposed to the heavier duties of the day.

I got off at Los Angeles and called immediately at the Under Sheriff's office.

Al Manning said Anderson and Lips were still on duty.

"They are keeping a close watch on the Furey home," he reported.

In answer to my question as to "what was doing out there," he explained: "No news of any kind."

I thought it best not to say anything to Manning about Furey being in San Diego. Of course, what "authority" had sent the wire to ＿＿ I did not know, but as Manning did not mention it I concluded it was not from his office.

I then went to see District Attorney Woolwine and told him of the wire saying, "Furey was now registered at the U. S. Grant Hotel in San Diego," and that I had come down from San Francisco to investigate it.

He made no remark about having heard anything of the wire, but this did not make me suspicious.

Woolwine sent Kirkman, one of his trusted detectives to San Diego with me that afternoon. Kirkman registered at the U. S. Grant Hotel and I at a smaller one. He found out that Furey was not at the hotel nor was any trace of him to be found in San Diego. Kirkman then returned to Los Angeles and I remained there for two or three days searching the town.

Even at this time I suspected nothing.

Crowds of people were flocking to Tia Juana (Tee-a Whanna) for the races. "Wine, women and song" were in full swing. As I was so near I thought it might pay me to have a look there. These places are the mecca of the confidence crews.

All the money I had was ninety-three dollars. In a measure, I was sorry I had come down here so short of cash, but traveling costs money and with the expenses of others here and there, I was getting pretty low in funds. This worried me, as it was always a question whether or not I could arrange for more.

As I entered the gate and took a program I saw the first horse entered was a Texas horse. My ranching and racing blood rose in me.

I love horses and claim to be a fair judge of them.

It would be a poor Texas horse who couldn't win a little money for a Texas cowman, I thought. Especially when he needs it as much as I do. I knew something of the ancestry of this horse and after going through the paddock and looking him over, I asked the jockey, "How is he feeling?"

The little rider was preoccupied and didn't hear me. I considered the matter and decided I had better keep what money I had.

Soon I found myself back in the paddock. The jockey looked a little closer to the earth this time, so I tried it again.

"What is Texas going to do?" I asked.

"He's going to win this next race if he can run fast enough," he answered.

This struck me as an honest opinion. I counted my money; ninety-three dollars to the cent. Ninety dollars of this I would risk on a horse from my home state. At the betting booth I saw the odds were six to one against him.

"But he is from Texas!" I said to myself. I placed my bet on him and walked back to the starting post. By the time I reached there they were off. It was a one mile race. Once around, win or lose!

He was in good company. They were all real race horses and evenly matched.

I climbed up on the fence to get a better view. Shading my eyes with my hand, I watched the cloud of dust out of which would come five hundred and forty dollars, or leave me with three.

They had gone half the mile and were coming on, neck and neck. They ran like a bunch of blackbirds fly, close together, gaining little on one another. A saddle blanket would have covered them all.

My heart beat with their hoofs.

Closer! Closer! Closer!

They moved like a solid body. All at once from the telegraph pole on which I now found myself I saw my little baby in the lead.

Only a quarter mile now! Soon the suspense would be over. His nose came along ahead of the others.

He had the rail. That would help some!

"On! On! On! Coming!" I cried out loud in chorus with the thousands of other voices.

"Come on, you Texas! Remember your State, boy! Look who's betting on you. Walk over the rest of that gang. You can do it! You're from Texas."

"Come on! Come on! COME ON! Stretch your neck, I need you. Oh! how I need you. Now or never, boy! Step ahead of those snails."

I guess he heard me. Within two feet of the wire he was still nose ahead, but as he reached the wire he stretched out his head and pushed that little white face under the wire a full neck ahead of the others.

My limbs trembled as I slid to the ground. I collected my money and stuck it down deep into my pocket, rolling the bills over and over in my hand to be sure I wasn't dreaming.

I now had carfare for somewhere.

Chapter Nineteen - Across the Mexican Border

On the way out I noticed an old gentleman sauntering through the crowd. His gimlet eyes scanned the faces of the people. He answered the description of one Bill For see who had the reputation of being one of the squarest detectives that ever lived.

"Having any luck?" I asked him.

He looked surprised. I introduced myself, saying I was sure he was Forsee.

He admitted he was.

We talked a few minutes, and he told me he had been watching this place as well as San Diego for six weeks and that none of the gang for which I was looking had been there.

This made me think that _____ had been misinformed as to Furey's whereabouts.

When I got back to San Diego I rushed for a taxi back to Los Angeles. I was burning up for speed. Murder welled up in my heart. Over and over I declared to myself that I'd get the whole double-crossing gang and when I got them, they'd pay! I'd make them pay! The rest I hardly formulated into words I was so frenzied with greed for revenge.

Across the street stood an empty car with a sign "For Hire." I went over intending to get the driver to take me to Los Angeles.

"I'm booked up for a Tia Juana trip, but I'll get you a car going into 'Los'," he offered.

I recognized the boy as the son of an old Hale Center rancher. I inquired where his folks were and he pointed up the hill.

"Mother's living up there. She'd be mighty glad to howdy with you," he said.

I don't know why I did it, but I turned and climbed the hill to the little vine-covered cottage. The mother in a quaint old fashioned gingham frock and big white apron came out of the front door just as I closed the gate behind me. I went up the three low steps to her.

"Frank! Frank!" Then she took my hand and covered it in her motherly ones.

I must have looked wild-eyed, for she passed her hand across my flushed face as a mother soothes her child. She drew me down beside her on a porch bench.

There I told her how I had been double-crossed and how it had crazed me. She said nothing but patted my hand and nodded understanding. I broke away from her and strode down the path into the street and back toward the taxi station.

I don't know why I just up and ran but something ugly, something bestial drove me on, mixed with a fiendish longing for these men who had tricked me. I felt a gentle hand on my arm. I was so lost in bitter thoughts I jumped as if a branding iron were pressed against my flesh. I turned and the mother stood there. She said no word but caught again my trembling hands between her own.

"Vengeance is mine sayeth the Lord! Vengeance is mine!"

I caught my breath and looked into her face. So benign, so full of suffering, so patient and pleading.

"Remember, Frank! Vengeance is His!" She turned and went back up the hill and into the quiet of the seaside garden.

"Well I guess the train'll get me into 'Los' soon enough," I said to myself.

Without wasting any time after I got into town I went to the Sheriff's office. Who should be there in full force but all of the "night watch" ...Lips, Anderson and Manning. They were deep in conversation. Undoubtedly watching the Furey home was being done by the man in the moon. If someone had dashed a pan of ice water in my face, it couldn't have struck me with more of a shock than I felt as I entered that place and saw the three of them, heads together, talking in low tones.

I knew at once I had been double-crossed. This thought was so strong I acted on it and instead of bracing them in my natural way I cupped my hand behind my ear after the manner of the deaf and said in faint, husky tones:

"Hello, boys! Has anything developed?"

"What the matter?" asked Manning. "Why all the husky voice?"

"Got tonsillitis," I returned in a loud whisper.

I kept asking them to repeat and repeat, trying to drive it home to them that I could not hear.

"No, nothing developed," they said. They guessed my tonsillitis was about the only new thing that had developed since I left.

This seemed to strike them all as very funny and they did a lot of horse laughing. They were concerned about my throat, however, and suggested a certain kind of salve as a relief.

I went out and bought a jar of the stuff and got a piece of flannel on which to spread it. It was a warm day and I shall never forget having to do my good neck up in this hot, itchy, strong smelling, vaporous mess. Wherever I went the turpentine in the stuff heralded my coming. I went back to the Sheriff's office.

Every time anyone would come in and I would talk to them I would again put my hand behind my ear and shout that I could not hear, that they would have to speak louder. This went for the Sheriffs, Anderson and Lips.

Something had happened that they were keeping from me, I knew. What it was I had no idea. The whole atmosphere was charged with mystery.

I figured if I stuck around long enough and my tonsils did not improve that after awhile they would become so used to my deafness they might "spill the beans," thinking that I could not hear.

While this did not happen, still they did refer to me on several occasions as just an "old damn fool" who was sitting around here trying to catch Joe Furey, and "wouldn't that old sap get a kick if he only knew the truth!"

From things like this and understanding glances which passed from one to another, I saw "my goose was cooked" as far as their getting Furey for me was concerned.

I went to see Woolwine.

He had heard nothing new. My trail had petered out and I wondered where I would turn next. All I could hope for now was that the elevator boy in the Stanford Court would let Lucille know when Furey got home.

The only move I saw now was to find out if any telegraph messages had been sent from Mrs. Furey at Glendale to Furey at any point, or if Furey from somewhere had sent any to her. Forthwith I set out to see what could be done in this regard. It took some maneuvering, but I obtained a promise that if anything came over the wire, one way or the other, I would be notified There was nothing to do but settle down and wait.

One, two, three days passed. The waiting was agony. Time, that precious belonging of the busy, was slipping away. So far I had heard nothing from any living source. I sat in my hotel room. I paced the lobby floor until I expected

106

to be asked by the clerk to leave the pattern. Most of my time was spent in the Sheriff's office, keeping in the way. Still I waited.

Then one night, I was informed over the phone that Joe Furey had wired his wife a sum of money for a Christmas present from Jacksonville, Florida.

My throat and ears had what is known in metaphysical terms as "instantaneous healing."

I glanced at the clock. It was 10:30 p.m. The next train for Jacksonville left at 2 a.m. Four hours with nothing to do!

I had noticed some bright bouquets of desert flowers in the shop of a florist not far from the hotel. I thought they would be fine to take home as we do not have flowers in West Texas during the winter months.

I had spent so much time in the hotel the past few days, I became acquainted with Mrs. Tinkle, the manager's wife. She introduced me to one of the guests, a Mrs. Street. I recalled having seen this little lady in San Francisco, but she said she did not remember me. We talked at different times during the days I was waiting for my message to come through.

I settled my bill and checked out, remarking to Mrs. Tinkle that I wanted to get a bunch of those straw blooms to take home and asked her if she thought it was too late.

She said perhaps not; that she would be glad to show me the shop as it was only a few blocks from the hotel. She invited Mrs. Street to join us. The three of us went out that winter night after the dried flowers. By this time it was after twelve and the place was closed. We returned to the hotel.

Mrs. Tinkle went on duty and Mrs. Street said she would sit up and talk with me until train time. She had traveled a great deal and we discussed the different American cities, then she took me on a brief verbal trip through Europe.

She inquired where I was from and I told her Orin Junction, Wyoming, to which place I said I was returning, in time for Christmas dinner with my family. She hoped I would have a Merry Christmas and bade me good-bye.

My train ran through Littlefield, only one hour's ride from my ranch. I purposely concealed the fact from everyone that I was going to Jacksonville, Florida. I planned to leave the train at Littlefield, get home for Christmas dinner, and by catching the next train on the Santa Fe cut-off, go through Fort Worth, collect necessary papers and get into Jacksonville as soon as if I had not stopped off for my turkey.

My program worked on schedule time.

I walked in on the home folks just as the first spoonful of dressing was coming out of the big Christmas bird. Shouts of joy arose at my entrance. What more bliss can a man want than a home-coming such as mine? My little daughter threw her arms around my neck; her mother, God bless her, flung herself into my arms and Pete, my boy, put a sympathetic hand in his dad's and wrung it with silent understanding.

It was worth everything in the world to me to have that visit. Snatched from precious time, it filled me with new courage and determination to keep on.

It was like a chess game. The world the board, men and women the pawns; being moved from place to place; jumping each other here and there, gaining, losing, and slowly being eliminated, until I felt in the final move I would clear the board.

What a Christmas this was compared to my last one spent in San Bernardino!

In Fort Worth, I was overtaken by Pete, whom my wife had instructed to go to Florida with me and not let a soul know where we were going. She made it known in our locality that Pete was to join his father at the Ellis County farm where he was to become manager for some time to come.

The first stop we made was at Tallahassee, Florida. It was fortunate for us that the train stopped here as I wanted to get a requisition warrant from Governor Hardee, of Florida. Armed with this I could take Furey out of the State without the interference of his friends or tripping upon the coils of red tape which wind around those who wish to do business in a hurry.

Luck was with us. We saw the Governor without any trouble. I have found it true that usually the only person in any important office, who has no time to see you or is too busy to be polite, is the office boy.

I explained to the Governor what I wanted. Said I expected to get Furey in Jacksonville and with a requisition warrant for him (or J. B. Stetson) I could take him out of Florida the minute I got him.

Governor Hardee had heard of some of my experiences and was more than anxious to assist me.

What success I had in Florida, aside from flitting in and out of death traps like a moth through a flame, was due to the hearty co-operation of Governor Hardee.

He made out the warrant, signed it with his official signature and stamped its face with the great seal of the State of Florida. This in my hand, I would not have traded for all the jails and penitentiaries in the Southern State.

When I left the executive mansion the Governor wished me the best of luck and hoped I would get Furey and not Furey get me.

We arrived in Jacksonville the next morning. And who was the first person to greet my wary eye in the station but little Mrs. Street, to whom I had recently said good-bye in Los Angeles.

I wanted to say "hello" to her but thought it best to keep my arrival in town as quiet as possible. I had to think quickly as it was necessary to pass directly in front of her to get to the street.

I yanked my cap down over one eye and pulled a wisp of hair over the other. At my feet on the station floor was an emigrant's bundle of bedding with a child half asleep on top of it.

Before I could realize that I might be arrested for kidnapping, I swept the dozing baby into my arms and caught up the bulky bundle of gay colored patch-work quilts, and as if direct from Ellis Island, I sailed past Mrs. Street, my face buried on the dirty blouse of the small "Antonio." Outside the station door I set down the child and belongings and fled.

Chapter Twenty - 4,000 Miles Straight to Furey

I bought myself a new cap and had my mustache shaved off. We did not register at any hotel but got a list of the leading ones. Pete took four and I took the other four. We agreed to report to each other every forty-five minutes as to what we had seen.

Pete had never seen Furey. The only thing he had to go by was a picture and my description. Prior to taking up our watches I cautioned him to be positive he had Furey, and no one else, before tackling him. Also I cautioned him to be equally certain when he did pick up a hand, not to lay it down for anybody.

I was to cover the Seminole Hotel and Pete, the Mason. After mingling with the crowd drifting in and out of the impressive entrance without success, I noticed Pete coming.

We stepped inside the lobby door, and he whispered that he was sure he had seen Furey come out of the elevator at the Mason Hotel.

The man was the exact image of the picture of Furey and answered in every detail the description I had given him.

We both hastened to the Mason, but did not see Furey in the lobby. We took stands at the two corners of the street and waited.

Soon I saw Furey pass. Motioning for Pete to follow I trailed in behind. He went a short distance and entered the Hilton Cafe, taking a seat at a front table in the corner opposite the door. It was my intention to wait until Pete came in then we would eat, keep an eye on Furey and arrest him after he had returned to his hotel.

When I entered the cafe I saw that nearly all the tables were filled. The head waiter motioned me to a seat at Furey's table. My eyes followed his indicating finger.

At this instant, Furey, opening his napkin, looked up and saw me. His eyes lingered on mine but apparently he had not penetrated my disguise, but my general features stirred in his brain some memory. He continued to look at me.

I saw recognition come into his eyes. His trembling fingers clinked the table silver against the china with a metallic tinkle. In another minute he had himself under control. He looked out of his eyes like one who sees but cannot comprehend. He gripped the table with his hands. The blood receded from his large shapely fingers leaving them as white as the table cloth. His face blanched. He pushed the table from him and half rose from his chair.

At this moment I reached the table and stood directly in front of him. As he opened his mouth to yell I "threw down" on him with my gun, exclaiming:

"You can't do it, Furey! You're my prisoner!" This had no effect, for he raised his voice and cried out in a loud appeal:

"Don't let him rob me, men! Don't let him rob me! He'll take my diamonds — Don't let him do it! For God's sake, men, don't let him!"

At this the dining room was in a panic. Men, women and children fled. Some ducked under the tables and others jammed the entrance in an effort to escape. Jewels were torn from slim fingers by their owners and stuffed into stockings and bosoms, in an effort to save them. Men clutched their wallets, watches and scarf pins.

"Robber! Thief! Murderer! Help! Don't let him kill me, men! Gentlemen! For God's sake — Help! Help!" continued to scramble the air throughout the restaurant.

Shrieking women, screaming children, and cries of "Police!" "Police!" filled the atmosphere.

"Shut up! I've got you good this time, Furey," I said. "Your catcall won't help you."

At this moment I saw an expression of relief come over his face. My back was toward the door. Help in some form was coming to him. I still had him covered but did not dare turn my head to save my back. A form pressed itself against me from behind and my wrist was caught in a vise-like grip. Snap it went and my arm was bent to my side.

Furey, seizing this opportunity to escape, kicked his chair back from him and started for the door. He had to pass between me and the wall to get out.

As he lunged past me I reached out with my free arm and clutched his coat lapel in a death grip. I sunk my fingers into the thick cloth of his expensive garment until they nearly met my palm on the other side. While my other hand was pinned to my side by an unknown assailant, I still retained my revolver but no longer had him covered.

Someone in the crowd grabbed the muzzle of my gun and tried to wrench it from my locked grasp. I could not see how many people were behind me but it seemed I had the world at my back. The room swam before my eyes.

The riot was on! I was dragged by the back of my coat collar toward the lunch counter. The knuckles of my assailant dug into my neck. Bang! Bang! went the overturned tables. As I was dragged from the back I grabbed Furey from the front. What tablecloths my feet didn't catch, Furey's did, dragging china, glass and silver to the floor with deafening crashes. Everything was swept into the maelstrom.

Furey tried to get his heels on the floor and wrench himself free, but I continued to haul him along face down. What a sight we were! I tried to tell the officers that I held a warrant for his arrest, but my voice was as a sigh in the roar of thunder.

At this minute a powerful knee was driven into my back, and an arm locked about my neck tight under my chin, cutting off my wind and forcing me backwards. Then another arm went across my shoulder clamping the other hand around my wrist.

I glanced down at the hand on my shoulder. Where had I seen that ugly five-fingered fist before? That big scarred paw! The hair on the finger grew the wrong way. In a flash, I was back in the country club on the hill! I saw Steel, crumpling in his great scarred hand a little scrap of paper.

"My God!" I said, "I wish I'd killed him that day on the road."

Furey had fallen forward and sunk his long white teeth deep in my hand between the knuckles.

I yanked the bleeding member out of his mouth. The blood spurted up, blinding him. It ran down my arm and marked the white tiled floor in a gory stream. If he thought his cannibalism would loosen my grasp of him, he was mistaken. I could have dragged him to Texas. Nothing could separate my grip on him unless some one had cut my hand off. Between his cries for help he would snarl at my hand like a trapped wolf snaps at the trap that holds him.

Both of us had been wiping up the floor for the length of sixty feet. I was making a desperate effort to save my hand from the frothing jaws of Furey, prevent myself from being choked to death by my old combatant, Steel, and from having my back broken by some confederate of Furey's. I could think of nothing that could save the situation. I was one against an army of enemies.

In the riot I had forgotten all about Pete, so accustomed was I to battling single-handed. But just as hope seemed gone I saw Pete drive his gun into Furey's side.

He had seen the confusion from outside, but the throng of escaping diners choked the entrance so he had had to climb over chairs, tables and people, fighting his way through the panic-stricken crowd, beating clown first one and then another to get to me before someone killed me. He kept yelling that he was an officer, and the crowd to some extent let him trample on them thinking lie would help quell the riot.

Pete cracked one in the head and kicked over another. Those at my back went down like chips, under the blow of his gun. On hands and feet, spurting blood from their nostrils, they crawled in between the stamping feet of the crowd. He turned his back to the empty end of the room and with one gun in Furey's side turned the other on the crowd.

I could have pulled the trigger of the gun in my hand at any time during the fracas, but was afraid of killing some innocent person.

When the officers and the crowd saw Pete's gun on them, they quieted down.

Furey was still megaphoning for the police and broadcasting "Murder! Robber! Thief!"

Most of the crowd thought I was a hold-up man and Pete my assistant.

In the semi-silence induced by Pete's guns he yelled again that he was an officer and held a warrant for Furey's arrest. This he punctuated with another jab in the fugitive's ribs.

A big police officer slid around the other side of the room and coming up behind Pete raised his club to cave in his head. I shouted "Noble."

His club glanced off and barely escaped taking a piece of my son's skull with it.

I said: "For God's sake! man, can't you see we are officers of the law the same as yourself. Do you want to have a murder right here? Here is a county warrant in my son's pocket. If you can't believe me, take a look at it!"

I ordered him to call Detective Captain Cahoon.

"He knows us and our business," I said.

The incoming police cleared the wrecked cafe and hustled the loiterers out. I passed Furey over to the grasp of the officer and bound up my bleeding fist with one of the linen napkins.

Furey and the police officer walked between Pete and me all the way to the police station.

The officer in charge of the station asked the police officer who had accompanied us what all this "stuff" was about.

The officer told him he had seen through the window the riot going on inside; saw Pete with one gun on the crowd and the other in Furey' s side. When the people began to pour out through the door, shouting "murder! murder!" he dashed in and attempted to stop the affair. Pointing to me he said:

"This old man had Furey by the collar and this young fellow had his gun in his side. I thought the boy was robbing Furey and I was going to lay him out.

"The old man explained that Furey was their prisoner. So I brought 'em all up here to finish it."

Furey and the sergeant looked at each other, but spoke no word though it seemed to me a flash of understanding passed between them. The sergeant motioned to Pete to come closer.

"What right had you," he asked, "to have your gun in this man's side?" indicating Furey.

"I was helping my father arrest him."

"Well!" snapped the officer, "what right have you two got to arrest this man?"

Pete showed him the county warrant.

"How do you know this is the man?" he said after glancing at the paper.

Pete backed up the warrant with Furey's picture, which was a perfect likeness. The sergeant looked at it defiantly, then sneered:

"Do you call that a picture of this man?" He gave a sarcastic laugh.

At this I stepped toward the officer just as Furey rose and walked assuredly up to him saying:

"My name is Edward Leonard. I never saw either of these men before in my life. I am here on some very important business. Name my bond, officer, so that I may attend to my business without further annoyance."

With this pretty speech he ran his fingers up and down his mangled trousers pinching the creases into place. Carefully he patted out the rumpled coat lapel which had suffered in my grip. Then he brushed one palm against the other as if he were wiping his hands of the whole tiresome affair. I started to explain the situation but was cut short by the uniformed tyrant who, with a dictatorial wave of his hand ordered me to go back and sit down, saying:

"When we want to hear from you we'll ask you to speak — see?

"You wish to make bond then do you, Mr. Leonard?"

"I do!" said Furey with impressive dignity. With these directions the officer swung around in his swivel chair, picked up a pen and started filling out the bond form.

I bowed my neck and demanded to know what he was writing. Before he could answer me, Furey spoke up in a superior tone of voice saying:

"He is writing out my recognizance bond for one thousand dollars."

"Ah!" I ventured in a pleasant tone, "I see you are among friends."

I knew of course that this confidence gang boasted of their own private "pipe-lines" to many political executives as well as police headquarters and I now saw that the writer of the bond was one of the sections in the pipe-line which I was coming to regard as a "sewer" line.

I had not expected to prove my suspicions as to "Joe" being "among friends" as soon as I did, but I started a little direct action and whipped out my requisition warrant signed by the Governor of Florida and pushed it under the sergeant's nose, saying:

"This is what I'm arresting him on" and, sticking my gun into Furey's stomach. "This is what I'm taking him back to Texas on! Not tomorrow, or the day after, but now! Get me?"

The officer read the warrant. When he came to the Governor's signature his eyes stuck out of his head. He handed the warrant back to me and said apologetically to my prisoner:

"Mr. Furey, I cannot do a thing for you."

When he called his friend Leonard, "Furey," I gave him a long, narrow look and burst out: "Why, what do you know about that? So you know Mr. Furey, do you?"

"Well, well, well! We're bound to meet up with old friends, aren't we?"

When this broke some newspaper reporters who were listening in gave the disconcerted gold-braided one the horse laugh.

"How do you get that way?" they kidded him.

"They don't get that way!" hollered one of the writing squad, "they're born that way."

While speaking of friends who should appear at that moment but my dependable acquaintance, Cahoon, head of the detective force, and his assistant, "Shorty" by name but long by nature. I was among friends myself. After a brief but hearty exchange of greetings, I showed him my exhibit marked "F" for Furey.

"Put the bracelets on Mr. Leonard," I told Pete.

"Then get a service car. One that can take us across the Georgia line."

I was in a fine humor by this time and was recovering with rapidity from my bats and bites.

"What's the matter with your hand, Frank?" asked Cahoon.

"Why!" I answered, giving Furey the wink — "This young man bit off more than he could chew."

While we were waiting for the service car, the Head Deputy came dashing into the room from the County Sheriff's office. We had met several times the winter before and had been most fraternal. He was eager to help me.

"Don't bother to get a service car, Norfleet, let me take you and your man across the line. My God! man, I am glad to see you and under such happy circumstances."

I called Pete back and he countermanded the order for the taxi. We put Furey in the car between Pete and me; the Head Deputy drove. Our suitcases had to be collected from the station but this would take only a minute or two and after that was accomplished I figured if "we stepped on her" we could make the Georgia boundary in a few hours. The ramifications of this gang of Furey's were so far-reaching that the sooner over the state line the better.

As we were about to turn in at the New Union Depot, our friend the Deputy, slowed down, and looking at his watch exclaimed in an apologetic voice that he had an engagement and was sorry but he would not be able to take us across the line.

This was the second time that officers of the law had taken out their watches and "just thought of pressing engagements" when I had outlaws to be arrested. The last time was when I led the Police Chief at St. Augustine to the three Bockerman swindlers. Evidently when they wish to evade making an arrest all they do is take out their gold watch and have an engagement.

"Here are long lines of service cars, Dad," the deputy said, pointing in both directions. "You can get a good one anywhere along here to take you across."

This didn't sound good to me. "By heck, if you don't get us another car and driver just as good as this one, your engagement can go and you'll take us across and right now!"

"Well, now don't get all tore up about it," he soothed.

"Fiji not torn up at all," I said. "But I know somebody is going to be if matters don't clear pretty quick. Furey's going across the Georgia line with me tonight — dead or alive!"

"Well, well, I'll go get a taxi. Just hold on a minute." He got out and walked off in the direction of the waiting service cars.

In a minute we saw him picking his way back through the heavy traffic in a Cadillac car piloted by a colored driver. We transferred Furey to the hired vehicle and directed the chauffeur to drive to the Dinsmore Flag Station, fourteen miles from Jacksonville.

Our friend had suggested if I took him there I could secrete him in the forest until the first train came along. By hiding him thus I could prevent habeas corpus proceedings or any other court procedure instituted to detain me. Also he argued that in this way I would lose no time.

114

It struck me as a good plan, and we started off in the direction of the little flag station.

Furey had remained silent during all the maneuvers and offered no objection to the conditions. Evidently he was considering a diplomatic tack when the occasion presented itself.

As soon as we were beyond the town limits he began to beg for freedom. He said he would make good to me every cent I had lost through him and his confederates.

"I'll give you twenty thousand dollars of it tonight," he cried.

For miles he kept up a steady fire of pleas and promises. I told him I would certainly like to have the money if I could get it for I certainly needed it, but —

"I wouldn't trust you if you were dead," I snorted.

"You don't know me," he sighed.

I told him maybe I didn't, but we would have a chance to get better acquainted on the way back to Fort Worth.

This made him wince.

"Oh! my God! have mercy, and let me pay you back and go," he moaned. "Don't take me back to Texas, Norfleet. Oh! my God! for the love —."

"I know all about the suffering humanity, and the rash acts, and I'm not going to take a brainstorm, so you may just as well save your breath. You're going back to Texas!"

A creek ran alongside the railroad bed and made a sharp bend about three hundred yards from the track and no more than one hundred feet from the main road over which we had come. The vicinity was well wooded. A dense forest had grown up but woodsmen had thinned the tall pines to some extent and left here and there a stump about two feet high. The broad, flat shielding palmetto shrubs were thick and provided ideal seclusion.

Chapter Twenty-One - As the Golden Sun Melted Into Red

I got Furey out of the car and set him on a stump facing the road and flag station.

He plumped his big body down with a fat sigh and dejectedly folded his handcuffed hands.

"Norfleet!" he wailed, turning his beady eyes on me, "can't we get down to business? I'll see that your son, Pete, gets twenty thousand dollars as soon as he can get to Jacksonville. I'll stay here with you" — this did amuse me — "And when he comes back he'll have that much — on — on account as we say in business."

"Where are you going to get twenty thousand?" I inquired without a great show of interest.

"My friends were there with me in the restaurant."

"Was Spencer there?" I cut in.

"Yes and others too," he replied. "Several of us are — er — were rooming together in the Mason Hotel. They will be there now. Our headquarters are in Room 1000 at the hotel. We were just closing one of the biggest deals that we ever pulled off in Florida. In another hour it would have been finished and I would have had my percentage of seventeen thousand dollars. You damned old trail hound! If it hadn't been for you butting in I'd have had it by now and been out of the rotten State instead of being chained here to a log like some animal." He puffed for breath and great round beads of perspiration coursed down his cheeks.

"I'll write out an order payable to Pete for twenty thousand dollars. Have him go back there at once and present it to Weintrot, the treasurer of the exchange, bring the money back to you, then you can do as you please until I pay you the balance of twenty-five thousand. Or I will give you a deed to my apartment house on the corner of _____ and _____ San Francisco, with an approximate valuation of thirty-three thousand dollars which is in the name of my financial agent, Mrs. Mabel Harrison, or," gasping for more breath, "my half interest in a 400-acre ranch near San Luis Obispo, California."

"Who owns the other half?" I asked.

"My financial agent," he said.

The thought of a partnership with the agitated female at Stanford Court Apartments made me laugh. He thought I didn't believe him and burst out indignantly that this wasn't by any means all he owned. My mind flew to my visit to the tax collector.

"No, I know that, Joe," I said casually. "Your Glendale residence isn't any dump!"

"Glendale!" he shot at me. "Damn your western soul."

"Now listen to me, Furey. I'm going to let you write out that order for the twenty thousand and I'm going to let Pete take it and present it for payment. But I want this to sink into you and sink deep. If you get Pete into any of your traps; if anything happens to him, or if he isn't back here by the time this sun goes down, your light goes out. Is that understood?"

"Yes," he answered quickly.

I felt that if he was not sincere he would have taken no chances, as he knew I would surely kill him if Pete did not return by sun-down.

I gave him a pencil and a piece of paper.

As best he could he wrote out the order and signed it.

I gave it to Pete who had heard the conditions.

He jumped into the car and told the driver to "step on it" all the way in to the Mason Hotel.

"I'll be back before the sun goes to sleep, Dad," he called to me, "and bring Spencer along if I can."

When I saw him speeding into, God knows what danger, I wondered if I had done the right thing. Still, I thought, Furey thinks too much of his own hide to take a chance.

As soon as Pete disappeared in the distance, Furey turned to me with an expression of curiosity on his face. "Well, you old trail hound, I never expected to see you out here. How did you get here? I thought we left you in Fort Worth, broke!"

"I was a trifle bent," I admitted. "But I lacked a whole lot of being broke." I had no desire to let him know how nearly he had ruined me completely.

"That's just it. I thought we had you strapped. I had no idea you could get hold of another hundred dollars to follow us with."

"Am I the first man you ever robbed that followed you up? What did you expect me to do?"

"What did I expect? Why, that you would do as the other old chaps have done, either get sick over the loss of your money and die off within a year or go 'nuts' grieving after it and take a shot at yourself. Either way you would have been unable to bother me."

I laughed. Evidently I was of a different breed.

The idea of giving up because I was broke! Why I had been broke a dozen times until climbing back up had become a habit, no matter what the odds were nor how hard a bump I had just had.

Joe was silent for several minutes then began muttering as if to himself:

"I told 'Goldie' this old man would be our ruin. I told him I didn't want to get tangled up with him. A fool that don't know when he's broke is bound to be dangerous."

"What's the matter, Furey? Talking to yourself?" I asked.

Furey shot me an appraising look from under half-shut lids.

"I wish to God we had killed you the last time you were in Florida! We planned to, but didn't go through with it. I have spent seventeen thousand dollars keeping out of your way. If ever there was a nemesis, you have been mine. I have lost through your damnable hounding as much money as I have made. Believe me, in my game, the best of them don't hesitate to shake us down. A lot of officials wouldn't have the guts to go out and take a man's money away from him, but they have no scruples at taking the money away from the fellow who risked his life to get it. It's a fine world," he complained bitterly.

This reference to his being "shaken down" by certain officials started a train of thought in my mind. I had realized for sometime that I had been double-crossed on the Glendale angle of my hunt. Lips and Anderson had undoubtedly done me out of Furey. I could not prove this, but I wondered if these "shaking officials" could by any chance be the ones Furey was referring to so acidly.

"How in the devil did you get here so quick? I left you only a few days ago in California. My God! you can get in the way more than any human being I ever saw."

117

"Well, Furey," said I, watching him narrowly to see the effect of my words, "those California Sheriffs gave us both a fine double-crossing, didn't they?"

He darted me a glance I'll never forget. The blood receded from his big face and left him chalk white. Then it rushed up into the roots of his hair, straining his face a deep red. Revelation came into his eyes.

"God Almighty, Norfleet!" he cried. "Is that, is this — this — did they squeal on me? I paid them twenty thousand dollars. They wrung it from me. They had me when I went home to Glendale and they put their price at twenty thousand dollars. I paid it! I bought my release and this is what those sons of snakes have done to me!"

He covered his face with his hands. Between his fingers I could see the heavy veins swell out until his forehead was seamed with ridges. His passion so consumed him, he was left weak and trembling. He rent the air with curses, calling down upon Lips and Anderson every known anathema.

"I know that, Furey," said I, trying to conceal my excitement over the news. "But I thought you were the one who always got the money," I continued.

He was breathing so hard from the shock of his betrayal I feared he would have an apoplectic stroke before I could drag from him the truth about Lips and Anderson.

"Oh! I know they got the money," I lied convincingly. "But tell me how they managed it!"

He drew in a long breath which caught in little spasms. He rubbed his hand across his brow, jingling the chain of the handcuffs.

"Norfleet! I have not had one minute's peace since I left you in Fort Worth. I have run over the face of the earth. But not one minute's peace have I had, except in Europe. To think of it, the first day I put my two feet back on American soil I find you on my trail, hotter than the fire of hell!

"Why before I got into my home in Glendale, when my little boy ran to me throwing his arms about my neck, and I was kneeling down on the walk to return his joyous greetings those 'bulls' ran out of my own house, down my own front steps, and pounced on me, coupling my hands like this!" He raised his manacled wrists.

"I made a desperate break for liberty. My little boy threw his child body between the two deputies and myself. This confused them and I leaped over one of the men and dashed up the steps, in through the house. My wife was coming down the stairway and saw me rush through the hall and out the back door into the yard, followed by the two officers. 'Joe! Joe!' she cried after me. But by that time I was out into the backyard. I made a high jump to lock my hands over the top of the eight-foot fence, which would have landed me into the orchard and from there I could have gained the park and had a fifty-fifty chance of escape. My hands slid off the fence on the other side and I would have followed them over but was caught in the middle and for a moment I hung across the fence top, like scales in balance. Finally I fell backward into the soft earth on the side from which I sprang. Bullets from the officers' guns hailed about me. I thought I was done for."

He shifted his bulk on the stump and said suddenly:

"Now I can see why their aim was poor. Oh, my God! if I had ever — ever dreamed they intended to sell me out!"

He looked into my face, then shifted his gaze far away over my shoulder and peered into space. I imagined he was mentally miles away, living over again the scenes that had led him into my trap. Suddenly I saw the muscles in his neck contract.

He flinched as if a blow had been aimed at him.

Terror came into his eyes.

Like a bolt of lightning illuminates the sky, it flashed across my mind that someone was behind me! Furey had been looking me straight in the eye. Now, his gaze shifted from side to side.

I jumped back, putting myself outside his reach, then darted a quick glance behind me.

I saw the muzzle of a sawed-off shot-gun not sixty steps from me. Instantly it was jerked under the broad, flat fans of the dense palmettos. I sprang behind Furey. putting his heart between me and the shot-gun. I pressed my old forty-five against his head just behind his right ear.

"Furey," I bellowed so that the palmettos could hear, "I am going to make an ambush out of you and this stump and sell out for the highest price I can get for myself. They are not going to take you away from me — not alive!" I waited to let this sink in. "You had better warn them to go back where they came from."

"Go back, men! Go back! For God's sake, go back!" he implored, raising his voice high in pleading. He begged them "for the love of suffering humanity, to go back! go back!"

The woods rang with his supplications.

Not a leaf stirred. Not a twig cracked.

The forest was loud in silence.

I knew I had seen the cold muzzle of steel.

I knew it was intended for my back but life all about us was so still, I wondered if I was having a brainstorm. I would soon find out.

Furey was writhing and throwing a fit on the stump.

"You sit tight on your little wooden stool!" I snapped, and drove my words in with a jab of my gun behind his ear.

I was afraid he would make a break into the underbrush and complicate matters. He kept up a steady flow of pleas for mercy and he wasn't the only one who thought it was perhaps the "last days of Pompeii."

"If you over there behind those palm leaf fans, don't show up, and pretty quick, I'm going to do some bombarding into your hiding place that'll make you either stand or lie down forever."

Like jumping jacks, four men sprang to their feet, showing themselves, heads and shoulders above their shelter. They were not woodsmen, but of the city type.

Between the time I had sprung in back of Furey and delivered my ultimatum, they had crept as noiselessly as the creeping creatures of the swamps, twenty steps closer to me and far enough to one side to have a broadside shot at me, had I still been facing Furey.

In a flash I calculated the distance between me and the shot-guns. Would they have the necessary range to blow me to atoms?

I knew what my forty-five could do.

It looked as if the time for battle had come. Furey evidently thought the same thing for he began afresh his cries to spare his life.

"Go back! Never mind who sent you, never mind what you were told to do or who told you, just go back! go back!"

The men stood like four soldiers in a row but never moved an inch. They stood and stared.

What their idea was in playing petrified I could not imagine, and it made me uneasy for fear they had reinforcements somewhere close.

"Men!" I asked, calmly as possible, "what is the nature of your business?"

One of them answered, prefacing his reply with an oath:

"Our business is to find out what your business is!"

"Gentlemen, I am an officer of the law. This man is my prisoner. I am holding him here for a little while, or until I get ready to let him go. I am attending to my own business and don't need any of your help! I think it is best for you all that you move backward!"

They bent their heads together and spoke in low tones. Then slowly they moved back to the roadside and halted.

Long shadows from across the creek fell upon us. The pine trees split the rays of the lowering sun. Deathly stillness hung over the forest. I wondered what time it was. I said to Furey:

"Pete could have been to Jacksonville and back again by this time."

"For God's sake don't worry about him, Norfleet! He'll be back again before sunset. The sun is still yellow."

"It will be black for you if he doesn't come back," I replied.

Furey put his hand to his ear. I had dropped my gun to my side but held it ready for action.

"Listen!" he exclaimed. "Listen! I hear him coming now. I hear the engine of the car in the distance. He'll be here in a minute. Thank God!" he cried, almost in tears.

His prophecy was true, in a measure. Almost as he spoke the words a car shot into view from the direction of Jacksonville. It ran up near to the group of men standing in the road, turned to the right, circled and backed into the woods with the car headed back toward Jacksonville.

Pete was not there!

Three men got out.

Each man had a riot gun. They walked up to the other four men and held a conference in muffled voices, every now and then darting furtive glances toward Furey and me.

Well! thought I to myself, the reinforcements have arrived. When does the shooting begin?

I saw little chance of getting out of this trap without changing the soft green of the moss under foot to red. The council by the road continued in session.

"Furey, if you have anything to get off your conscience you'd better begin to unload!"

"What do you mean, Norfleet? You aren't going to kill me, are you?" he cried in trembling tones.

"I mean if there is anything you want to make right with your God, it looks like now is the time to do it."

I was thinking about a few little matters I wanted to square with the Almighty and felt I could afford to give Furey the same opportunity. He could use his own judgment about taking it.

The golden sun had melted into red. Slowly it slipped down behind the trees. Soon it would meet the horizon; then sink from sight on the other side of the earth's rim.

It was the biggest, the reddest sun I have ever seen.

As I looked at the blood-red disc hanging in the sky, it brought to my mind the picture of the siege of the Alamo, and the blood-red banner the Mexican soldiers unfurled just before charging the intrepid Texans who had barricaded themselves in the old mission in the "War of Independence," in 1836.

Chapter Twenty-Two - Some: Negro Chauffeur!

'Twas dawn when the gallant Travis
Gazed down at the Mexican foe
Whose numbers ever increasing
Surrounded the doomed Alamo.

"Our time has come," he quickly cried.
"We must conquer or die today!
See that blood-red banner hoisted?
It means 'no quarter' in the fray!"
* * * * * *

— (From "*The Battle of the Alamo*," by an anonymous author.)

I pointed my thumb across my shoulder. "Furey," I said, "look at that sun!"

He turned and looked at the great crimson ball. A slice of its circular base had been cut off by the earth. Down, down, it sank as if drawn from sight by unseen hands. My heart skipped.

There was no sign of Pete. My senses were quickened for the sound of a car. The country about us was dipped in the red rays. The pines were dark striplings against the flaming sky.

My God! I thought, would Pete never come. Before me sat the man whose life I had sworn to take if Pete did not return at the setting of the sun.

Furey turned his head and jerked it back again as if averting a blow. Half of the deep ball of fire was gone.

The shadows crept closer and wrapped us in their mystic folds. I wiped my clammy fingers on my side.

"Norfleet!" groaned Furey, "He will come! He will come! I know he will! I hear him now, I hear him now. Don't you hear it? Listen! Listen!"

I strained my ears until I thought they would drop from my head. It was the unmistakable hum of a Cadillac.

A greater fright clutched my heart!

If Pete had come from danger, was he not riding directly into greater danger? The seven marksmen in the road had heard the approach of the car. They arranged themselves as if under command, three on one side and four on the other, guns in hand.

My heart rose into my throat, choking me.

"Furey!" I exclaimed, "I am afraid those thugs are either going to kill or kidnap my son! If they do either, I'm going to treat you just as I promised."

The car rushed on toward the firing squad. Four of the men turned their attention to its approach and the other three kept their eyes on us. The machine was within one hundred yards of the men in the road.

I wanted to yell to Pete to be ready for action, but that was impossible.

I lived years from the time I saw the car until it came along the road between the armed flanks.

I put the gun behind Furey's ear again and waited while my boy rushed headlong into this army of thugs.

The least mistake and God knows what the result. It seemed as if all that lived in me left my body. I was suspended between action and inertia.

The whole situation came to me in the winking of an eye; a long story visioned in the space of a heartbeat.

Furey was quick to get the drift. He waved his shackled hands aloft and shouted the same old instructions with slight variations:

"Men! Men! for the love of God! Don't start anything! Don't start anything!"

As for kidnapping Pete the fear was an idle one. The negro chauffeur took one look at the men and riot guns and couldn't have stepped on the gas harder if he had been a centipede. Like a shot from a cannon the Cadillac zipped past the guards, crossed the creek and kept on its way at seventy-five miles an hour. He was a scared colored gentleman!

Pete leaned toward him and flung his hand back in our direction, shouting to him to turn the car and go back. But the African continued to feed the gas. Pete stood up, lunging from side to side as the great car rushed over the rough road. He tried to take the wheel from the negro's hand but the black boy was bent double over it, his eyes on the next town.

Pete pulled out his little persuader and stuck it against the darkey's head.

"Now you turn back!" he roared.

The car slowed up.

"God! A'mighty! Boss, doan do dat!" he implored, trembling from head to foot. "Doan do dat! Dey got de Cap'n now, our turn am next!" he chattered. "Let's go back to Jacksonville, Boss, and tell de story dar! — Foh de love of God! Boss, don't make me turn around!"

Pete and the gun were too much for the boy. He swung the car round in the road and came slowly back to the bridge. They drove across, but instead of continuing on the road to the men they swung at right angles from the road and the car plowed its way down the little slope, stopping close to Furey and me.

Pete looked amazed at the increased number of friends and leaped to the ground.

"Dad, what is all this about? What does it mean?" indicating the seven co-nundrums.

"Mean!" I responded as mystified as he. "Don't ask me what it means. But I have expected hell to break loose ever since you left here."

I saw the chauffeur was making stealthy preparations to back the car out of the creek and speed to safety.

"Here you! cut that out! If you can't stand up to it, get out and lie down to it! Get under that running board."

He stretched himself full length under the board and burrowed his body into the sand until he was even with the ground. He was so near the color of it I had to look twice to see if he was there.

I told Pete to get Furey into the car.

"Put him on the back seat on the right side. You sit on the left, and when I give the signal drive slowly past me with the front door open and I'll get in. We will have to make it quick, too, if we are to reach the station and flag the train. It's a chance and we'll have to take it. There is nothing else to do. If nothing slips, we may catch the train."

I walked half way from the car to where the men were standing to prevent them from springing a surprise on us while Pete was getting Furey seated.

I looked back. Pete and Furey were occupying the right and left sides of the back seat and the driver had forsaken his dugout for the wheel.

I beckoned them to come ahead.

They drove up to the road.

I jumped in and we passed them by. We were so seated that had they tried to plug us, Furey's life would have been endangered.

We reached the flag station in one minute. I could hear the train coming. I jumped into the road and ran to the track. The train was in sight.

Waiting at the crossing were a man, woman and two little girls in a buggy. When the man saw me standing in the middle of the track waving my arms like a scarecrow, he explained that the train did not stop.

"It's a limited and does not pay any attention to flagging/'

"Why the Deputy Sheriff at Jacksonville told me to come out here and flag the train. He said it would stop and I could take this man aboard."

123

"Well, I live right near here and I know it wouldn't stop if you waved all night. It's a 'through' and absolutely stops for nothing at this point."

This struck me with the full force of a blow.

I looked at Pete. A grim smile was spreading over his face.

"Kind of looks like we got helped off on the wrong foot, Dad."

His words were drowned in the roar of the passing train. The man was right.

I walked over to the family in the vehicle.

"Sir," I said, "my son and I are officers of the State of Texas. This man in our car is our prisoner. We have gone through hell to get him. The Deputy Sheriff at Jacksonville advised us to bring him to this point and signal the train and get aboard. We followed his instructions. You see the result. I cannot understand any more why he should have misadvised us in this regard than I can understand why those seven men with riot guns (which are usually the property of police departments only) have followed us here, especially as the Deputy Sheriff was the only person who knew of our destination. Life is strange, isn't it? However, I am telling you this for the reason that we will have to go back the way we came. If anything happens to us on the return trip you have the information and can relate the circumstances to the proper authorities."

I got back into the car.

The driver said he thought there was a train leaving Jacksonville on another road that could be caught if we hurried.

I asked him if he could take us across the Georgia line from where we were parked.

He said the road was impassable, but that he would do his best to get us to Jacksonville in time to catch the other train. This train would go direct to New Orleans, connecting there with one to Fort Worth, Texas.

He stepped on the gas again. We circled and faced our gun squad once more. It seemed we would never get out from under the scrutiny of firearms.

"Well, here goes another chance, Pete!" I said resignedly.

We were seated as before; our hands clasping our guns. It was necessary to pass between the two cars of artillery; four men in one and three in the other. The cars were headed toward Jacksonville with engines running.

This looked to me like a race. As our car darted between the other two, they flanked us.

I looked back.

"How fast can this bus go?" I asked the driver.

He said he didn't know but this was a good chance to find out.

The trailing machines were rocking with speed. We gradually gained on them.

The wheels became wings.

I glanced at the speedometer. It registered seventy-eight miles an hour! It didn't seem possible.

I dreaded to think what would happen if we hit a rut.

124

No sooner thought, than I saw the great form of Furey rise and jump full force on the driver's back. He grabbed the steering wheel, jerked it to the right, plunging the huge car off the dump.

The barrel of my gun met his forehead with a crashing blow and sent him senseless to the floor of the tonneau.

The impact of Furey's weight crushed the negro's body against the steering wheel, throwing the big car out of balance. It shuddered and dived off the dump at the side of the road, rose in the air on the rear tires, then leaned and swung over on one side until I thought the next instant we would be pinned beneath its roaring body. The driver righted the wheel, threw the weight of his big form on the rearing side and rode it like a bronco never was ridden. Unseen pounds of might he seemed to throw into the balance.

Slowly the giant piece of machinery returned its four wheels to the ground but was still tearing its unlawful way through the forest of small pine trees, stripping the bark from their young trunks for a distance of forty yards.

Furey's inert body slid from one side of the car floor to the other.

With scarcely slackened speed, the chauffeur guided the pulsating car back into the road and we continued our race from death, still in the lead of the pursuers and without loss of more than forty yards.

Chapter Twenty-Three - Furey Stages a Get Away

We made Jacksonville without further mishap.

At the station the driver took the suitcases, Pete took charge of Furey, and I hastened to get a drawing room to New Orleans. "All aboard" was being called as we shoved Furey up the steps and into the vestibule.

I sank down upon the seat of the private compartment and wondered if we were really on the train or simply dreaming. The let-down was a relief, and it was all I could do to keep awake now that the strain was over.

Pete then told me about his trip to Jacksonville. He had gone to the Mason Hotel and to Room 1000 where he found seven men busily engaged in packing and crating all kinds of paraphernalia, consisting of bulletin boards, telegraph instruments, etc., showing that the "headquarters" of the gang had really been another fake stock exchange.

As Pete entered, one of the men came forward. Pete asked for Weintrot, to whom Furey had addressed the note.

"He is not here," the man said. "I think he is downstairs. I'll go get him for you."

Several minutes passed, but the man did not return.

Another man, noticing Pete standing at the door, asked his business, and again Pete inquired for Weintrot.

"I'll go get him," this second man replied. "I think he is downstairs."

This was repeated at intervals for perhaps an hour until only one man was left in the room, and Pete realized his time was up if he was to keep his appointment with me by sun-down.

The landlord of the Mason Hotel told me afterward that twelve rooms were vacated that afternoon, the occupants grabbing what was easiest to handle and leaving behind toilet articles and soiled linen in their mad get-away.

Furey was furious when he heard Pete tell me how his friends had deserted him and began walking up and down the stateroom wringing his hands.

"Dad, we'd better put an extra pair of bracelets on Joe, don't you think?" asked Pete.

I said I thought we should.

All during the time Furey had had on the handcuffs, he kept working with them in an effort to get the chain attached to the two swivels into a position where he could snap the link that locked one hand to the other. This action gave him the appearance of wringing his hands. Men have snapped their hands free, so I figured an ounce of prevention would be worth the pound of cure.

Our prisoner was pacing the length of the drawing room. I could have bound him to the seat which would have been the cautious thing to do, but his strain was as great as ours. He was like some trapped animal, and I felt I could not deprive him of exercise.

Suddenly he side-stepped through the door into the aisle of the train. He stood at the head of the car and began whining and pleading for sympathy.

"Women! Men! Oh, women!" he begged, his face reflecting agony and torture.

He was a sight to arouse compassion and certainly master of the method.

This cry for help, of course, drew every eye in the train to him.

"Why don't you help me? These men have abused me! I am suffering. All day I have not had a bite to eat nor a drink of water to cool my scorching tongue. For God's sake help a dying man!"

His voice rose to a dramatic height, then broke under perfect emotional control. I really believe if anyone had passed the hat, he could have collected enough to pay back what he had stolen from me.

Two dear old women rushed to his side.

While he was talking I saw at the extreme end of the car, my old friend, Mrs. Street, of the Alhambra Hotel, Los Angeles, whom I had seen in the Jacksonville railroad station. Apparently she did not see me and I had no time to inquire of her health just then.

"You poor man!" cried the female Samaritans in unison, shooting looks of contempt at me that would have done justice to wildcats.

Pete, unfortunately for the sufferer, interrupted the offered ministrations of the ladies, grasping Furey's supplicating hands in an iron grip forcing him backward into the compartment. He sat him down on the long couch which faced the window, then sat down beside him on the seat next to the door.

I stood in the doorway between the onrushing females and their object of solicitude.

At this moment the news and fruit vendor came through with a basket of magazines and oranges, grapes and bananas.

Feminine fingers lifted great purple bunches of the luscious fruit of the vine, others selected juicy oranges and still others chose bananas for the abused one.

I stood with both hands held out accepting their offerings and thanking them profusely. The pile of fragrant fruits grew into a small mountain on my hands.

I looked like a "horn of plenty" at an autumn food show. As contributions were made with appropriate slams at Pete and me for our inhuman treatment of our charge, the conductor came through and joined the "sisters of mercy," looking over the marcelled heads of the ladies to see what all the excitement was about.

Pete, hearing the verbal grenades hurled at us by these tender-hearted women, looked up at me and laughed.

'Tis said: "He laughs best, who laughs last."

Furey must have known this, for while Pete had relaxed his watchful waiting to see the comedy in the doorway, Furey crossed his hands before his eyes and took a high dive through the car window, staging a head-on collision with the projecting end of a railroad tie, cutting a three cornered canal in his head from temple to temple.

I heard the splinter of glass and turned just in time to see the soles of his shoes follow his head through the jagged opening.

The conductor pulled the bell cord. The train slowed down and Pete flung himself through the exit cut by Furey.

I raced to the window and looked out, throwing Pete my gun.

The last I saw of Pete he was racing down the tracks after Furey.

I fought my way through the jam in front of the door and rushed for the steps. I swung to the ground and caught the suitcases hurled after me by the porter.

In another instant the train was on its way. I stacked the luggage to one side of the track and ran toward Pete who was beckoning me to hurry.

"Dad," gasped Pete, "a switch engine picked Furey up and he is gone!"

This was astounding news. I had no idea there was so much bad luck in the world. I am not superstitious, but I found myself wondering if after all, it was intended that I should get Furey.

"Which way did he go?"

"That way!" pointing down the track which made a sharp curve and hid the runaway engine and rider.

I saw we were standing almost under a tall square signal tower built on narrow steel stilts. I shouted up to the signal man. He stuck his head out one of the windows.

"Say!" I called up to him through my megaphoned hands: "Can you wire in to W. B. Cahoon, of the City Detective Bureau, Jacksonville? Tell him to look out for Furey — Joe Furey — who jumped off the train and caught a switch engine probably bound for Jacksonville! Tell him Norfleet sent him the word."

How much of my message the man got I do not know, but he nodded his head, pulled it in and shut the window.

A little way down the track another engine snorted and blew off steam. We asked the engineer if he could catch the engine that passed his a minute or two ago.

We explained about the escaped prisoner.

"You bet your life we can catch him!" he exclaimed enthusiastically.

"Jump on!"

We did and he gave orders to uncouple the two cars from the locomotive.

He threw the throttle wide open and in another instant we were thundering down the steel rails. We swung around the curve and sighted the other engine in the distance.

"There she is!" cried the engineer, cocking the throttle way back and giving the great hissing, shrieking creature a new speed.

We leaned far out of the cab window. The terrific heat beat in our faces.

The heavy iron wheels pounded on the glistening rails and ground down the distance between us and the locomotive ahead.

"We're gaining on 'er!" yelled Pete.

The great boiler trembled and shook. It took deep hot breaths and let them out with the hiss of Hades. I could not understand why under the great steam pressure the throbbing black body did not blow up.

The race kept up for five or six miles with us gaining on the truants ahead.

The engineer blew several shrill blasts. We were almost in the railroad yards of Jacksonville.

The locomotive in front of us stopped.

We caught up with it in time to see a policeman hurry through the gates from the street and go up to the cab.

He spoke a few words to the engineer and Furey stepped down into the officer's charge.

Pete and I reached the two of them at this moment. Explanations were made to the policeman and Furey delivered back into our hands.

His curses rivaled the noises of the freight cars.

However, we were used to these. With Joe it was either prayers or "swears."

We decided to leave him in jail for the night then proceed on our journey the next evening, hoping for better luck en route.

It was well on its way toward midnight. We had not eaten during the day.

On our way from the jail in search of food, we ran into the same officer who assisted in escorting Furey and us to the Jacksonville Police Headquarters the day before.

He was the officer whose blow was aimed at Pete's head. Sight of him brought back the bloody scene in the restaurant.

It seemed like it had happened years ago instead of less than twenty-four hours before. Time had been so crowded with death-dealing adventures that this part of our battle had been forgotten. Now after the strain had been let up and Furey safe behind bars, a flood of fraternal feeling swept over me at the sight of the officer, like one who greets with pleasant memories the comrade with whom he has "gone over the top."

We said "Howdy" all around and launched into a graphic account of our wild day. I told him I was a little skeptical about leaving Furey in the jail as most peculiar jail breaks have been recorded, but added I saw no other way out as I disliked parading him through the streets all night.

I asked if he could think of some trustworthy person in whose house we could keep him until train time the next night.

He said he would try to think of someone and while we were eating, he would go home and get his Ford. He directed us to a little restaurant and agreed to meet us there in a few minutes.

The cafe was a small, dingy chop house with the usual arsenic green ceiling, high glaring lights and greasy dishes. To us, it was a banquet hall.

It must have been about an hour from the time we left Furey within the confines of the jail when our friend returned in his car to gather us up.

He burst in through the door, rushed over to us and exclaimed in guarded tones that we must hurry back to the jail at once,

"What's up?" I cried, knowing that some more bad luck was in store for us.

"Why!" he blurted out excitedly, "Furey has a lawyer and he is preparing habeas corpus papers to serve on you. If we can get there within the next few minutes, we can get Furey out and beat it before they serve them."

Well, when things go bad enough, it gets to be just a round of pleasure. Things had about reached this stage with me. I took just as much interest in the affair as if it were a stroke of fortune. If we succeeded in getting him out of jail, it would be.

At the jail we claimed the right to remove our prisoner, momentarily expecting to be pounced upon by a process server. But either he was late or we were early, for we receipted for Joe, and led him, still manacled out to the car. We piled him in, followed suit ourselves and drove off under the shelter of the night.

We drove and drove and drove. It seemed we covered almost the distance between there and Fort Worth. Everything was strange and quiet. Furey's groans and other manifestations of suffering were all that could be heard in the stillness. However, he drew little sympathy from our friend.

We stopped in front of a colonial residence; an immense old mansion in the center of spacious grounds.

"I think we can find a harbor here," said our friend.

We were greeted at the door by a slender, timid looking little woman.

She evidently expected us, for without hesitation, but trembling a little, she directed us up the great wide stairway.

We climbed three flights of winding stairs past rooms of comfort and elegance. Thick velvet carpet underfoot muffled our tread. Up, up we went in solemn single file, Furey pulling one heavy foot up after the other. Finally we reached the attic. In one corner was a room partitioned off.

We made our way to this through a maze of trunks, boxes, barrels, and old clothes suspended from lines attached to the rafters. Different sized oil paintings were stacked against the walls. I even imagined I could see the stern eyes of departed ancestors roll in horror as we filed past.

This was where we were to spend the night. The partitioned part of the attic was a bed room. It was plainly furnished but had two strong iron beds. Things were clean and inviting.

Like keepers of a zoo we chained the big bear flat on his broad back, to the bed; his head to the headboard; his feet to the footboard.

He began to moan and cry for a doctor. I certainly wished we could have given him a dose of chloroform to hold him over until morning, as neither Pete nor I had had a wink of sleep and the strain was telling on us. Now with his loud howls for medical assistance, I knew we would get no rest.

Our guide left us, giving his word to return the next night in time to get us to the train. He promised to try to restore the transportation we had lost, also to search for our luggage, which I had left in the weeds beside the railroad tracks.

He said, "Trust me! I'll not fail you!"

All through the long hours until daylight, Furey kept up an infernal moaning and groaning and howling.

I told him to shut up, that he had brought it on himself, and that I had ridden the range many a time for only a dollar a day in worse condition than he was in.

At day break the little hostess crept up the stairs with a tray of breakfast. We were so dog tired it was almost impossible to swallow.

However, the hot coffee tasted mighty good. She brought us our luncheon and dinner in the same manner, but of it all, the coffee was best. At no time did we get more than a half cup apiece. The good little thing's hands shook so that most of it went into the saucer. But she was game, if ever anyone was.

We put in the next day with nothing to do but wait. The day dragged out into the longest hours I have ever known. It became necessary for us to beat our heads and tear our hair to keep from toppling over asleep. At length the shadows of dusk fell across the strange scene in the attic prison where two human beings were watching over another human being, chained like a wild animal to a tousled bed.

The train was due to leave about eight o'clock. Twilight would have melted into darkness by that time. I had no desire to take our captive through the station crowds in daylight.

About seven o'clock I heard footsteps coming up the attic stairs. I poked my head out the door.

An instant later the head and shoulders of our good Samaritan rose above the balustrade of the narrow steps.

We said little but could have spoken volumes of gratitude for his faithfulness.

He said it was time to break camp and get to the station.

We brushed Furey off, slicked back that proud hair and adjusted his disheveled clothes until he presented a fairly neat appearance. In spite of cold baths on our faces, our eyes were red and swollen. We both looked like a couple of "morning glories," after a hard night.

Mr. Padgett had our tickets for us and had recovered the luggage. In the car was a young man whom we could absolutely trust, said our friend.

We all drove to the station together. Mr. Padgett had arranged to have Mr. Quattlebaum go with us as far as New Orleans, so Pete and I could get a little sleep on the train. I was afraid if we did not we would be unable to cope with any situation which might arise.

Mr. Quattlebaum guarded Furey through the night, never once slackening his hold on the chain.

Furey slept some and Pete and I dozed. In the morning we were refreshed and ready for the fray!

During the day trip Furey seemed to realize that this time we had him for better or worse. He appeared resigned to whatever fate awaited him and became more manageable and talkative.

After luncheon I decided to take advantage of his communicative mood and asked a few questions which might tend to clear some tag ends of previous episodes.

I took out my leather billfold and from among the contents extracted a torn, rumpled scrap of paper. I handed it to Furey, who was sitting on the drawing room seat opposite me. He took it in one of his bound hands and read it.

"Furey," I remarked with a dry smile, "they nearly got me that time."

He looked sheepish and handed the paper back to me.

"How did you manage to get that note to Steel, and how did you know Johnson had taken me to the club house on the hill?"

He waited a minute before replying, then turned to Pete and said:

"Pete, your daddy bears a charmed life. If he did not, he never could have escaped from that place or from eight of the best men there are in our game that ever came from New York."

I did not have to prod him further for information regarding that death trap. He told me quite willingly that when Johnson, Steel and I were in the automobile on our way to the club house, they purposely passed the Sea Breeze Hotel slowly in order to give him the opportunity to see their victim, as the general operations of the club house were under Furey's direction.

He had no way of getting the information to Steel that I was Norfleet except by the messenger who brought it in the motor boat. He peeked out through the window curtains and saw I was the victim.

So he hurriedly wrote the note, got one of his trusted employees (he smiled at this designation) and sent him racing to Steele in the speed boat.

"What would have been my final end," I inquired, "had I not escaped?"

"That, I cannot say," he answered with all the dignity of an expert technician in ways and means of disposing of people. "Johnson might have strangled you with that rope; Steel might have shot you; or they might have bound and gagged you, then weighted and dropped you from a boat a mile or so out at sea; all depending on the circumstances, and the originality, imagination and resourcefulness of the one doing the job."

I took a long deep breath to make sure I was not back on the hill. The scenes coupled with my intended death floated past my eyes, causing me to pinch myself surreptitiously.

"Yes," he added reflectively, a little sadly, "I thought that little note I sent would be your funeral sermon."

"Motor boats seem to be a fad with you," I said. "What became of you that morning in Key West when you and Barney King, the fake policeman sent me by the sheriff, got into the little motor boat and sped out to sea?"

He burst into a genuine laugh. His great sides shook.

"Why!" he said between spasms of laughter. "We got aboard a yacht anchored a little way out and from it we boarded an ocean liner bound for England."

"I thought perhaps Jonah had you swallowed. I knew he would throw you up as soon as he found out who you were, so I spun around in a sea-plane waiting for you, then went on to Cuba."

"I was out of the country by that time." He sighed a big fat sigh. "I wish to God I had stayed there. It's the only time I have drawn a free breath since I ran into you."

Chapter Twenty-Four - From the Lack of Early Training

"Pardon me," I broke in. "Since I sat down on your wallet, you mean."

"Yes, I guess that's right," he agreed. "But there is one thing about doing an Englishman. When they've taken the dose, they keep it down, while an American howls his head off. There is something superb about the poise of the English. Fine people!"

I could almost see King George nod his approval.

"By the way, Joe, now that we are out of range of riot guns, what about the finish of the Los Angeles deputy sheriffs, Lips and Anderson? You remember you stopped off in your story where you had just fallen back into the yard, when those friends of yours interrupted our conversation by trying to shoot me in the back."

"Well, instead of shooting me as I feared, they picked me up and took me around back of my orange grove to a waiting car. This was not the one they came in, but another one driven by a third deputy from Los Angeles, who assisted the pair.

"I was driven to the Long Beach Hotel at Long Beach and kept under guard. One of the men returned to Glendale and picked you up in the little jitney. You were waiting, he said, near the garage about five blocks away, for them to report."

"What happened then?"

"Well, they began to shake! And they shook hard; me, my wife and even my little boy! Curse them!"

"How much did they get?"

"My wife and little boy together gave them twelve thousand dollars, but they demanded twenty. At this time we couldn't dig up that much. My wife had refused, ever since the birth of our boy, to assist me in any way in my business. I suppose she was right. Mrs. Furey had only four thousand dollars in cash at the time. My God! I didn't know what I was to do. I begged her to help me think of some way to get the rest. Finally one of us, I don't recall which, thought of little Mark's money. My wife had saved nearly everything I had given her and put it in the bank for the baby.

"But, well — hell! I just had to have that money! Mrs. Furey went with one of the sheriffs to the school where the child was. They took him out and drove to the bank where they inquired the exact saving deposit of the boy. 'Eight thousand dollars,' said the teller.

"They had the baby sign a check for the entire sum. Anderson told little Mark to write his name on the line."

Furey paused a moment, caught his under lip between his teeth and bit into it until a small bead of blood welled out — then went on —

"They returned the kid to school and came back to Long Beach. I still had to get the balance of eight thousand. You remained in and around Glendale for several days and I was kept a close prisoner in the hotel room, always guarded by either Lips or Anderson. This was one reason why you never could find them on duty at my home. Then you went up to San Francisco looking for me. I told them if I could get to San Francisco I could get the balance of the money. So they took me up there. Do you remember the message you received saving I was registered at the U. S. Grant Hotel in San Diego?"

"Yes!" I exclaimed. "A member of the San Francisco Police Department read it to me and said he had been advised by the authorities that you were there and then he did everything but throw me out of town in an effort to get me to San Diego."

"Well, I'll tell you, Norfleet," half patronizing, "we were in San Francisco at the time you got that wire. In fact, in less than an hour after you left, we occupied the very room in the hotel you vacated. Fast work, wasn't it?"

Then he waxed eloquent on the methods of the officers in helping him obtain the rest of the money to buy off the law.

"The two sheriffs and I took _____'s car, crossed the bay to Oakland Cemetery, where it was arranged to meet Mrs. Harrison and _____ in Mrs. Harrison's car. We met there among the green plots and tombstones. God! it was lucky for me that I was not born superstitious, for not five feet from me yawned a long open grave into which I looked indifferently while we waited for the arrival of the others. Presently they came up the long winding drive. The eight thousand was delivered."

"Do you think _____ got his share?"

"I don't know, but I am damned sure my money was split three ways in Los Angeles!"

(This was ambiguous, but just what he said.)

"I got into the car with Mrs. Harrison a free man."

"What became of your three liberators?"

"They got into _____'s car and drove off. That was the last we saw of them."

"It's a funny thing to me," continued Furey, "how damned easy it has been for you to get and keep my trail. It looks like to me I have been given the double-cross in more places than one. Why," he burst out into renewed wrath, "your own officer, _____, right in Fort Worth promised me absolute protection when I stung you. But of course I had to pay for it, and I did too. The second time I got you it wasn't my own idea at all. It was the suggestion of that crooked officer, _____ of Fort Worth. The first time I did you, I paid him ten per cent of my er — earnings. This was to include two bodyguards. The second time he came to me and said:

"'Go get Norfleet again. He can dig up more money and I need a new Cadillac car'."

The storm of anger that rose in me was almost uncontrollable. It is one thing to be the victim of an out and out bunco man, but to be victimized by a minion of the law, paid to protect citizens, is a situation that stirs the blood to battle.

"Well," went on the captive, "after we got the second money, I paid $2500 and paid one hundred dollars apiece to the FOUR 'plain clothes' men he had insisted upon my having for a bodyguard when I tried to get out of pulling the deal. This is the truth. I would not tell you, only it looks like I am done for. I never had a stronger hunch in my life than I had just before we took that last money away from you. Spencer will tell you the same thing, how I tried to get out of it. I told them this was the deal that was going to put the Indian sign on all of us.

"'Goldie,' I said, 'this cash is our funeral.'

"They laughed, but you see I was right."

134

My emotions ran riot as I listened to this broken leader of confidence men and I thought of what a wonderful success this man should have made in the world had he devoted his talents to legitimate instead of unlawful operations.

What a politician he would have made! With his superb powers of eloquence and his marvelous organizing ability, he could have been anything he chose.

I know I should have hated him, but even after he had robbed me so outrageously, I was still aware of his personal magnetism and had to hold myself back to keep from sympathizing with him in his adversity.

Master crook he was, yet whenever he referred to a woman it was always in the most delicate, respectful terms. Strong drink for him had no allure and profanity was ordinarily absent from his speech.

A feeling of pity, mingled with regret, swept over me — regret at the loss to society of a great soul, gone wrong. Earnestly I asked:

"Joe, tell me this: Why, with your brains and education; your marvelous self-control; your uncanny gift of leadership, why are you not today Governor of New York, instead of a criminal on the way to prison?"

Like a giant oak, crippled by the storm, poised in mid-air for a moment, then falling to earth with a resounding crash, Joe Furey, Master Crook, struggled a moment, then collapsed.

Tears in rivulets sprang from his eyes and coursed down his large fat face. His great body swayed with the violence of his emotion.

"It all came from the lack of early training," he sobbed. "My God, Norfleet, what wouldn't I give to be able to start all over again!"

For a minute he was quiet.

"My baby," he cried out. "What will become of my little boy? Norfleet, for God's sake, promise me he shall never know the kind of life I have led. What chance can he have knowing his daddy is in prison?"

I was deeply moved by the grief of this misguided father for his innocent child.

"Why didn't you quit the game when your wife did, and get into some honest business?" I asked.

"I don't know why I did not. It would have been far better if I had. Somehow, the excitement had become necessary to me. I had to keep on from one thrill to another to keep from remembering all the things I had done. *Memory is a luxury that only those who go straight can afford.* I believe that three months with no new thrills to quiet my memories would have driven me screaming 'bug house.' I had to go on."

He thought for a long while like one who watches past events pass in review, then said:

"If you want a man to be good, you've got to start him young. No use trying to work him over after his habits are formed. When life steals a youngster's youth, he just naturally turns crook to get even. I never had a fair chance."

Then he went on to lament his lack of early training, his youthful association with professional crooks, and at last bewailed his prospective punishment.

He pitied himself a-plenty.

One thing certain, Joe was awfully sorry for himself.

At Pensacola we had to change trains, with a wail of two hours at the station.

I began to wonder about those habeas corpus proceedings, as we were not yet out of the state of Florida. I did not "crave" having my prize snatched from my hands at Pensacola, and there was no telling but an aeroplane had been commandeered to carry the process server. They might even be on the train waiting for me to alight. There was only one place in Pensacola I could think ot where I could hide until train time. Church! They would never suspect me of it! So as soon as the train drew into the station, I dropped off over the observation platform, leaving Pete to exercise Furey in the station.

I went to church and enjoyed one of the best sermons I have ever heard. I don't know whether it was all in the sermon or a little in the fact that I knew I was safe.

After the last hymn I left and walked back to the station. Just as the train was about to pull out, I climbed aboard and re-entered our improvised prison.

Late in the afternoon, a tap! tap! tap! sounded on the drawing-room door. My heart stopped its beating for a minute.

There they are! I thought.

I got up and asked through the panel who was there.

A sweet feminine voice answered:

"It's I."

Some more of those angels of mercy, I groaned to myself.

"Who is I?" I sent back through the door.

"Your old friend, Mrs. Street!"

I opened the door, and to my utter amazement there she stood.

"It certainly is curious how our paths cross, isn't it?" I said delightedly.

I closed the door and we went into her section to have a little visit. She was an attractive, bright little person, and I always enjoyed talking to her.

She said she had something very important to tell me. In a whispered voice she informed me that only a few minutes ago in the car beyond, she had heard two men talking about killing someone on this train and that they intended to do it tonight.

I was used to murders and other forms of amusement and while I was interested, I guess I didn't act very surprised for she leaned close to me and said:

"Oh! Mr. Norfleet, I am sure they mean you or your boy!"

This was not an impossible thought at all. I became more deeply interested.

I stepped over to our compartment and told Pete what she had said.

136

Pete was busy wrapping cold towels about Furey's head and extracting bits of sand and gravel from his skull, driven into it when he met the railroad in his head-on collision.

I told my son that we were nearing New Orleans and for him not to stick his head out for anybody until I came back for him.

"Mrs. Street says she would recognize the men if she saw them and we are going through different cars and she'll point them out to me. When we get into the station I will get a wheel chair and some 'red caps' and have them stationed at our car. You let the porters carry all the luggage and keep your hands ready for action."

The train carried twelve coaches.

One by one we ambled down the aisles, rocking from side to side with the motion.

Mrs. Street scrutinized closely all the occupants, including those in the smoker. But we could see nothing of the two men who had been plotting. She became rather confused and looked chagrined at not being able to spot them after telling me of their conversation and expressing so firmly the belief that either Pete or I was to be the target. We were in the smoker and she was apologizing for making me so much trouble.

At this minute the train ran under the shed into the New Orleans station.

We got off the train at the front. Pete was the full length of the train at the other end.

It was dark except for the electric lights in the station. It was misty and the atmosphere heavy and oppressive.

I asked Mrs. Street to watch out for the men and if she saw them to tell me at once. Then I called to the red cap telling him to get three other red caps and a wheel chair and go to the rear end of the train.

I wore my overcoat. It was unbuttoned. I crossed my arms so each hand grasped a six shooter under my armpits inside my coat. Mrs. Street was hanging on my arm.

I said nothing to her about being armed.

Together we fought our way alongside the coaches through the crowd in the direction of Pete.

Twice she whirled me 'round and exclaimed with a little shiver of fright:

"Oh, look! What are they going to do?"

Each time I looked but saw nothing except friends greeting arrivals, couples kissing and other forms of affection. She peered into the face of all those whom we passed, doing her best to find the intended murderers.

As we drew near the last car it began to dawn on me that if anyone did expect to plug me, he would probably dart around the end of the last car from the dark side of the track and get me face to face. As the thought crystalized, we neared the end of the last Pullman.

Out of the darkness stole two men bent forward in a skulking attitude. They eased stealthily around the observation platform. As the light from the electric lamp shone on them I saw them glance quickly at me and Mrs. Street.

They flashed their hands to their hips.

I threw Mrs. Street from me and uncrossed my hands, a gun in each, and flung them down on the two figures, crying out:

"Stick up your hands." Then backed myself up against one of the huge cement pillars that supported the train shed.

"Who are you, and what do you want?" I demanded.

Each one of my revolvers was covering a man. They had thrown up their hands, but as I asked this question one of them exclaimed in what he intended to be a threatening tone:

"We are railroad police and are going to arrest you!"

"You are not!" I challenged.

I stepped out from the pillar and moved toward them describing a semicircle.

"Now you two fellows just walk up to the cement pillar and hold your hands flat against it. If you're railroad police you won't mind doing it, and if you are not, you'd better."

They moved up to the support and did as I told them. I now had them where I had been standing and I was in their former position.

I looked to see what had become of Mrs. Street. She was nowhere to be seen. Evidently she was frightened almost to death and had fled.

At this point in the game the red caps came alongside wheeling the invalid chair. Still keeping the men pinned to the pillar, I ordered the boys to go to the drawing room and help get Furey out. They brought him out, and when he and Pete were well lost in the crowd, making for the station waiting room, I backed away for some distance, then turned and left the two accomplices.

I joined Pete in the station where the police met us with a car and took us over to the city jail.

We deposited Furey there, then went to the Planters Hotel for the first relaxed sleep we had had since the beginning of the Florida chase, three days before.

In the morning after an early breakfast, we went immediately to reclaim our prisoner. The night sergeant was on duty. We went up to the desk and asked him how our man got through the night.

He arose from his chair, began to shake the kinks out of his legs and stretch his arms. He yawned and patted his mouth. He mumbled something about not knowing just where the man was, as he dug his fists into his sleepy half-open eyes.

"It seems to me," he swallowed in the wake of a growing yawn, "that sometime in the night somebody came an' — an' got him." He finished closing his mouth and batting his eyelids.

He continued to shake his sluggish form and was not the least bit concerned with the whereabouts of Furey.

"Somebody came and got him?" I yelled. "My God!"

It seemed the jail floor would slip from under my feet. After all our hardships in getting him across the line, now some fool had allowed him to be whisked out from under our noses while we were peacefully snoring. It was too much.

"Who took him out and where is he?" I shouted.

"Well." — beginning some setting up exercises, "I think if I remember right, somebody from the Humane Society took him in charge. The Humane doctor said he had something to do with it."

"Humane Society!" Pete and I gasped. "Where is it?"

He told us and I rushed out and covered the four or five blocks in two jerks of a lamb's tail. Pete went to get a car and was to meet me there.

I did not wait for any information-desk ceremony but burst into the place like a bomb.

A door was standing open a little way down the main corridor.

I heard the chatter of female voices. I looked in.

There was Furey!

He was half lying, half reclining on one of the beds. Around him were a half dozen fluttering women.

They spoke in soothing tones and ministered unto the suffering one like grey doves of peace.

I dashed into their midst.

They scattered as if someone had thrown a brick into their crumbs of mercy.

I felt a wave of relief sweep over me at the sight of Joe.

"Hello, Furey!" I said. "How did you get down here?"

Belligerent glances were focused on me.

"How did he get down here?" the spokeswoman repeated. "Why we went up and brought the poor man down here where he can be kindly cared for. He is a poor suffering man and we are going to defend him with the last drop of our blood!"

"That will be appreciated by Mr. Furey, I am sure. He is quite used to bloodshed!"

Furey sent me a sarcastic look.

"Well!" continued the mother bird of the "Humane" ones, "our doctor says he is a very sick man and in his condition it would be at least fifteen days before he could travel! You cannot touch him!" the chorus cried, and moved to surround his bed.

I followed them and stood on tiptoes looking over the white caps of the noble nurses at Joe, who lay in state on the white cot surrounded by the wreath of invincible protectors. All the denied maternity came into their service and I half expected them to give him a bottle of warm milk to drink through a nipple and a rattle to play with.

Much to the irritation of the women, I tossed conversation over their heads to him.

I asked him how he had slept, if they had fed him yet and inquired playfully what his power over women was. I said:

"You have taught me one thing, Joe! That's this: when a man wants sympathy from women all he's got to do is to jump out of the window of a moving train, swindle the widows and orphans or murder somebody!"

"Aren't you ashamed?" sneered one of the white-robed guard.

I laughed out loud. I have never in my life seen a funnier sight than that one. His handsome shirt studs were missing as well as his diamond scarf pin and jeweled cufflinks.

"Where'd they go, man?" I jibed.

"Don't pay any attention to him!" warned another of the foster-mothers.

Their heads turned in unison toward the door.

I looked to see what the commotion was all about.

Pete stood there. He had a six shooter in one hand and the handcuffs in the other.

"Step right in here, Pete!" I ordered in a firm voice. "Put those handcuffs on this prisoner and we'll just walk him right out to the car. And," giving the staff a meaning look, "we'll not be put to the trouble of shooting to get him there."

Pete made his way into the group of ladies, who fell apart at the mention of shots.

Furey offered no resistance.

The handcuffs clicked and out we three walked without even a detaining hand or a backward look.

The dear souls, however, fell into line and followed us. Like a stately wedding procession we moved out to the sidewalk right into the arms of two policemen. All that stood between us and the waiting car was the law.

"Look here! You can't take that man out of this institution without paying his bill!" one of the officers declared, stretching forth his hand for Furey. I reached out my right and shook his hand heartily.

"Good morning, officer!" I said pleasantly. "There is no bill for us to pay. The Society came and got him of its own accord. I have no money to pay it and have a pressing engagement with the train leaving for Fort Worth. See you again," I promised.

They stood and watched us shove Furey into the car and drive off without arguing the matter further.

The trip from there into Fort Worth was uneventful. That night Furey was delivered at the Tarrant County jail into the keeping of Sheriff Sterling Clark, where we knew that the devil and all of his assistants could not get him out.

We had after fourteen months of ceaseless searching at last found our man and had promptly fulfilled the requirements of the requisition warrant, issued by the Governor of Florida five days before, to deliver the body of J. B. Stetson, alias Joe Furey, inside the jail door of Tarrant County, Texas.

Chapter Twenty-Five - The Creed of the West

After the long months of tension which taxed even my iron constitution, I was only too glad to return to the ranch and there with my loved ones, turn my attention again to paths of peace.

Never had my wife and children appeared so precious to me; never had the sweet breezes of the plains breathed such messages of quiet sympathy and inspiration.

Here in this environment it was difficult to realize I had actually been through such discordant experiences. Like one awakened from a deep troubled sleep I rubbed my eyes and drank in the beauties of nature exhibited in the broad panorama that met my vision.

Surely those strenuous months were but the fantastic recollections brought back from the dream world.

Slowly those old plans formed before my fateful encounter with the members of the bunco ring, began to troop back into my conscious mind and demand attention.

There to the left lay the gently sloping tract of fertile loam where I had intended to have my cotton patch — one thousand acres in the fleecy staple, planted from the best high-bred, pedigreed seed that I could procure at any price, with every stalk exactly like every other stalk in uniform height, color and productivity.

For the moment I visualized this same great plot after "Jack Frost" had visited the tender stalks and stripped them of their foliage, transforming at a breath, as it were, this immense sea-green garment to a titanic robe of whitest ermine.

Becoming practical for a moment I wondered if it were possible, by using the very best seed money could buy, to compel this deep chocolate loam to yield one bale (500 lbs.) of lint cotton to the acre. If it were possible so to harness the mysterious life-giving force present in such vibrant degree, then the proceeds from one crop would erase all losses sustained from my recent experiences.

With lint cotton selling at one hundred and fifty dollars a bale, my profits should amount to almost that sum for each acre, as the sale of the pedigreed seed should bring enough returns to pay the expense of growing and ginning the crop.

A pleasant picture indeed!

One hundred and fifty thousand dollars! One year's income!

This surely should satisfy any reasonable man!

Even as I thought this, a memory of the cotton fields in the Imperial Valley of California, came stealing across my mind. I remembered the yield in that country was far in excess of a bale to the acre. How could that be?

"Irrigation," I thought out loud. "That is the answer! I believe this land of mine is underlaid with 'sheet water' at about three hundred feet, with force enough to get flowing wells on most of the land."

I could see this water running in sparkling ribbons down the mile-long rows and doubling the fruitage of the prolific plants.

Two bales to the acre! That would be three hundred thousand dollars a year from one thousand acres!

One moment I was left to enjoy this thought of peace and prosperity, then I saw my little daughter coming. In her hand she waved something which proved to be a number of letters and telegrams.

"Daddy," she cried excitedly. "Look at the letters and things Pete just brought from town."

I looked at the telegrams first. They came from all over the country filled with congratulations from friends and from many I did not even know.

One was a cablegram from Paris, France, in which my good friend Angus, of the Burgers Detective Agency of Miami, Florida, sent heartiest congratulations for the capture of Furey and announced his own success in capturing the notorious Roy McMullin, another member of the international gang of swindlers who had pulled off a big $100,000 swindle a few months before.

Hundreds of letters from a radius of one thousand miles, many of which were from women, were awaiting me at the house when I returned.

My daughter took more interest in the situation than any of us.

"My dear old Dad," she exclaimed. "Just think of it, Sherlock Holmes No. 2. My it's great to have a famous father! Don't you think so, Mother?"

A shadow passed for a moment over my wife's face.

"Yes, Daughter," she calmly said. "But where will it end? If I could know that your father would be able soon to settle down to his work here on the ranch, I would be far better pleased than that he should make a million dollars and become the most famous detective of all times. I sincerely hope this trip to Los Angeles will not keep him long."

At the mention of Los Angeles, I came back to earth. I had forgotten for the moment my duty to return to California and help prosecute the deputy sheriffs who had double-crossed me.

Before I left my little daughter looked me over with questioning gaze.

"Dad," she asked, "what is the 'Creed of the West'?"

"To treat everybody right, then make them treat you right," I replied.

"All right. Make them do it as soon as you can and hurry home."

At 3:30 in the afternoon of the next day I took the train for Los Angeles. Two days later I arrived in the City of the Angels, as it is known, though angels were not associated in my mind with it.

I went to Mr. Woolwine immediately and told him all that Furey had told me; explaining, of course, that I had allowed Furey to think I had known the story all the time.

Mr. Woolwine's usual dignity suffered itself to be momentarily set aside. He exclaimed:

"Norfleet, if what you say is true, we will go the limit with these two deputies!"

Then he proceeded to unload to me a few things that had reached his executive ears.

We put two and two together and decided that instant action in the matter would be the policy.

"If you will give your personal and undivided attention to this case, I will give it mine!" he declared, and was as good as his word.

At once the wheels of the law were set in motion to bring to a belated justice, Lips and Anderson. Without warning, warrants for their arrest were issued and served on them. They were summarily yanked from their own official desks, and unceremoniously locked within their own jail.

They employed as counsel Schenck and Kitrells, who proved to be very able in every respect except in getting their clients off. The Sheriff's office was thrown into a panic. Such a thing as arresting the two uniformed gods of the community was nothing less than a crime in itself.

I believe one of the factors which helped us most was the over-assurance of the officers. Had bets been placed on the outcome of the trial they would have been about one hundred to one in their favor. Their pictures were frequently flashed on the screen in the moving picture theaters, telling the natives how many daring deeds both performed nightly to guard the lives of the citizens. Their position in this direction was so well and consistently organized that their faces on the silver sheet invariably met with approving handclaps. Little did they dream the next pictorial exhibit of their manly beauty would be held in the rogues' gallery.

One of the most significant facts pointed out by Mahoney in the trial was the unswerving industry of Anderson in his efforts to uphold the oath of his office. He had killed no less than five men and one woman in what he termed his line of duty.

Their trial was set several months ahead on the calendar. They furnished bond in the amount of twenty thousand dollars each.

In the meantime I returned to Fort Worth and attended the trial of Furey, which came up on the 14th of March. This was about two months from the time we brought him in.

Nothing of a sensational nature attended his sentencing. He pleaded guilty and asked for the mercy of the court. Judge George Hosey gave him twenty years. For the time being his spectacular career closed. He went to Huntsville Penitentiary, Walker County, Texas.

As soon as Furey was established as an inmate of the prison his executive nature began to crave expression. Naturally avenues of self-expansion were limited in Huntsville, but a born leader will always find an outlet for his talent and Joe was resourceful. All of his former and oft repeated pleas for "mercy," his "for the love of suffering humanity" and his "Oh God's," at last found a proper channel.

Joe Furey elected himself superintendent of the Penitentiary Sunday School, which became the largest Sunday School in any penitentiary in the world. He organized it; preached in it and in every detail of its sacred functioning, his hypnotic influence was felt. How many of the striped lambs he led into the fold, I have no idea, but if Joe Furey promised them a future seat on the right hand of the Lord they evidently fell for it. Joe's administrative capacity was of no mean order and while he was extremely busy with his "flock" he found time to organize his disciples into a general jail escape.

On the eighth day of May, less than two months following his conviction, I received a telegram from District Attorney Woolwine, of Los Angeles, warning me that a wholesale jail delivery was scheduled to be pulled off at Huntsville on the following Sunday.

Woolwine had been tipped off that Mrs. Mabel Harrison and Mrs. Furey had gone down to Huntsville.

When he heard this he immediately sent one of his men, Norris, down to trail the pair and see what they had up their sleeves besides their arms. Norris reported there was a man connected with the deal who answered the description of my old enemy, Steel.

As soon as I received the wire from Woolwine I get in communication with Jesse Brown, District Attorney of Fort Worth, and asked him to take some action toward preventing the jail break.

Brown called up the Governor and succeeded in having him communicate with the warden of the penitentiary and instruct him to transfer the Sunday School superintendent into a dungeon. The warden doubted that there was anything in the rumor of the planned escape, but carried out the Governor's orders and put Furey in solitary confinement.

Sunday dawned and directly after Sunday School, minus the beloved leader, pandemonium broke loose.

It seemed that Mrs. Furey and the "financial agent," Mrs. Harrison, had been paying frequent visits to Furey for several days preceeding the fateful Sunday. Captain Coleman, the warden, told me that he supposed the two women had smuggled little vest pocket automatics to the prisoners. The women always carried small handbags about big enough to conceal a feminine powder puff but also large enough in which to hide the diminutive pistols that killed and wounded some of the guards. Armed with these little death dealing "gats," the prisoners forced an entrance into the arsenal and obtained guns of bigger proportions.

The penitentiary became bedlam. Shots rang out from all directions on the soft Sabbath air. Convicts, resembling stampeding zebras, ran amuck, leaped from the high prison walls and, shooting down obstructing guards, fled north, south, east and west. Blood stained the courtyard and jail corridors.

When the roll call was held, forty-two were missing.

Some distance from the prison walls two women stood. Some distance from them in the field an aeroplane waited.

In the dungeon Joe Furey wondered.

144

A few days afterward I went to see Furey. He wasn't singing "Hallelujah," though he was glad to talk with me and lamented that his athletic figure was on the decline.

"It's too damned hot for me in this climate. I can't last long in this hot 'hell hole'," he snorted.

"If you will go to San Francisco and see Helen Harrison, Mrs. Harrison's daughter, and tell her to see W. B. Spencer and get thirty-five thousand dollars from him and dig up elsewhere enough to make up to you what we took, including your traveling expenses hunting us, I will instruct her to pay it to you. All I ask in return is that you see that I am taken out of this hell and transferred to a sanatorium somewhere in Colorado. I will trust to your honor to do this."

After ascertaining from Captain Coleman that Joe's health really was failing, I laid Furey's suggestion before him.

It met with his approval and he said if I could get all or even some of my money back, he would indorse the removal of Furey to an institution in Colorado; one in which his health might improve but where his liberty would be just as restricted.

This plan found favor with Governor Neff. On his promise to assist me as far as the law allowed I left for San Francisco to hunt up Helen Harrison, the young lady who had conversed with Lucille Carson regarding the little dog that day in the Stanford Court Apartments.

Before calling on Miss Harrison, who was then living at the Cliff Hotel, I employed the legal firm of Sheffey & Johnson. Johnson was the young son of Senator Hiram Johnson, former Governor of California.

I gave Sheffey all the credentials and property documents that Furey had given me to enable me to collect the money from Mrs. Harrison. He looked them over and made out other necessary papers to be served on Mrs. Harrison which would necessitate the converting of some of Furey's San Francisco real estate into cash to pay me.

The papers were to be served the next day; following that, I was to see Miss Harrison and make arrangements for her and her mother to get the thirty-five thousand from Spencer. I prayed things would mature without mishap.

As it was a simple matter for either Miss Harrison or her mother to get in touch with Spencer I was naturally hoping to get a line on the slicker for myself. Perhaps they would let slip some hint of his whereabouts that would save me future search. I wished to avail myself of every clue as I was not at all sure that the money would ever find its way into my hands no matter how near me it came.

The hand of death had a longer reach than mine. The next day Sheffey learned that Mrs. Harrison was, indeed, very ill. While in Huntsville with the real Mrs. Furey, whose husband's affections she shared, a heavy cold fastened itself on her. By the time she reached San Francisco she was on the verge of pneumonia and two days afterward the doctors declared she was in a dangerous condition. It was at this stage in the affair that Sheffey sought to serve her with the papers.

I could only think how I would feel toward anyone taking advantage of my wife in a similar circumstance. They said she was tossing and burning in the flames of fever. I could not let him serve her.

"She had a fighting chance to live," said the nurse, "but she has not the will to get well! When Furey did not escape in the Huntsville break she returned home a broken woman and lay down to die."

So that was all there was to it. She died, and I was not able to continue the matter as at present the real estate holdings and all of Furey's property passed into the estate of the "late Mrs. Harrison."

Not one cent did his legitimate wife and little son get. They were left practically penniless while Helen Harrison, her brother, and other minor heirs, came into the fortune of stolen gold. What good this wealth will do these young people will be interesting to observe.

I had a brief talk with Miss Harrison, thinking that, perhaps, when the estate was probated, she might be willing to help Furey to the extent of carrying out his wishes in the matter of the return of my money and his removal to more healthful quarters.

At first she lapsed into a brow-beating attitude.

"When I first met you," she began scornfully, "I expected to meet a brilliant man."

I fear I did not measure up to Joe in any sense of her scale.

She told me I ought to be ashamed of myself for the grief I had brought on innocent people.

"You are satisfied now, I suppose!" she cried dramatically. "Now that you have succeeded in jailing Joseph Furey, one of the noblest men God ever made."

I began to suspect, perhaps, she too was good at acting.

"Not only have you ruined him, but through his arrest and conviction you have caused the death of my beloved mother."

After a little more of hearing how the Furey and Harrison households felt towards me, I explained to her that it was many times considered a privilege to die on the outside of a prison. I then told her that I had the numbers of both her and her mother; had had them for a long time and could have made it extremely warm for them had I chosen.

"When did you ever see my mother?" she flung at me.

"At the Stanford Court Apartments, following a little dog episode. I saw you and her get into your luxurious limousine and sweep like queens through the entrance arch to the street. I have danced with you when you thought I was some green hick from the country. Would you like to know more about yourself?"

Her dark eyes glittered. But her mood underwent a change for the softer.

Finally we got down to business. I outlined the proposition that had been intended for her mother. She agreed to fulfill Joe's instructions and said she would advise with her counsel and meet me in Los Angeles on the following night at the Alhambra Hotel.

I reached Los Angeles Friday and conferred with Woolwine regarding coming events.

Saturday night Miss Harrison called me on the telephone and said she was out at the Vernon Country Club and asked me to come there.

I refused. She then consented to come to the hotel.

I waited and a few minutes later she called me up again; this time from the Elks Club, so she said.

She asked me to come there. I refused and again she consented to come to my hotel.

That was the last I heard from her. Evidently her counsel thought it best for Joe to continue to languish in discomfort at Huntsville.

Chapter Twenty-Six - A Female Judas

I remained in Los Angeles for the Lips and Anderson trials, which were the most sensational the State of California has ever seen. It was proved that both Lips and Anderson not only shook down Furey and his wife for the money, but also shook the cradle. The last cent of the savings account of little Mark Furey was confiscated.

The mills of the gods grind slowly but surely! On the person of Anderson a receipt to a safety deposit box was found by Malcolm McLaren, Woolwine's head investigator. This furnished the clue to his box. It was searched and there reposed most of the money that had been taken from Furey while they had him prisoner at the Long Beach Hotel.

According to the testimony of the banker who handed out little Mark Furey's savings to Mrs. Furey on the day the mother, child and deputy sheriff called at the bank, it was the same money. The bank markers were still on some of the packeted bills.

The box was rented under the name of W. J. Stafford but all the contents were in the name of W. J. Anderson. This fact served to pretty conclusively prove the guilt of Anderson.

Anderson admitted catching Furey and not turning him over to the law. This action Anderson said was taken because Furey agreed to point out Spencer to them. So they took him to the Long Beach Hotel in an effort to get Spencer. He then admitted taking him to San Francisco as Furey said Spencer had gone up there. It was in San Francisco that he said Furey got away from him. He denied ever having received any money from Furey for a bribe.

He accounted for the money being in the safety deposit box in this way: When he and Lips were in their private room in the jail, talking over Furey's escape, Anderson claimed he said to Lips: "Well, it's too bad he got away!"

FRANK ELWOOD NORFLEET
"PETE"
A CHIP OFF THE OLD BLOCK

"I HUNG MY HAT OVER MY THUMB
AND GRASPED MY GUN."

"Yes!" Lips had replied. "But he left something behind" and he then tossed the roll of bills on the bed. During the trial Anderson was more than eager to give Lips full credit for everything.

Lips was convicted on my sworn testimony, backed up by the statements of Furey, which were proved absolutely correct.

I had gone to the Nurses' Home, formerly the Furey residence in Glendale (the Research Hospital having purchased it from the Fureys). In the front yard were several of the nurses drying their hair. I fell into conversation with them, saying I had seen this house sometime ago and had returned to look it over again with the intention of buying it for myself.

"Why the Research Hospital across the street has bought it!" one of the girls said.

I appeared surprised and said I was sorry as I should have liked to own it.

"Well, maybe you wouldn't be so crazy about it if you knew the history of it," another one put in from behind a screen of wet hair.

"History?" I asked.

"I should say so!" exclaimed several of them. "Sometimes it gives us the jim-jams too, to think of all the tragedy that took place in it."

"Do tell me about it."

"Why this used to be the home of that millionaire bunco king, Joe Furey. There is a big trial going on now in Los Angeles of the two deputy sheriffs who arrested him and then accepted a bribe of twenty thousand dollars to let him go!"

"Well! well!" I gasped. "Do you suppose they did arrest him?"

"Sure they did!" laconically replied the speaker, jabbing at her tangled locks with a comb. "You know they did!"

"Did you see them arrest him?" I asked and my heart skipped a few beats.

"No! I didn't. But my friend, Mrs. Coover, who lives only a few blocks away, saw Sheriff Lips when he got Furey in his own backyard."

"Well, well, well," I said as quietly as I could. Then I took another breath and asked where Mrs. Coover lived, hoping the Lord had not seen fit to call her home in the meantime.

She lived some little distance away from the house. At the time of the Furey episode, she was figuring on buying the lot next to the Furey home, and on the day Furey fell backward into his own garden and was caught by Lips, Mrs. Coover and some of the contractors were in the next lot discussing plans for building. Had Furey plunged over the fence instead of see-sawing back and forth on the top, he would have fallen almost at her feet.

I called on Mrs. Coover and the next morning she appeared in court as State's witness, accompanied by the two contractors. The three made oath to the fact that they had seen Lips arrest Furey, then spirit him away in an automobile. This was what entitled Lips to a home in San Quentin for fourteen years.

The only other unique feature of the trial was the return of my old friend, Mrs. Street. She again entered the arena of my fight, and I finally learned she was a wolf in sheep's clothing.

It came about while I was waiting at Los Angeles for the first trial to begin. The court was occupied with the case of O. C. Berry, a banker of Los Angeles, who was being tried as an alleged accomplice in several bunco deals which netted him a fortune and impoverished others. He was found guilty, convicted and sentenced to the penitentiary. As soon as his case was out of the way the Lips and Anderson case would come up.

I had only been in Los Angeles a few days when one night in my mail box at the Alhambra Hotel, I found a cordial note from Mrs. Street. It read:

"Do come down to our room and tell us all about everything. That night I left you in the New Orleans station, when you pulled your guns on those two men, I ran away into the crowd. I was so afraid you were going to be shot. Charlie (my husband) and I are eager to see you again. Come down this evening if you have no other engagement"

I was glad to have their company as I was alone most of the time. I went to their room, and we three had dinner together that night and for the next thirty-three nights at the Los Angeles Y. M. C. A. They were both interested in my affairs and I told them all about what had happened since the night I had so rudely flung her down on the station walk. She laughed about it and said she had picked herself up and run into the crowd.

They both were deeply interested in the coming trial. We talked it over freely. One night she introduced me to three or four young people who were dining in the restaurant. Some of them were musicians. It was said that we must all get together some night and have a musical evening. This suited me and they promised to set the time another day. Three weeks passed and nothing further was said. The Streets kept harping every day that we would go out to the young people's house.

Two days before the Lips trial was to start Mrs. Street said that the next night we would go out to the people's house for dinner. We were not to meet her and Mr. Street as they had an engagement which would take them right up close to the dinner hour. They gave me the address. It was the night before the morning of the trial.

Mrs. Street called me up on the telephone and asked me to hurry on out — "We are all ready and waiting for you."

I ordered a taxi and gave the driver the address. We rode and rode until I thought he must be taking me back to Hale Center.

Finally I asked him how many more miles out it was.

He said we were nearly there, but that it was a long way from town in the farthest outskirts of the city. I saw there were not many houses in the district and practically no street improvements.

A minute later we stopped in front of a large house. I got out and told the driver to wait. There was a little light in the house, but I figured if there was any mistake, or if they were not at home, I didn't want to be without a conveyance to get me back to civilization.

I rang the bell. In a minute the door opened. I motioned the driver to go on and stepped inside.

The door apparently had been opened by magic hands. I was in a small square. The stairs shot up a steep flight.

As I stepped inside the door banged shut with a resounding slam behind me and the lights went out.

There was not a sound. I felt for my gun which was as much a part of me as my nose.

Mentally I raised on tiptoes. I would have liked to suspend myself in mid-air.

The little space under my feet might be a trap door letting down into some form of purgatory.

Still no sign of life. I looked up the stairs. I could make out a turn at the top. It was barely dusk and the light from an upper window shone on the top landing. I wondered why my friends did not appear.

In a minute the strange weak voice of a woman floated down from the regions above:

"Is that you, Mr. Norfleet?"

"Yes I" I called back.

Well anyway I was expected, I thought, on hearing my name called.

A woman I had never seen came down the stairs saying I should come right up, the table was ready.

I mounted the stairs. Before starting, I had taken my right hand gun out of my back scabbard and stuck it into my belt almost in front of me. I cocked the trigger ready for action; took my hat off and hung it on my thumb so that it covered my hand on the gun.

We met half way up the stairs. I felt apprehensive. Things certainly were not regular looking, but I thought, of course, the Streets would be waiting for me upstairs.

The woman took my free arm and said she was so glad I had come and would I be her friend for the evening?

I said I supposed I would.

"We will have such a good time," she said.

By this time, we had reached the top of the stairs and turned into a large living room. The place was bare save for a rickety little card table in the middle of the room with a bottle of whiskey in the center from which a small amount of the liquid had been poured.

Six glasses filled with whiskey surrounded it. I noted that not more than two scant glasses were missing from the bottle.

In the corner of the room was a set of double box springs on the floor. A dirty, torn rug lay across it. This completed the household furnishings.

I realized a house-warming of some sort was due. In the middle of the room hung a low chandelier with several dangling bulbs and many glass prisms. It looked like a bouquet of crystals. The sun was dying. A crimson carpet of light overspread the western sky and lighted the room through a group of wide windows.

Apparently we were the only two living creatures in the house. It echoed in that strange way vacant houses do. There were several doors leading into other rooms.

She pressed me gently forward to the table. With her left hand she raised a glass of the liquid to my lips.

"You will have a little drink with me, won't you?"

I drew my head away from the rim.

"No!" I said, "I never drink whiskey. If I should it would spoil all my fun."

She grasped my arm again and let out a piercing scream.

Instantly three men sprang, crouched like animals, into the room through a door at her back.

She darted to the box couch and fell on it in a heap.

The men closed in on me, one in front, one on each side. I have never looked into a meaner face than the malicious one opposite me. Shivers went racing up and down my spine.

"What's all this about?" they demanded.

"No cause for alarm as far as I can see!" I retorted, forcing a laugh.

My hat still covered my cocked gun. I began slowly to back toward the wall in the direction of the electric light button. It was my idea if possible to get a little more light on the subject.

The men moved one step forward for every one of mine backward.

The woman lay crouching on the springs watching our little act with tigerish eyes. The men spoke no word and in order to fill in the silence I kept laughing and declaring there was no cause for alarm.

When I got within arm's reach of the button I stopped. I saw I was up against it for fair.

I could not think what to make of it all. They were three to my one.

While I was backing toward the wall I saw the woman lie flat on her back on the bed, toss the whiskey from the glass over her shoulder on the floor. Then she suddenly sat up.

She began to smile, and tipping the glass to her lips with one hand, she shielded the bottom with her other so I could not see that the glass was empty. She appeared to drink the fluid with satisfaction and at the last drop, even gave a little gassy cough such as novice drinkers do.

"Well, if you won't drink it, I will."

Walking toward me, she put the glass down on the table and took up one of the full ones.

I could have flashed on the light and illuminated the rapidly darkening room, but I was afraid to move a muscle until I knew what the game was.

The woman put her arm about my neck and placed the glass to my lips for the second time. I gently but firmly pushed her hand away, repeating my first statement that I did not drink.

"We thought we invited a sport here. You're just a damn piker!" cried the middle guard.

The woman's hand pressed tighter about my neck. I could feel her fingernails sink into the flesh at the back.

There was just one chance!

I caught hold of the brim of my Stetson in my free hand, let out a wild warwhoop and jumped into the air crying out:

"I'm no piker, let's start something, now!"

152

On the "now" I swept my huge hat off my thumb, brought it with a terrific flourish up into the delicate crystal chandelier, at the same moment finishing the sweep by pushing on the button. One globe remained intact and lighted.

There was a frightful shattering of fine glass. They had followed with their eyes the movement of my up-flung hat. A shower of splintered glass rained into their faces.

They ducked their heads to avoid being blinded. This confused them for a minute and in that flash I had my other gun out and one of them covered and drove the muzzle of the other gun into the stomach of the man on my other side.

"Throw up your hands and hold them up high!" I shouted.

I sent it home so hard, it sickened him.

He looked greenish white and shook as if palsied. His hand dropped to his side.

The woman rushed shrieking to the bed and ducked under the rug.

"Is that your Packard out there?" I inquired, trying my voice to see if I was still alive.

"Yes!" volunteered the virulent-faced creature who had dropped several feet back and looked the picture of indecision.

"Well, are you all ready to go?" I asked.

At this invitation to leave, my solar plexus victim whined in a choppy voice, cutting in two every word with his chattering teeth. "Nettie! — oo-o-o — Nettie! Let's g-g-g-go, Nettie!"

Nettie cried out from under her "Sheik" costume on the bed.

I ordered them into line and turned the whole party around as if we were all on a turn table.

"Op-p-e-e-n-n the fron-n-n-t door, Net-t-t-i-e!" continued the nauseated one, trying to keep his appendix from coming up.

Nettie went furtively into the nearby closet and pulled back a lever.

I could hear the front door swing back and hit the wall.

Picking up my hat I began my backward march down the stairs, the four strangers of the night following. When the man at the first of the line reached the front porch he said he had forgotten his driving gloves and might he return to recover them.

I said, "Yes."

He stepped back into the little square catch of hall when, like in "Ali Baba and the Forty Thieves," the door slammed shut, with them on the inside. I got out of range of shots from the windows and hustled my steps for several blocks. Soon I skirted a wild oat field. I plunged into the fragrant grasses and lay down to consult with some of the wilder oats.

After resting a few minutes I studied the heavens. I do not suppose I expected to see any street cars running in them, but I was so far from my old haunts that I imagined I might get my bearings. Way in the distance I saw a faint streak of light flash every now and then. This, I figured, was some suburban electric line. After walking for miles and miles I found it was.

153

Early in the morning I went to the Streets' and inquired if they were in.

"Sorry, Norfleet," the clerk replied, "Mr. and Mrs. Street checked out, bag and baggage, just before daylight."

"Did they leave a forwarding address?"

"No."

I gave him a generous tip and asked him if he ever had a line on them to let me know. He signified his willingness. Within a few days he notified me that a cleaning establishment had returned some garments for the Streets and he had received a letter from Mrs. Street asking that they be forwarded to her at

_____.

This address later on led me indirectly to Spencer.

Chapter Twenty-Seven - The Legislature Almost Helps

Instead of Anderson's trial proceeding as we expected it was postponed until it was known whether or not Lips would get a new hearing in the higher courts or a reversed decision.

Judge McCormick ordered Lips transferred from the county jail to the penitentiary annex.

I had known of so many prisoners escaping in these transfers that I went personally to see that it was safely accomplished.

The court bailiff got two deputy-sheriffs to assist him make the change of abode and I accompanied them.

When I left the penitentiary Anderson and the officers were talking to Lips through his cell bars. They were whispering to one another, their heads as close as the bars permitted.

As I walked out I had the impression that they followed. This must have been true, for when I gained the sidewalk Anderson and his friends were right behind me but turned and went half way up the steps where they met another man with whom they stopped.

Anderson looked back at me. His quick glance had the "trouble sign" in it. I had come to recognize the look in the eye that reflects evil intent.

I slowed my gait and crossed the street to the corner, where I stood close to a building and watched them without being seen. They then did a queer thing. They walked right out into the middle of the street and stood there in a little knot, talking and nodding and gesticulating.

Twice Anderson started away from the group in my direction. Both times someone crooked a finger at him to return to the executive session.

Finally the third time he broke away and made directly for me.

I walked up the street for half a block. He began to overtake me. I turned around in my tracks and bowed my neck for whatever was coming. My gun was tucked in the front of my belt, and as in the case of the shattered chandelier, I hung my hat over my thumb and grasped my gun.

Suddenly he began to curse me:

"Damn you. Norfleet! How long are you going to stay in Los Angeles?"

"Why I expect to stay here until after your trial is over!" I answered, cocking the trigger under my hat.

"Yes/' his hand shot to his hip, "and a damn sight longer!" he cried, with his revolver half out of his scabbard.

But he had to go after it and bring it out, and I was out and ready. My hat fell to the ground and he was covered. His hand trembled and let the gun slide down into its leather holder. He raised a restraining hand and whined:

"Oh, my God! Norfleet, don't take a brainstorm; don't do a rash act like that, my God I"

"I know all about the rash acts, Anderson; about the brainstorms and all about the suffering humanity, all about the poor wives, innocent children and aged mothers, but don't you ever tempt me again! Don't you ever tempt me again. Do you hear that?"

"Oh, my God!" he panted.

"Now then, another thing, don't try that old stall about self defense either. Be original. And if you and your little witnesses have any business to attend to, you had better hurry right along."

He edged off toward them, uncertainly trying the ground under his feet as he went.

This was my last encounter with either of the two double-crossing deputy sheriffs.

From here I went directly to Austin, Texas. I had received several telegrams asking me to appear before the Legislature in session there in regard to being reimbursed for my traveling expenses, inasmuch as the State of Texas had benefitted so much through my operations in rounding up the swindlers.

I had, of course, borne all the expense out of my own pocket. My funds were getting lower and lower and I thought if I could get State help I would be very glad, as I still had Spencer to find and had no idea how long it would take me. While he was the last of the gang, still it might take as long to get him as it had taken to get the other four. There is no telling about these things.

I stopped off* at Fort Worth on the way there and gathered up the court records and other necessary data with which to support my claims for recompense. Just as I was ready to continue my journey to Austin I met District Attorney Brown.

"Hello, Norfleet!" he cried. "Heard the news?"

"No!" I exclaimed, thinking that probably Spencer had been caught.

"Well, Reno Hamlin has forfeited his bond and is gone again!'"

"Reno Hamlin gone!" I exploded. "Now I've got to go after him again!"

155

I suppose when I was congratulating myself that Spencer was the only one left to get I should have knocked on wood. Now Hamlin was roaming "round wild. I wondered if by the time I got him would Furey be out and then when I could catch Hamlin again if it wouldn't be Gerber's turn for freedom and when he would be safely landed back in the pen, why Anderson and Lips would have their chance.

It was like trying to hold down six keys with five fingers — every time I press one down another pops up. However I decided to get the Legislature business out of the way first and then take up the trail again.

I saw Governor Pat Neff and appeared before the various committees at the Legislature. They all seemed more than eager to repay me for my expenditures. Mr. Lee Satterwhite was chairman of the Appropriation Committee.

I put my claims before him through the co-operation of Mr. Burke Mathis, my home representative. We then laid the matter before Mr. Stephens of Ballinger, chairman of the Claims Committee. The idea of rebating to me the amount spent was favorably looked upon by both the Claims and Appropriation Committees. It then went before the House. They made an appropriation to cover my traveling expenses. It was submitted to the Attorney General for his approval. Here it was turned down for illegality.

The State Constitution provided that the Legislature in general or called session has the right to make an appropriation for services to be performed, but it has not the right to make an appropriation for services already rendered.

I then had a conference with Assistant Attorney General Jones, Governor Neff, Satterwhite, Stephens and Burke Mathis.

I asked them if the Governor's law enforcement fund could not be swelled to an amount sufficient to offer me a reward for the capture of Spencer and Reno Hamlin. I told them ready cash was a little shy, and I hoped they could see their way clear to have the State reward me after I had delivered the goods, in either Hamlin or Spencer. I suggested giving me half the reward when I brought in the first fugitive so I could use the money to keep on the trail of the second.

They thought the matter over and decided this was an equitable manner in which to show the State's appreciation for my services in clearing it of so many two-legged rattlesnakes. It was agreed that a contract to this effect should be drafted. Assistant Attorney General Jones and I got busy on it.

Before it was completed Judge Adrian Poole of El Paso introduced his friend Willis Holman to me, begging Holman to tell me his story.

Holman was a young chap of about twenty-eight, from Austin. His story was the same as that of many others.

He had met a young man in Colorado Springs. The two became friends.

Tales of easily made fortune soon followed. Holman's friend explained he knew how to manipulate affairs and suggested they go to Denver and make some quick money.

Holman fell in with his friend's idea and they went to the western city. There they met a third man who told of large amounts of money he had made in stock speculations and offered to give them the inside tip. It was accepted.

Holman had thirty-seven thousand dollars coming to him as his portion of profit when it was, as usual, discovered he was "not a member", of that particular Board of Trade.

As usual they could not think of paying him his earnings until he could confirm his bid by placing twenty or twenty-five thousand dollars in cash in some bank in Denver.

At the time Poole introduced us Holman was arranging for the money to "confirm the bid" and was going back to Denver in the morning. He had accidentally met Poole and told him of his sudden riches.

Poole, who knew of my financial misfortunes from this method of swindling, told Holman he was being robbed.

Holman scoffed at the information and Poole had to almost bodily drag him to me to hear my similar tale. I told it with all the conviction I could bring to bear. But Holman refused to believe such a fate was waiting for his money. He believed implicitly in his newly-made friend.

When he reached the point in his story about having to "confirm the bids" because he was not a member of the Board of Trade I interrupted him saying:

"Now let me finish the story for you."

I then told him each and every step that had been made in his deal. He looked astonished and inquired how I could have known all about it. I told him how, to my sorrow, I had found out.

"This is the gang that has got you, Holman," I said.

However he still refused to believe his friend false and declared he was going on to Denver and see it through.

I told him if he was going to do this thing that I was also going on to Denver and see that he did not lose his money.

From the descriptions of the "friends" I felt sure they were the remaining members of the bunco ring. If Spencer was not there at least I had located another fake stock exchange and might possibly get a direct line on him.

When Holman saw how earnest I was about the matter he became disgusted and said he was going home, that perhaps there was something in it after all, and by morning he decided not to return to Denver.

I told Governor Neff, Satterwhite and Jones that I had this new red-hot tip and that I felt, in the State's interest as well as my own, I ought to act on it before it grew cold. I told them I wanted to leave for Denver that night and asked that my contract for rewards for the capture of Hamlin and Spencer be completed and my interests protected in my absence.

This was agreed upon, and I left that night for Denver feeling that I would be fully covered in the matter.

While on the train I began to think affairs over. I was without a direct lead except what I had heard from Holman. Scheming had gotten to be a daily, if not hourly, occupation for me. I now had to get not only Spencer but Reno Hamlin as well. Being running mates they would probably be together.

My original swindling charge against Reno Hamlin was still on the Fort Worth Court docket. As long as this remained there he would probably keep more or less under cover. But if it was dismissed he would not use as much caution in covering up his whereabouts. Also if he felt free to operate more publicly this would result in Spencer also following suit under the semi-protection of Hamlin. Therefore it seemed a wise move for me to stop off at Fort Worth and have the case against him dismissed.

A little publicity given in the newspapers to the effect that the old charge had been cancelled would soon reach Hamlin. He would then pat himself on the back and say: "What a smart boy am I!"

I did this and cut out several of the clippings, as well as mailing entire editions to various of Hamlin's cronies that I knew would immediately apprize him of his good luck.

After doing this I went before the Grand Jury at Fort Worth. They returned a new and much stronger indictment against Hamlin, but this charge was not given publicity. I saved it for a little surprise.

I had heard that Mrs. Hamlin, Reno's wife, was somewhere near Oklahoma City.

I wrote an old friend of mine, Will Flynn, an old time cowman and sheriff, for his help. Will and I were life-long friends. It was one of those long-enduring friendships that are born of pioneer days and hardships. I told Will I was sure Reno would join his wife there and for him not to let him get away. I enclosed Reno's picture and told him of the dismissed case and that Hamlin was sure to take advantage of his apparent freedom.

I went home to get more money to keep up the grade and while there received a wire from Flynn stating that the next day after getting my letter, he spotted Hamlin and now had him in jail awaiting orders from me.

I went immediately to Oklahoma City and there found my old "mule buyer" safe behind the bars.

His spirits were high and no suggestion of defeat was reflected in his smiling face. He immediately informed me that I could do nothing with him. To back up his assertion he pulled from his pocket one of the very clippings telling of his dismissed case, which I had caused to be written and then mailed.

"Norfleet," he explained kindly, "you see there is nothing against me in Fort Worth. You cannot hold me here!"

I said: "If this is true, Reno, and there is nothing against you there you are right. But, see here!" I flashed a letter from John A. Boykin, solicitor general of Atlanta, Georgia.

Reno's face went white.

"You see Boykin says you are wanted in Atlanta for the same kind of a gag you worked on me. Now what are you going to do about that? Atlanta is offering a reward of one hundred for you."

This seemed to get him. "If it is as you say, there is nothing against you on the Fort Worth docket, why when we get there I'll certainly give you your freedom. But," I continued, "Boykin's man is on the way here for you. He will arrive in a few hours."

Hamlin turned to the Chief of Police and said he would waive requisition and go to Texas with me as soon as we could get a train out.

The report of Hamlin's arrest had been circulated in the newspapers. Boykin had seen it and wired the Chief that a man was starting out at once to claim him. It was through me that Hamlin's arrest had been brought about, and although I had no reward up for him I felt that I should have him. It was going to be "nip and tuck" to see which of us got Hamlin, because Boykin had the lure of a reward and I had none.

I called over long distance to Governor Neff asking him for the necessary money to bring Hamlin back. Said I had him and was in a rush to get him away before the Georgia authorities claimed him. Being strapped for ready money and looking on the advance as a portion of my coming reward I did not think it out of the way to ask the State to make it possible for me to bring the fugitive back.

The Governor said he would let me know at four o'clock.

Later that afternoon, the Chief of Police notified me the Governor had phoned him that he believed it advisable to allow the Georgia authorities to claim Hamlin.

When I heard this it went straight through me. "Let the Georgia authorities claim him!" I shouted at the Chief. "What does he think I'm made of? Before I'll let anybody else have him I'll walk to Texas and lead him!"

I was desperate. I telephoned to District Attorney Jesse Brown and asked if he could offer any reward to help me get Hamlin back to Fort Worth or if he could offer any suggestions that would be helpful to get him back. He replied that he couldn't offer any reward and had no suggestions.

"Well, have you got any room in the jail for him if I bring him back!" I shouted and slammed the phone up.

I stamped out onto the street in a rage. What could I do? I must get the money somewhere and put up an equal reward and pay our fares back to Fort Worth.

"Let the Atlanta authorities have Hamlin?" I snapped aloud.

"Talking to yourself, Frank?"

"Hello, Flynn," I cried, relieved to see his friendly face and hear the sincere ring of his voice.

I recited how deeply interested Governor Neff and Brown were in helping me to bring back my prisoner, now that I had him.

Flynn swore like a good cowboy, plunged his big rough hand down into his trousers pocket and brought up one hundred dollars.

"It's yours, Frank, for as long as you need it."

I couldn't speak for a minute. Old Bill Flynn, my old pal! I could feel again that comradeship of the range, not gone, not changed!

"Thanks, Bill."

"Now then, Frank, we'll step into this dry goods store and tap the till for another thirty-five. They know me in there and it'll save time."

In we stepped and Bill "Howdy'd" with all the girls on the way to the cash drawer. Here he successfully obtained the loan and off we rushed to the jail.

I paid the one hundred dollar reward, Hamlin signed the requisition waiver, and the bottoms of his feet itched for travel.

Flynn had left me at the jail door but was on hand to help me get Reno aboard the midnight train.

"Never can tell what a bird'll pull," he remarked.

He rode as far as the first station south with us but when we reached it, he exclaimed:

"Pshaw! I haven't got a lot to do at home, Frank, I'll just keep going till I hit Fort Worth with you."

I was mighty glad to have him as we had not seen each other for a coon's age; besides I thought between us we might get some idea of the whereabouts of Spencer out of Hamlin. But probe as we did, we could not extract a word out of him regarding Spencer's hiding place. Every time Reno would get close to the point he would shut up like a clam. He certainly was loyal to his partners in crime.

The next morning we arrived in Fort Worth. We took him handcuffed to the Metropolitan Hotel and kept him in the private waiting room. He wanted to get in touch with his attorney, A. U. Puckett, of Dallas, but he couldn't be gotten, so we waited until late that afternoon and led him, handcuffed, up to the jail. I knocked on the door of the Sheriff's office, and giving a rather gloating laugh, I asked him if they had room there for Reno Hamlin.

Before going to the Sheriff's office I took Reno up to Brown's office and introduced him to Brown and several of his associates. Of course Brown had seen Hamlin before, but I thought it would be a good thing to let him know he was back in town.

When the door of the Sheriff's office closed behind us, Hamlin said to Hardcastle, the head deputy:

"Why, Hardcastle, there are no charges against me here — see this clipping. It says the charge was dismissed." He rattled his handcuff as if ready to have it unlocked.

"Yes I know that indictment was dismissed, but there is another one, No. 1007, which is still in force and effect. It's a later one returned by the grand jury."

Hamlin stared a minute. Then his head sank and he looked like a punctured balloon. Throwing himself into a chair he cried:

"I ought to have known it! I ought to have known it!"

Just then Judge Hosey entered and placed his bond at twenty thousand dollars.

As soon as Hamlin was bedded down for the night and then some, I took the night train to Austin to close up the unfinished contract and claim the reward for Reno.

I saw the Governor and told him I had put Hamlin safely in the Fort Worth jail and had had to borrow the money to take him there.

He said he would see that the State reimbursed me for the borrowed money. And a little later I did receive that and repaid Flynn. But as to my reward for capturing Hamlin the Governor said he would take it under advisement.

It is probably *still under advisement* for it is the last I have ever heard on the subject.

Chapter Twenty-Eight - First Aid in Montreal

It seemed I was not to go to Denver just then. Every time I started to find the fake stock exchange there something more tangible came to my hand to take me elsewhere.

Just now I headed for Wichita, Kansas. While I had Hamlin in the private lounge of the Metropolitan Hotel in Fort Worth I overhead a conversation between him and an acquaintance who happened in.

What I heard assured me that Spencer's father-in-law, Sam D. Stover, was living on North Emporia Street, Wichita, Kansas.

This was the first time I had heard anything about Spencer's people. For all I had known, Spencer might have been the only living member of his family. Now I had someone to tie him to. It was a new and very important lead. Again, Denver must wait.

I took Pete with me in order to cover more ground in less time. In many cases two can operate more efficiently than one.

In Wichita Pete made a practice of going to public dances. Most of the younger set patronized them, and as Stover had a young daughter Pete was hoping to meet her at one of these places. One night he did. They became good friends and through that association, we found out that her sister, Mildred, Spencer's wife, lived in luxury.

"She is in Montreal now, but usually spends the winters in Florida," the sister said.

On this information we pulled out of Wichita, expecting to end our hunt in Canada.

We stopped off in Kansas City and visited a few days with the various city officials and police department heads. We searched the archives of the Kansas City rogues' gallery for Spencer's picture. So far we had never been able to find a photograph of him anywhere.

The department said they had none of him under the name of Spencer or any other name as far as they knew.

Through the sister of Spencer's wife we found out that Spencer had married her under the name of Harris, so we inquired carefully for him under that name, but they disclaimed any knowledge of him.

I employed and paid expenses of two city detectives to go with us to Excelsior Springs, Missouri, a few hours trip from Kansas City, to comb that town for Spencer. The police declared the Springs was a great hangout for confidence men.

We found nothing but an automobile thief wanted in Kansas City. The two officers picked him up and we returned to Kansas City with the thief.

It was a funny thing but the man resembled Spencer enough to have been his twin brother.

I pointed this out to the policemen, but it roused nothing in their memories.

From there we went to Niagara Falls and came down to Buffalo, New York.

In one of the railroad stations I noticed a very familiar looking masculine back. The man had on a hunting suit and was leaning forward kissing a woman. Her pretty face was held between his hands.

I pretended to read a railroad map and walked right up behind him. He was patting her cheeks and telling her that when he returned he would bring her a nice piece of venison. I heard his voice and knew I was not mistaken.

It was my old friend of the Country Club, Johnson!

The celery farms of Sanford, Florida, Daytona Beach, Steel, with his important telegrams, the Country Club on the summit of the hill, the motor boat, the stranger with the note, and the rope intended for my neck in the hands of Johnson, flashed through my mind.

There was another woman with Johnson's friend, and they parted and walked off. As Johnson moved toward the ticket office he ran into an acquaintance and said:

"Well, what they don't know won't hurt them, will it?" They both laughed knowingly.

"I'm going off to celebrate!" explained Johnson. "It's too cold for me to go hunting, this weather, so I'm just going out on a little spree!"

I motioned to Pete. "There!" I pointed to Johnson, "is a friend to Steel, a friend to Furey and a friend to Spencer! He is Johnson. Follow him, and don't let him get away!" Pete found it easy to engage in conversation with them.

He told them he wished he could go hunting. This seemed to amuse them and they talked to him in that patronizing way elders so frequently do to children.

They said they were going to Montreal, Canada.

I waited until train time, and when I saw the three of them on board I followed a few coaches behind.

Pete still stuck to them.

They did not mention hunting anything but whiskey and wine in Montreal. These interests, as well as other important ones were calling them to Canada, they explained.

Pete sat in their section and listened to their plans for getting the booze out of the storehouse and selling it.

Pete told them he lived in New Mexico and had just sold out his sheep and seven carloads of cattle on the Chicago market. He said that as long as he was so close he had been taking a holiday and had visited Niagara Falls, Buffalo, and now had decided to run up to Montreal and get a little of the "hootch" for himself.

When we got to Montreal I trailed the trio to the Windsor Hotel where they all registered. I did the same, after giving them time to get upstairs.

Pete and I then got together for the first talk since boarding the train at Buffalo.

He said they were very nice to him and especially interested, after hearing that he had collected on seven carloads of cattle. Stocks and bonds were, he said, the chief topics of conversation.

They had the same old line out. How much easy money was being cleaned up in this game. They said they had a friend who was coming very soon to Montreal to meet them there. He was a very important personage in the financial world and they could not do much in a business way until he arrived.

While Pete was clinging to their parties, I prowled the town for other clues. There was no doubt in my mind that the friend they expected was other than Spencer.

The American consul took me before the head "law" of the city, Chief P. Ballinger and Captain La Page.

Both were splendid to me and treated me like a prince. They duplicated my American warrants for use in Canada and also warned me not to pull a trigger in the "Great Northwest."

They offered every assistance but impressed it on me not to shoot!

"You southern men in the United States are too quick on the trigger for this country."

I appreciated the tip as I saw it was meant in good faith and for my own well-being.

Two or three days had elapsed and we were still waiting for their friend to show up. Every night, Pete, Johnson and his friend would go into the bar room. They kept a watchful eye on Pete and continued telling him as soon as their moneyed acquaintance showed up they would put him onto a nice little piece of change. In the bar room Pete always sat facing the heavy plush curtains that separated the bar from the lobby. In this way I could watch through the slightly open curtain.

We decided on certain signals. I could stand facing him and he would give me the high sign. One signal for "nothing doing, go to bed," another for "stick around," and so on. In this way, I could get a fair idea of how things were progressing. They were very reasonable about Pete not drinking any liquor and never pressed him to take anything stronger than ale.

It was some task with our scant bank account to make up a showy "roll" for Pete to flash every night. It was necessary to look like money as they believed him a wealthy young cowman.

Day after day we waited for the financial genius to appear.

One morning they told Pete with much satisfaction that they had had a wire from their guide and he would arrive early in the evening of that same day.

On this night the noted "Human Spider," Bill Strother, was to climb the walls of the magnificent Windsor Hotel Building.

The city was agog over his chances of accomplishment. I had known Strother and his manager, Mr. Hill of Houston, Texas.

Along toward dusk the crowds began to gather in the Dominion Square in front of the hotel.

I had been in the lobby talking to Strother and his manager and told them jokingly that if he was the magnet which was drawing Spencer to our trap, and we got him, that we would all celebrate tomorrow.

As usual Pete and the others were in the bar room. I motioned him to come out and talk to me. He tipped his chair against the table and excused himself.

He went out in the opposite direction and came around and met me on the other side of the curtains.

He gave me a significant smile and hurriedly explained that their friend, "Mr. Spencewood," would be in on the train which arrived in fifteen minutes.

"I had better stay with them, Dad," he said, "because I think he will come directly here from the station if he can get through the jam of people outside. And believe me if he does come in here I am going to coldknock him so quick he can't move for some time. You be on the lookout because we may have trouble!"

Pete's hand rested on the curtain. Just as he went to part them to go back into the bar room they were flung quickly apart and Johnson, who had become nervous at Pete's exit, looked me full in the face.

Instant recognition shone in those same gander eyes. He flung his arms out wide and clutched at the curtain as he fell over his own feet and dashed out through the bar.

There was no use in following him as we had nothing on him. But he had recognized me and would try to warn Spencer, or Spencewood. He had become aware of my presence.

Pete and I leaped into the crowd and fought our way through their midst in an attempt to be at the station when the train pulled in. But our progress was blocked every foot of the way. Huge bulky forms threw themselves in our way, and time after time we were forced out of our course by the impact of the watchers.

After we did gain an open road we saw four men running across the street. As they passed under a street lamp on the Dominion Square side which was entirely parked Pete cried:

"There he goes! That's Spencer now! Watch him walk. That's him!"

164

We had been too late. The train had come in. However not one of the other three was Johnson or his friend. We crossed after them and tried to overtake them before they lost themselves in the vast crowd of upturned heads. We caught up with them just as they plowed into the jam, tearing their way right and left; knocking men, women and children aside.

We did our best to follow in the furrow they had cut in the crowd but those whom they so roughly thrust aside closed the path with angry gestures and exclamations of surprise. We could see them plunging ahead through the heads and shoulders of the watchers. We fought our way after them, never losing sight of them for a minute.

While I had been unable to get a close-up of Spencer, yet I was sure it was he.

The four lined up at the curb like pals at a bar. They stood looking across the street at Strother whose spider legs were slowly but surely creeping up the smooth side wall of the hotel.

I was standing at the right hip pocket of Spencer and Pete was behind the man standing at Spencer's side. They were unaware of our proximity.

At this instant a big burly Canadian came floundering up behind me. He had his eyes riveted on Strother's ascent and, not looking where he was going, crashed into me, throwing me into Spencer.

This, of course, startled Spencer. He swung around with raised fist and looked into my eyes.

There was no longer doubt as to who he was. One look at that crooked nose and it was settled.

He recognized me as quickly as I did him.

"Come on!" he exclaimed to his friends and swung one of his companions between him and me.

They started to paw their way back through the mob of thirty thousand people, Spencer in the lead, the others following, and Pete and I after them. Pete was ahead of me. As they opened up the trail, we followed in it.

After battling our way for fifty yards, Spencer checked in his flight and whispered something into the ear of a tall heavy-set man.

Instantly the man threw his hands into the air and uttered strange idiotic guttural noises. He reeled in the small opening, and just as Pete ran alongside of him the fellow crashed down on him, mashing him into the snow.

It was a strange tableau! I kept my eyes on Spencer, who was taking advantage of our blockade and beating his way from us as fast as possible.

I jumped over Pete and the man who was rolling on him in this peculiar sudden frenzy. As I leaped them I intended to kick him with my foot, but I was not certain that he was an accomplice. I thought it better to let a thug go unkicked than to maim an innocent or afflicted man. So I brought my last foot clear over his body. I tore after Spencer who had gained on me. As I left, I saw Pete and the man still wallowing on the white ground.

I pursued Spencer for fifty yards. By this time we had reached the outskirts of the vast throng and had more room. I yelled at Spencer to throw up his hands. He heard me and swung around in his tracks, facing me.

"Hold up your hands, Spencer! You're my prisoner!" I shouted.

"That's not my name!" he retorted, as his hands shot into the. air.

Then he proceeded to tell me I was mistaken. While he was explaining one of the men with him jerked a card out of his pocket and held it towards me saying:

"This is his name on this card. He is not Spencer."

I had no time to look at the card, I was too busy shouting for the police. As I reached to my hip for my handcuffs I received a sledge-hammer blow on my jaw.

Whoever the slugger was, he must have been a left-handed one for he hit me on that side. As I went down under the blow I locked the left corner of Spencer's overcoat tail in my left hand. It was the same grip I had sunk into the lapel of Furey's coat that day in the Hilton Cafe.

Spencer kicked me in the face with the round toes of his rubber overshoe which fortunately for me softened the impact.

I wanted to kill him. I was almost blinded with agonizing pain. Canadian law or not, I thought, I'll kill him this time.

I reached up from where I was sprawled and with my right hand punched him in the groin, intending to shoot him straight up through lengthwise. As I angled my gun for fire I saw the form of Bill Strother clinging to the icy wall at the top-most point of the tall building.

In that instant I realized the crack of a pistol-shot might confuse him, knowing I was out for my men, and plunge him to his death. This was all that kept me from blowing Spencer up the middle.

Like a frightened animal Spencer leapt into the air with the pain of my blow. He cried out and screamed horrible oaths from the hurt of it. He broke into a prancing run and dragged me after him still clinging to his coat tail like a sled. This rapid transit continued for twenty or thirty yards until suddenly the coat tail gave way and I was left flat in the road with a piece of it in my hand. He broke into a wilder run and I sprang after him.

The blood was dripping from my face and left round scarlet patches on the white snow.

On! on! he ran, like a whipped bull quits the roundup. He dodged and shuttled; he shot in and out alleys, up and down; he was gaining on me. Not much, but enough to serve his purpose. I was still calling for help but to no avail.

Two husky young lads about eighteen years old came in sight. I beckoned to them and pointed at the fleeing figure.

"Catch that thief, boys! Catch him!" I cried.

They turned in their path and like two young greyhounds sped after the swift moving Spencer. They got in his way and checked his speed. But after doing this they became nervous and hesitated to lay hands on him.

He took this opportunity to run into the Strand Theater on St. Catherine Street. By the time I reached the inside of the place I saw him making the last turn at the top of the long flight of stairs leading into the gallery.

I took the steps three at a time.

When he reached the top gallery he kept on up into the attic of the play house. A door stood open, and in a flash he had banged it between us and pushed the lock across.

Hearing the beating of feet on the stairs, the house detective had followed in my winged footsteps. He demanded to know what the commotion was.

I told him I was an officer of the law; that my prisoner sought escape up these stairs and was now barricaded in the attic room behind that door.

"I want you to help me get him!" I said, wiping the blood, which had frozen in nasty clots around my eyes and mouth.

I must have been an ugly sight. Battered and bruised from the blow in the face, torn and dirty from my ride through the streets at the end of Spencer's coat.

The detective forced the door and dragged Spencer out. When he emerged from the door in the clutch of the man's brawny right he held a roll of bills so big that his hand wouldn't reach around it.

"Men, oh, men! don't let him take my money! Don't let him rob me!" pointing in my direction.

The house manager appeared on the scene. Of course he also wanted to know what the trouble was.

Spencer was shrieking to them in French which I could not understand. The stairs became alive with onlookers. The detective and manager began to beat them back.

I tried to show my warrant to them but they had been so impressed with the foreign words uttered by Spencer that I could not command the slightest attention.

The manager ordered my hands bound down to my sides and that I be taken to jail.

"He is disturbing the peace in my place of business! Take him to jail!" he ordered.

Two volunteers from the crowd on the stairway officiated.

As I was led back down the stairs I begged and pleaded to them at least to bring my prisoner along with me. But Spencer stood there with an evil smile on his face and was allowed to watch me march to jail in his stead.

On the way to the jail we ran into two policemen. My escorts turned me over to them. As soon as I showed these officers my warrants with Chief La Page's name signed to it they exclaimed:

"We'll get him!"

The three of us rushed back to the theater accompanied by the two men who had just brought me down.

"You go into the theater!" I cried, "and I'll watch the fire escape at the back."

I stood on the street, my eyes riveted on the metal stairway.

My horrible appearance drew a crowd of spectators.

Two traffic officers came up and saying that I was stopping traffic, pushed me roughly into a nearby cigar stand.

I explained to the officers why I was observing the escape and they permitted me again to take up my station. But in the meantime, as would be expected, Spencer had come out on top of the building, run down the steps from flight to flight, and just as I stepped again onto the sidewalk I saw him run up the ally and turn the corner.

I shouted out to the officers that I would give a reward to the one who captured him.

Like dogs circling for a trail of their game, the men ran through the snow.

Chapter Twenty-Nine - Ward's Tragic Fate

I had forgotten all about Pete. When I reached the hotel I met a man by the name of Scott, the head of a large detective agency in Montreal. While we were talking Pete and two policemen came in.

I told them about my skirmish with Spencer in the theater and they left for headquarters to make a formal report of the fracas. Pete got in touch with the department and soon the lobby was swarming with official uniforms.

Voluminous information was given them, and they left in another swarm to spread a dragnet for Spencer.

There was a doctor from Rochester, Minnesota, stopping at the hotel in the room next to mine. He cared for my injuries which were more serious than I supposed. For ten days I was wrapped in bandages-.

During the time of my convalescence I was daily in communication with the police, but while they did their best to get track of Spencer, no success rewarded their efforts.

Just before we were ready to leave the city a large Shrine ceremonial was to be held. We waited over for this, and into the pocket of every Noble we put a little circular giving a brief story and description of Spencer and his operations,.

The newspapers also gave us help in the way of widely circulated news reports of the street battle.

One of the circulars yielded substantial results.

The Potentate of the Temple at Albany, N. Y., who was also the Mayor, got in touch with me and tipped me off to some inside information that a deal similar to Spencer's was being pulled off in Albany.

Pete and I left that night for Albany to follow the lead. By the time we arrived in town the police had arrested Harnon and Trent, two of the most notorious confidence men in the United States.

They were old timers at the game.

We were given to understand that Spencer had been in on the deal and got away with the cash before the police could nab him. We heard later that the two received long sentences.

From Albany we went to New York City. Since Spencer had quit Albany in such haste we thought probably he had gone to the industrial base of the organization.

This base we knew to be located in the City of New York. We had the address of Ward's lawyer, Joseph B. Rosenback. We located him at his office, 306 West 54th Street.

From him we learned the tragic end of Ward in the prison at Washington, D. C, where he had been confined since his removal from Fort Worth following his dramatic meeting with Mr. Nee.

Rosenback said Ward was being held in Washington on the "Nee" charge of a thirty-five thousand dollar swindle. Rosenback, it seems, was on his way to Washington with the cash to square the deal. He arrived there and found that Ward's body was not yet cold in death, from suicide, committed as freedom was rushing to him.

Those who were in touch with Ward just before his demise, declare remorse over his past life and the hopelessness of the future, brought on a melancholia which drove him to suicide.

He had made arrangements, it is claimed by those in his confidence, to make good to all of those he could, the money stolen from them. Large amounts were to be transferred to him through his attorneys for this purpose, but when they reached the transfer point between his Fort Worth attorney and himself, the money was never again heard of.

His thwarted desire to make amends so depressed him that he cut his own throat.

Just out of curiosity, we looked up the training school for student swindlers. Furey had given us the address as the corner of Street and Broadway.

This, we found to be in the heart of the "Great White Way," or "Rialto." The number was a highly ornamental cabaret with lights, wine, women and song in full swing. The club house or schoolroom, as Furey called it, was located above.

I had once asked Furey why he did not destroy my fateful contract with him. This was the one found in the suitcase of telltale data discovered in San Bernardino.

He replied that he had kept it to show the boys at the "school" how he had beaten an old cowboy in a new way.

It was quite evident that Joe was proud of his originality.

We found nothing in New York which looked like a ripe lead, so took the train for Washington, D. C, where we had a conference with William J. Burns, head of the U. S. Department of Justice. When I entered the room, Mr. Burns turned to me and viewed me as a newfoundland looks at a fox terrier.

"What can I do for you?" he asked quickly.

"My name is Norfleet," I answered. "Perhaps you can advise with me."

𝔇epartment of 𝔍ustice

𝔅ureau of 𝔍nvestigation

𝔚ashington, 𝔇. 𝔒.

November 3, 1923.

Mr. J. F. Norfleet,
"I.X.L." Ranch,
Hale Center, Texas.

My dear Mr. Norfleet:

      I beg to acknowledge your letter of the
25th and want to convey my hearty congratulations
on your wonderful victory.

      I saw by the paper that Mr. W.B. Spencer,
alias Charles G. Harris, Rose, etc., had been arrested
in Salt Lake City, and I was as well pleased over it
as you were. I am glad you succeeded in getting the
last of these criminals, and I hope they will put
Spencer away for a long time.

      I think you have rendered the country a fine
service in running to earth these criminals. I hope
I may have the pleasure of seeing you soon to personally
congratulate you.

        Very sincerely yours,

              Director.

He showed surprise.

"Norfleet?" he queried.

"Yes," I repeated.

"Well, well, I wish to congratulate you, Mr. Norfleet. You have accomplished one of the most wonderful achievements that has ever come under my observation, in my lifetime of experience."

I couldn't help laughing. To me it didn't appear so extraordinary.

"I repeat it!" he declared. "To thinly that a man without a bit of experience pitted his wits against those of that organization; has been double-crossed at every turn, and then went on in spite of everything and secured conviction! We have marvelled at your success. But," his heavy mustache lifted in an ingratiating smile, "now that I see you, I can understand what has brought you this success. It is your insignificant appearance!"

This was unexpected. However, not being sensitive, it made no impression other than one of amusement.

I wanted to tell him that I had not come to Washington to discuss my beauty, but fearing he might misunderstand, I strangled the desire.

"What can I do for you?" he asked again.

I told him I wanted W. B. Spencer. I gave him his several aliases; told him of my Montreal experiences and asked if he could offer any suggestions as to where he might be operating now.

Burns knew nothing about him he said, but called in his stenographer and dictated two letters. One of them was to a son in New York and the other to another son in San Francisco. The young men were managers of the Burns' Detective Agency in the two cities.

Both letters asked that a special effort be made to get Spencer. Burns further stated in them his feeling of personal obligation to me for my activities in breaking up the bunco organization. He also instructed his sons to disregard expense as he stood ready to shell out if it was necessary.

This seemed a great favor, and I felt that before many moons had waned Spencer would be among those present.

Before leaving Washington, Pete and I called at the home of Mr. and Mrs. Nee. We were made very welcome and given a splendid time. Pete had a great time with the two young daughters and their two brothers. This was the last time I ever saw Mr. Nee, for he died a short time afterward.

Our next stop was Chicago.

Everywhere we went we would search the rogues' galleries. In no place were we able to get a picture of Spencer. Of all of the cameras, kodaks and picture making contrivances in the world, it did seem as if one should had been trained on his crooked nose some time or other. But hunt as we did, none had come to light. Verbal descriptions of people are far from satisfactory.

Up to this time there were only two rogues' galleries left in the United States of any size that we had not searched. Pete went to Sioux City, Iowa, to go through their files, and I remained in Chicago to see what I could find out. I was associated for the next few days with the head of the Finger Print Department and the Jail Photographer. I saw more revolting pictures of brutality and foul murder than I ever dreamed existed. And as for stories of crime, the gentlemanly game of swindling paled into insignificance.

At the end of a week Pete and I met in Kansas City. He had news for me. In Sioux City, the rogues' gallery had yielded nothing, but from there he had gone to the Omaha, Nebraska, gallery, the last one of any size in the U. S. to come under our microscopic eyes.

There Pete found the first photograph of Spencer. It was filed under the name of Charles G. Harris, alias Gus Schultz No. 3317. On the reverse side was a notation indicating that the same picture was on record in Kansas City No. 6334, Chas. G. Harris, alias "Whitley" Harris.

This was rather a reflection on the efficiency of the Kansas City files, as on our previous trip there the police had declared there was no photograph of anyone by this name.

We went over to the police station at Kansas City and requested to see the records again. There was no picture on file of Spencer, Harris or Schultz.

We called the attention of the Captain of Detectives to the photograph which bore the notation that there was one on file in his office. He studied it with bent head.

Then he walked over to a little filing cabinet and from a pigeonhole took a small metal box, turned a key in the lock and opened the lid. From the box he took a bunch of photographs, and from among them he pulled out one of Spencer; a duplicate of the one Pete brought from Omaha.

"I guess we must have overlooked this the last time you were here," was all he said.

On the reverse side of this picture the record showed that Spencer had been arrested by their department and turned loose. Also one of the two officers who had gone to Excelsior Springs with us had made the arrest.

I stopped in Wichita, Kansas, and had a number of Spencer's photographs made. These I circulated from one end of the country to the other, asking those who received them to notify me if they saw anything of Spencer. Then I went back to the ranch to rest up from my strenuous trip and await results from the distributed pictures.

Within a few weeks, I received a communication from a Mr. West, whom I had known in Wichita. West said that Spencer and two other men were known to have boarded the train at Galveston, Texas, bound for Denver.

I left immediately for Amarillo and watched the trains passing through there for days, thinking I might head them off at that point. The Santa Fe officials and detectives assisted me in searching their trains for them.

Nothing was seen of him along the Amarillo route. He evidently had gone to Albuquerque and from there into Denver by automobile.

On the road to Denver I took in Colorado Springs to see what I could dig up. While there I was notified by Captain Bruce of the Colorado Springs Department, not to go on to Denver. He said he had just returned from there and that Colonel Phillip Van Cise, district attorney of Denver, was laying plans to round up a big ring of "confidence men," operating in that city and that it would be better for me to lay low and not butt in on the game.

Captain Bruce intended this in good faith, I am sure, but as I had had little help from any official executives of any police or civic body, I was not inclined to consider their plans any more important than mine.

I did not go directly to Denver, but stayed around the Broadmoor Hotel for several days. By talking to different persons, I got a fair line up on previous "confidence" stunts pulled in the State of Colorado.

From what I learned I concluded that the Denver bunco stock exchange was the same outfit into whose claws young Holman at Austin was being enticed.

It did not seem fair that any officer of the law should, ask me not to hunt my men in Denver and I felt if they understood my position they would not ask it. I had previously corresponded with Colonel Van Cise and had offered to share with his office whatever information I got that would be of use to it.

So when I reached Denver I called Roy O. Sansome, chief investigator of the district attorney's office, on the telephone.

"This is Norfleet speaking," I said. "I just called you up to let you know I'm in town."

He warned me against speaking to anyone or letting anyone know I was in town until after I saw him.

I went right over.

Sansome told me to lay off the town and informed me that Colonel Van Cise was in the mountains.

"We are trying to trap this big ring of 'confidence men' operating here," he explained, "and we don't want to run the risk of having our plans spoiled by you."

"I won't spoil your game intentionally. I'm only trying to enforce the law. I think I know my business and perhaps I can be of some help to you."

He seemed to appreciate my motive but appeared doubtful of my ability, but I was out for myself and told him so.

I inquired when Col. Van Cise was expected back.

"In a few days," he said.

During the time I waited for Van Cise's return, I looked around the town to see what was doing in a general "confidence" way and what members of the gang were in town.

I got together a new disguise and spent my spare time in adjusting it, and accustoming my body to its new demands. It was hard to recognize myself in the glass. I always tried to act at home both mentally and physically in a new disguise. My face had to be changed as well as my clothes. For this occasion I chose a light weight and light colored palm beach suit. It was the hue of straw and had one of those little pinchback belt arrangements that strap the spine cross-wise. As I planned to represent a "country rube" in city clothes, this style o£ garment was of great aid. I decided to adopt a posture of bending forward like a cotton picker grows from his leaning position. The little strap across the back heightened this humpy appearance. The coat was such light weight material that it was extremely difficult to hide the gun on my hip. Therefore I simulated a stiff-waistedness and walked with a stiffened hand upon my hip after the manner of rheumatic old men.

I became a willing victim of the beauty parlors and their blonde, brunette and titian operators. My grey mustache had grown long. This I had dyed a dark brown, thinned out the ends and curled them up until they gave the appearance of pointing to the corners of my eyes. My eyebrows these young women also dyed to match. The hairs were long and bristling. Their shagginess gave me the feeling of peering out from under a thatched roof. My hair was dyed to match, and cut bowl style. It bushed in the back and stuck out in a thick roll from under the brim of my cocky little panama hat which rode uncertainly atilt my head. In my hand that was not on my gun hip I clasped the bowed handle of a crochety cane. When I spoke I achieved a high thin tone and cracked it in the middle.

When Van Cise arrived, I was notified. I had a consultation with him in his executive offices in the West Court. He told me of his great interest in the closing in on the confidence ring.

"The citizens of this town have made an appropriation of $15,000 to pay the expenses of this special capture," he said. Imported suckers, experienced in playing the boob, were employed to play into the hands of the swindlers to effectively cinch a capture.

On the day we talked he had been informed that several of the known bunco gang had had their baggage taken to the depot preparatory to embarking for other fields.

"Just think of it! And we have not one single bit of substantial evidence to tie them to so far!" he lamented.

He asked me not to be seen in the vicinity of the district attorney's office. Also he requested my absence from all prominent hotels, the civic center and other public gathering places, including the capitol grounds; which in all capitol cities, is the nesting place of this brand of criminal.

I handed him Spencer's picture as well as photographs of some other swindlers and asked him to distribute them among his detectives. I told him I firmly believed Spencer was in Denver working under a good cover.

He told me not to speak to any officer in the police or sheriff's department:

"There are some trustworthy officers, but you won't know which ones they are."

I said good-bye to him and promised to let him know if anything developed. He was very uneasy at having me loose in the city for fear of detective inability and its consequent scattering of the bunco forces before his office could get them.

I saw his mental reaction to the situation and I did my best to relieve his mind as to the possible harm I would do his organization. I guaranteed that if I could not serve his office constructively, I would not do so destructively.

He laid special stress on my not even calling his office on the telephone. For this emergency he gave me another number.

As I left the office I wondered what the final outcome of this one event would be. Strife and combat were in the air.

I put on my disguise and hit the trail for the post office.

The same blind man was tapping the side walk with his hollow sounding cane. I had seen him there every time I had been near the building. He was a well dressed, middle-aged man. He tapped his way but managed corners and obstructions with surprising ability for the "sightless" eyes screened by large, dark blue glasses. An unmistakable gash across his high cheek bone stamped him as "Bill Mooney" whom I had seen in Memphis, Tenn., where he was associated with the "confidence" crew.

I pursued a direct course to the general delivery window. Rap! Tap! Rap! Tap! came the blind man behind me.

Chapter Thirty - Another Stock Exchange

"Any mail for L. A. Mulligan?" I cackled, in a voice pitched to reach Mooney's ears. "None!" said the clerk.

I stepped out on the broad sidewalk and stood there watching the traffic; my attention focused mainly on the letter seekers, pouring in and out of the big Federal building. I eased up against one of the tall columns just as an officer approached me belligerently.

"This is no place for loiterers!"

I wondered what other business he had neglected in order to move me on. I walked over to the corner of the street where a big display sign of the U. S. Marine Corps was doing recruit duty. Highly colored posters plastered its slanting sides.

I stood looking at these. Rap! Tap! Rap! Tap! came the cane of Mooney. He passed on.

From across the street in the direction of the Denham Theater Building, I saw approaching another familiar face. When he reached me he stopped and looked at the picture with a satirical flicker of the mouth, remarking to me:

"If the real thing was as attractive as the picture it would be a beautiful life, wouldn't it?"

So Fred Soloman was also among those present in Denver! Well, well, well, I thought. Smiling Soloman! I called him this because of the perpetual radiance he exuded no matter how bright the sun nor how gloomy the sky. I recognized him as a Salt Lake product. His picture was among those in my personal rogues' gallery. He smiled from the front, he grinned from the side, even the wrinkles in the back of his neck laughed.

Like old Sol, he beamed. We had never met as they say socially, but I knew him. His remark soon ripened into a full blown conversation destined to lead into important paths of progress.

"Whatley is my name?" he smiled.

"Mulligan is mine," I replied.

"What part of the country do you hail from, my friend?" he followed.

"I am from the biggest cotton county in Texas, Ellis County. I own one of the finest cotton farms in the whole darn country."

"Whatley, Whatley!" I repeated, reflectively.

He caught this instantly and countered with an amendment.

"Not Whatley, Whitley!" he reconstructed cleverly.

I suspected he was genuinely familiar with this part of Texas and I took the cue to caution. If he is from my portion of the State, I thought, I'd not get very far fooling him, so I stepped lightly. Evidently he suspected I knew some Whatley s, and adroitly changed my seeming auricular error. Points were even so far.

We launched on a campaign of everything but the truth. I think the final score was a tie.

Soloman had a criminal record and was no doubt scouting for prospects for the higher-ups in the fake stock exchange.

While I was sure I could play into his part of the work and ultimately find my way to the Exchange as in the previous frame-ups, still I was afraid of this fellow. He knew Texans and I could not afford to play the game through a man who knew enough about my type to see through many of the lapses an impersonator is bound to make.

Soloman asked if I had many friends in Denver.

I replied in the negative. Then began the same old line which included the invalid wives. Soloman's better half was invalided along with the rest. At present he had her in a Rochester Hospital of fame getting "patched up," as he tenderly put it.

Soloman had some lovely "lady friends." His wife was absent.

Mine, I told him, had failed to join me.

He said there was no reason to be lonely. There were beautiful mountain drives, fast motor cars and congenial companions to be had.

"Why not a drive of scenic beauty tomorrow morning?" he suggested.

I fell in with his offers pending time to think matters over. It was agreed that we meet on the corner of 18th and California the next morning at nine o'clock.

During our conversation, we had drifted toward the Columbia Hotel on 17th Street.

Here I stopped and bade him good-bye. I gave as an excuse for parting, necessary business letters to be written to my wife. We separated in front of the Arbor Cafe, directly across from my hotel. I hastened to my room and peeked out through the lace curtains.

Old Sol was standing where I had left him. He was staring at the hotel entrance, which showed he was not entirely positive of me as a legitimate prospect. This investigating attitude of his strengthened my hunch that he and I had better not try to do business.

While I stood watching him, the heavens flashed with lightning and bellowed in long rolling peals of thunder. Rain fell in sudden torrents. In a minute the streets were running rivers. Soloman waited until the storm broke into a fury of hail, then smilingly turned up his coat collar about his throat and ran down the street out of sight.

I went to the telephone and called the emergency number Colonel Van Cise had given me.

The party who answered said if I had any important news they would connect me with Mr. Van Cise's head investigator, Kenneth W. Robinson. Robinson's voice came over the wire.

In guarded terms, for fear of wire tappers, I told him I had a "good trade" for him.

He replied he was interested and that there was to be a little party held within a few minutes at a certain address.

"Come down there Mulligan, and we'll invite you into the game!" he said.

I redressed myself in ordinary attire and started out for the party.

Such a night! such a storm! The streets were submerged in tides of water. The heavens cracked and split with zigzag slits of light and boomed with the roar of cannons. Wires were blown down, tracks torn up, trees felled to the ground and man and beast were swept into a welter of wind and water.

That night the homeless and injured totaled five thousand. The American Red Cross cared for fully this number and Overland Park, where the tourists were camped, was washed as clean of tents as a desert island.

The place where I had been instructed to go was beyond the carline.

I rode as far as possible then waded the rest of the way. The water rushed past me to my knees. Boxes, bicycles, signboards, chairs, umbrellas and spare tires barked my shins in their surf riding. I was drenched to the skin from the top of my head to the soles of my feet.

Finally I came to the house. It was the residence of Roy Samson. Inside it was warm, and I dried out enough to keep from getting a severe cold.

Colonel Van Cise, his deputies and detectives were in conference.

I told them of Soloman and the general lineup.

They were delighted.

"I've got the runners of the stock exchange on my hip and will be into the real game within a day or two," I promised.

They said they were depending on the "Rangers" for making the raid when the nest was discovered.

I expressed my unqualified approval of this fine arrangement and chuckled to think how the police would look when this "red-blood crew" got busy.

I offered my services to them under the condition that I be allowed a free rein and an unrestricted hand in dealing with the situation. I made it clear that I wished to act on my own judgment entirely, but would depend upon their support when the time came.

This was freely granted and it was decided I should go ahead and work, communicating progress to them. Several methods of reporting my moves were discussed, but it was left up to me.

The storm abated and some of the fellows drove me back to the hotel.

The rest of the night was spent in writing letters to my wife; some bona fide and some for display use. I also wrote one to myself from her and put them all in my pocket for future use. Even today, I consider it one of the finest I ever received from her. I wrote it in a fine, small and what I considered a truly feminine hand, far different from my own large lettering. It was as follows:

Ferris, Texas, August 17th, 1921.

Dear Husband:

I am very sorry I could not meet you in Denver as you expected. I know you will be greatly disappointed, but you know as well as I that one of us ought to remain at home to keep the pot boiling. By the way, I collected the $15,000.00 on the hundred acre oil lease that we signed up before you left home. I deposit-

ed $2,000.00 in the bank at Ferris, the balance I deposited in the bank at Dallas. Is that the way you wanted it distributed?

The drillers have struck oil in the corner of our field. They have quit drilling, and the company is leasing every acre of land they can get around this well. I am now holding down a lease on 236 acres of our land with my signature and I recommend that you come home at once and sign this lease so we can get the money and then you can go back to Denver and stay as long as you please. That will leave us the 19 acres where the buildings and the big tank of water are located and we can get our own price for that, if we want to let it go, as the drillers want the water for drilling purposes.

At the end I wound up with a tender little message of love.

The next morning at the appointed time in my disguise I watched from a protected place Soloman's arrival on the corner named for our meeting. I had decided to shake him.

On the strike of the clock, he arrived with a woman. They stood on the corner and looked up and down the street, evidently for me. After waiting about fifteen minutes, they started off down the street.

I followed after them and got a good look at the woman. She had on "a million dollars' worth of clothes" and, while rather well hand-tinted, was certainly good looking.

Soloman knew how to pick faces as well as pockets.

I did not trail them long but instead turned back and went into the Brown Palace Hotel. I entered through the 17th Street entrance. As I stepped inside the wide corridor which led into the main lobby, I espied two more of the gang. They were Leon Felix and big Robert Nash, alias Robert Knowles.

They sat facing the door watching for victims. In order to reach the lobby, it was necessary for me to pass between their chairs. They lounged in easy attitudes and turned to scrutinize all who passed their web.

When I was almost between them, I said in my best hick voice: "How'de do!" and grinned in an awkward, self-conscious way.

They both returned my salutation with amused, tolerant nods.

Often on the trains or during long waits, I would fill in the time studying the photographs of different fugitives at large. This was time well spent as it enabled me on several different occasions to recognize members of the holdup fraternity I would otherwise have passed up.

Felix was a medium sized sleek Jew with a small, dark, close-clipped mustache.

Nash was a two hundred pound, dark and prosperous appearing individual. Lolling in the deep chairs both looked the picture of leisured prosperity.

As I was "howdying" to the men, I saw a man with two little girls coming in from the Broadway entrance.

I felt that I had been well inventoried as I passed. They could not miss my country makeup and being true crooks, would spot me as a prospect. I could not keep on going and yet give them an opportunity to speak to me. There-

178

fore I went up to the man with the two little girls, held out my hand in that familiar country manner and exclaimed in a high pitched voice:

"Well, well, I thought I knowed you. You're Mr. Woolridge from down my way in Texas, ain't you?"

"No, no," he responded, allowing me to raise and lower his gloved hand. "No, you have made a mistake, stranger, I'm Jennings of Nebraska!"

"Wall, now I am sorry, Mr. Jennings, I was certain you was my old friend, Woolridge."

"No harm done, Fm sure," he replied pleasantly, then gathered the small ones by the hand and passed on.

"Are you looking for some one? May I help you, sir? You seem to be a stranger!" said a smooth voice at my elbow.

I turned and Felix stood there all solicitation for my comfort.

"Why, yes," I answered gratefully. "I am lookin' for a friend of mine from down Texas way. I'll go over here to the counter and ask the man if he stayed here last night."

He walked over to the desk with me and stood off a respectful distance while I inquired if Mr. J. C. Woolridge, of Texas, had a room there.

"I heered that last night's storm scattered them tourists all over town. 'Spect I might have a lot of friends bunkin' here if I only knowed it."

The clerk smiled in a superior way, as clerks so often do, and said there was no such person registered with them.

Felix then joined me and we strolled about the lobby; I, gazing at the ceiling and voicing amazement at the grandeur of the big hotel.

He introduced himself as A. C. Davis and I told him I was R. C. Mulligan from Ferris, Texas.

"I am from Texas myself!" he said.

"What part do you hail from?"

"Houston! — Houston, Texas, is my home."

But he pronounced it "Hooston," which no Texan of the lowest breed ever said.

Then I tried him on another.

"Say, now what is that there town where they always have the Cotton Palace, down near to where you live?"

"Oh, you mean Waco!"

But he called it "Wocco."

When he said this, I could have picked the street he lived on in New York City.

I was relieved to know definitely he did not come from Texas. I saw I would get on with him much safer than with Smiling Soloman.

"Can you please tell me, Mr. Davis, if there is any place up here in town where you can buy your tickets? I'm a wantin' to go home."

He told me where it was and followed it with a question as to how long I had been in Denver.

Three district attorneys and two sheriffs who helped corral the crooks — upper left, Col. Philip S. Van Cise, Denver; Upper Right, Thos. Lee Woolwine, Los Angeles; Center, Jesse Brown, Fort Worth; Lower Left, Sterling P. Clark, Fort Worth; Lower Right, Sheriff Walter A. Shay, San Bernardino.

I said I had been in town only a few days, that I had expected my wife to join me, but she could not and had written asking me to come home.

"Have you seen the parks or taken any of the scenic mountain drives?"

"No," I said. "I haven't seen nothin' much on this trip." Then I appeared eager to get my railroad ticket and said I must be going after it.

He didn't want to lose me yet.

"Why not let me drive you down to the office? My doctor recommends a certain amount of driving for me every day. He says that motoring in traffic is good for my nerves."

He was gently but firmly leading me back toward the 17th Street entrance through which I had come in.

"You're in no worse shape than I am, friend. My wife is in Joplin, Missouri, where my folks are. I'm here alone, too. Guess we Texans will have to throw in together."

Things were certainly working up pretty. I was now familiar enough with their game to know before they moved which way they were going to play. Therefore I usually helped them out without their knowledge.

"We're not as fortunate as my friends here," indicating Nash and another man who had shown up in our absence. "Their wives are along with them."

We walked out to the curb and got into a Cadillac touring car. He took the wheel and I sat at his side.

At the ticket office, he went in with me. I felt that it was the best policy to buy a ticket to assure him that I had been sincere in my declaration that I must go home to Ferris.

I saw he was fairly familiar with Texas transportation systems, so I discussed with him the advantage of not purchasing the ticket straight to Ferris, but instead to Fort Worth, and then taking the Interurban to Dallas and doing a little business there and then "Interurbaning" on down home.

I looked up at the clerk as if he were the information chief of heaven and explained that I was goin' down to the Western Union office an' if I got a telegram from my wife tellin' me not to come home right now and asked if he would "swap" the ticket with me for one of a later date.

He took me in from head to foot and smiled archly, imitating my rural delivery and said:

"Oh, yes, I'll 'swap' with you." Then he gave Felix a sympathetic glance.

We got into the car again and started for the telegraph office. While he was steadying his nerves in the traffic symphony, he remarked he was surprised that he saw no grease on my clothes.

"My! but that is a great oil country. Lots of money been pumped out of that ground."

"Wal, I'm a fixin' now to go home an' get some oil on me. Just got this here letter from my wife tellin' me to come home regardin' the oil. I believe I've got to be there by a certain date. Believe I'll make sure."

I took out the letter which I had written from my wife to me. I read stumblingly and ran my fingers along under each word. This gave Felix an opportunity to read it over my shoulder, which he did.

His shifty eyes skimmed the page and after that he worked with renewed vigor.

I went into the office and faked an inquiry for my message. When I returned empty handed, I said as I had gotten no word from my wife I guessed I would stay in town a day or two and take in some of the sights with him.

Off we spun. The lovely city park, the municipal zoo, the museum and other drives of interest occupied the morning. He was a courteous host if ever one lived. He was deeply interested in Texas cotton growing.

"But it's too slow waiting for your money to grow!" he decided. "Not for me. I like mine quick!"

Then he related how his father had made huge sums of money in the stock market.

Chapter Thirty-One - $3,000 Quick Profits

"Bucked the Board of Trade!" he stated with a modest vanity.

Ah! Now we were getting down to business. The old familiar "stock market" was again in sight. My pulse throbbed.

No mistake — I was into the ring this time.

I stilled my own thoughts in order to listen to his spoken ones.

"This reminds me of something that happened to me last year in Kansas City," he was saying. "My father sent me over to Kansas City to see a Judge Brady, an old time friend of my father's who was engaged in the private practice of law but had formerly sat on the Supreme Bench. The Judge owed Dad a note for eighteen thousand dollars which he sent me over to get something on, if convenient for the Judge, and if not to renew it.

"When I went into the Judge's office, he was in close conversation with a young man. He didn't pay much attention to me but invited me to have a seat in the adjoining room. The door was left open. Well, I waited and waited and waited.

"I was so mad — you can imagine how mad I was. It must have been two hours that he kept me waiting. I sat right where I could see the young man's profile and I had all I could do to keep from rushing in and pounding and slamming him out of the chair.

"Right then I made up my mind the note would never be renewed if I had anything to do with it. I decided he would have to pay it for keeping me waiting so long. Lord! I never will forget that young man's face!"

This evidently was the main lead up to the same old stock gag. I cut in with proper exclamations of surprise and appeared to be drinking it all in as the gospel truth.

"Finally the fellow got up and left. I was so mad I could have kicked him down the hall-way to the elevator. I went into the Judge's office. I banged the note down on his desk and informed him in no very polite terms that I had come over to collect the note and expected the money right now!

"The Judge got out his check book from the pigeonhole in his desk and without saying a word made out a check in full for eighteen thousand dollars and handed it to me as if it were a mere laundry list.

"Of course I was a bit surprised. Then he opened a box of expensive cigars and offered me a smoke. I took one and we both lit up. Knowing him to have considerable means, but not riches, and being a spender, it struck me as funny that he could part with eighteen thousand bucks and not turn a hair. This interested me, and I sat down determined if possible to find out where he got all of this flushness. Finally he opened up and said, "Young fellow, you probably have heard about the young man plunger who has been written up in all the papers recently as the 'mysterious young man' who has taken such fortunes out of the stock exchange."

I wondered if his picture had been published and if he had torn the top of the head off and if he was afraid of newspaper reporters and if he was overworked and read rafts of yellow telegrams and sat on logs — but I sat tight and just listened to the old "phonograph record" as it continued:

"Why he took one hundred and twenty-five thousand dollars out of the stock exchange in one day. His picture was published in the paper. Then I recalled the story and told the Judge I believed I had read all about it. I was certainly glad I had taken such a good look at the man. The Judge told me this same chap had given him a tip on the market and since then they had been working together and had cleaned up a pile of money."

I wondered if the money was piled on a table and guarded with carbine rifles. But still I said nothing except that it was wonderful to be able to know people like that.

"Do you reckin you would know the feller if you was to see him again?"

"Know him?" he cried. "Know him! Well, I should guess I would know him. I looked at him long enough. I could pick that bird out in hell!"

We turned a sharp corner on one wheel and for a minute I thought perhaps Mr. Davis was going to have an opportunity to do some picking.

He continued the story:

"I gave my father's regards to the Judge, put the check in my pocket and said I must go. The old man sent his best to my Dad and asked me to drop in again. I was glad by this time I had not started any rough stuff."

Davis turned the car into the Capitol Grounds. Under a spreading shade close to the curb, we parked the car.

I expressed a desire to look through the museum. Davis didn't care to look at the relics and when he saw I was preparing to get out of the car, he threw his whole soul into a new campaign of stock talk.

Money! Money! Money! was his topic. The mysterious man was again brought into the plot.

By this time I was sure I had spotted the mysterious stranger. I probably saw him before Davis did.

There he came like visions of old; the self-same sheaf of yellow telegrams in his hand. On he came, walking slowly toward me. His attention was riveted on the messages and he passed us as per schedule with never an upward look. It was all the same except he had cement under his feet instead of a beach.

As he reached the rear tire Davis grabbed my arm. His eyes were big with surprise, and he looked the picture of astonishment. In a whisper he poured into my ear that "there he was!" He clutched the wheel as if to support himself from the shock.

"Speak of the devil, and his image appears! There he is — the mysterious stranger. I can hardly believe my eyes. But it is true!"

"What would you do?" he asked.

"Tackle him! Tackle him!" I urged. "Find out how he does it! Get him to learn you how."

"I believe I will," he said. "I'll try anyway!"

He sprang from the car and followed after the man who was now well up the sidewalk. For a moment they stood talking, then broke into a hearty hand shaking festival. They gripped palms and shook and beamed and smiled and turned and walked back to me.

When they came even with me, Davis introduced him as Mr. Miller. The Miller gentleman was fairly tall, blonde and well groomed. He was young and sported white flannel trousers and a dark blue coat of snappy cut. His straw hat was becoming and he knew it.

"Mr. Miller, this is my friend Mr. L. A. Mulligan," said Davis in the most approved introductory manner.

I extended my hand, but before I could inform him how delighted I was to make his acquaintance I saw his face cloud with anger. He dropped his right hand to his side, stepped back and surveyed me as if I had been a bad piece of repair work. Then he glared at Davis.

"Why this man is not Judge Brady. You told me my friend, Judge Brady, was in this car!"

Davis floundered in a sea of apologies. He explained that Mr. Miller had misunderstood him, that he had said he, Davis, had seen him in Judge Brady's office and there learned of him. That Judge Brady was an intimate friend of his father's, and therefore he felt at liberty to approach Miller by way of the mutual friend. He was so sorry and hoped Miller would understand.

Miller's face began to clear, but he added:

"Why would I want to come back to meet a stranger?"

"This is my friend Mulligan, and I'll vouch for him."

"Well, well, I suppose he is all right then. But I am trying to avoid strangers."

He leaned in under the car top to dodge the sun's rays. As he did so the crown of his straw hat knocked against the top. He gracefully tucked the hat under the crotch of his arm and dipped his head lower and well under the protecting shade. This action disclosed that "old man Baldy" had stamped his trade mark on the top of his head. The blond hair was very thin and showed his pink scalp for a space the size of a dollar.

He passed an initialed linen handkerchief across his perspiring forehead. "I was afraid at first Mr. Mulligan might be a newspaper reporter."

I wanted to ask him if he also had had "so many good deals spoiled by too much publicity, if he was overworked and doing the labor of six men."

"I hope Mr. Mulligan will pardon my seeming rudeness, but I have to be very cautious of those I meet. I have had so many good deals spoiled by newspaper reporters giving my operations too much publicity."

Davis stepped into the tonneau and invited Miller to occupy the front seat beside me. Miller thanked him but declined, saying:

"No thank you, Davis, I have not the time. I have a very busy day ahead of me. I was just reading my telegrams which outline my work for me."

He pulled back his coat and showed the messages in his inside pockets.

"Then I take it you're in the same line of business?" put in Davis.

"Oh, yes, yes! Still the same little game. To be honest with you, gentlemen, I am with the J. P. Morgan Company. Of course the old man himself is dead but it's the same outfit. They are offering a prize to the man doing the greatest volume of business and I hope to win it. You can see now why I am so rushed. There are twenty-four of us competing, so it's a hustle for honors."

He took out a morocco leather folder.

Here comes the newspaper item with the top of his head missing, I thought.

"Probably this is the particular point Judge Brady made when you talked with him in his office that day," he said, extracting the worn looking clipping with the photograph at the head.

Davis glanced at it.

"Yes, that's it!"

Miller handed it to me. "This is the sort of stuff I have to fight against! You'll see the top of my head is slightly torn. I did this to prevent the papers from recognizing me should I lose the clipping. Of course in this picture I had on a soft collar which changes my appearance, but you can see from the collar down it's me all over!"

I pretended to read the report.

"My! young man, that sure is a powerful thing you done. Just think of it! You took one hundred and twenty-five thousand dollars out of the stock exchange in jest one day. Land! that sure is some money. Wish I could get a chance to make a killings like that!"

"My friend and I are stopping for a few days at the Brown Palace Hotel," said Davis indicating me. "Would you mind taking a little money out of the exchange for us? Or if you wouldn't want to do that, you could give us a tip!"

"Why," agreed Mr. Miller, "anyone who is a friend of Judge Brady's is a friend of mine. I could not refuse such a request."

He glowed with pleasure at the opportunity to serve on the altar of friendship.

Miller fumbled for his watch, glanced at the time and exclaimed that he must tear himself away, that he had already lost too much time.

"Just hop in and let us drive you wherever you want to go. We are at your service," cried Davis.

Miller had important matters to attend to at the post office. We drove him there first. Then we fought the traffic down 18th Street and parked the car in front of a barber shop. This was the same one in which I had been reconstructed into my present disguise. I was uncomfortable lest some of the beauty specialists might come out and recognize me.

I sank as low as possible into the seat and crossed my hands over my cane-handle and bent my head forward, resting my chin on them. I must have resembled a little terrier asking for sugar.

Davis gave him forty dollars. We remained in the car while the amazing deed was done.

In a few minutes Miller came back and handed Davis eighty dollars.

How delighted Davis looked! His eyes shone like new gold twenties. He was the personification of astonishment! He took the money with eager hands, insisting that I take half.

"We Texans! It's fifty-fifty!" he cried out.

I accepted the money, trying to look as much mystified and indulged as a child with a stick of candy which has been produced from behind a magic back.

Davis appeared so overcome with excitement that he handed Miller his forty dollars back again and asked hesitatingly if he would place this forty for him.

Miller smiled, took the money and disappeared rapidly around the corner. While he was absent Davis chattered about our great luck, the undreamed of meeting with this "tower of financial intellect."

It was once that he had stopped the car in the right spot, and so on until Miller appeared on the scene from the back of the car. I was watching for him to return the way he had gone, but evidently he had made a quick trip around the block.

Breathless from the stress of business he handed eighty dollars in bills and his original forty to Davis.

Now, thought I, he will be too busy to keep this charity stuff up. We will probably be invited to go to the exchange.

"Gentlemen, I don't mind helping you to make a little money, but I am so busy I haven't time to keep placing the bids and bringing the earnings back to you. If you wouldn't mind, you could accompany me to the exchange and place your bids just the same as I have done for you. It certainly is a pleasure to assist you."

"That would suit me! How about you, Mulligan?"

"Oh," I squeaked in a rube voice, "That would tickle me plum to death."

We three then drove to the exchange.

I was almost afraid to think for fear they would divine my thoughts. Evidently this Denver exchange was running along high powered lines with the best of the worst talent the New York training school had turned out.

The exchange was in the Denham Theater Building.

We left the car about two blocks from there and walked to the side entrance. We turned in so unexpectedly that I had no time to see what building it was as I had never seen anything but the front of it.

We took the elevator to the second floor. We stepped out and turned the corner of the hall.

From there the two men made a bee line for a door at the end of the hall. The doors on each side of the hall were heavy solid panel doors with a small opaque glass on which the occupants' names or firm names were inscribed.

This door we were making for was a queer affair. It had a deep, clear glass panel. On the inside, delicate, white, lace curtains were hung and draped back with colored bands. The window shade was drawn half way. From the appearance one would think it a bedroom window of a private home.

Miller opened the door.

I expected to be ushered into a room in keeping with the window treatment. Instead, the space beyond it was merely a continuation of the small hall. It was one of the cleverest and most misleading pieces of work I have seen.

Any stranger approaching would never in a thousand years think of opening the door. In this adroit manner, a natural privacy was enjoyed. On the other side of this division were three doors on the right.

The last one was 224. We entered this.

It was a well furnished, typical office. A large, darkwood table occupied the center of the room, several chairs were placed against the walls, various papers, drafts and bid slips littered a desk and the table.

The connecting room desk was at right angles with a low table. This furniture arrangement fenced off a small corner in the office. Behind this sat a medium sized man with coal black hair, florid complexion and glossy mustache, waxed to a curving fineness. He had an impressive dignity and a deep resonant voice which seemed to complete his personality.

"Mr. Mulligan," said the bland Miller, "I want you to meet my friend Mr. Zachery. Mr. Zachery, Mr. Mulligan, and also Mr. Davis."

Davis shook hands with Zachery first. While he was doing so I saw a pile of ragged-edged green backs piled up on the table at Zachery's right. In size, it rivaled the pile on the table in the Club House in Florida, only there were no visible guards attending this heap.

"Glad to meet you, Mr. Mulligan, I'm sure!" declared Zachery reaching for my hand.

It flashed into my mind that now was my chance to get some of this money away from them. Evidently the resolve was so strong it ran out at the ends of my fingers for Zachery said later that when I shook his hand, without betraying the least show of force, I almost dragged him over the top of his desk.

"These friends of mine want to place a few bets on the market just as I did a few minutes ago for them," said Miller to Zachery.

"Mr. Zachery, gentlemen, is the secretary and treasurer of this exchange branch. This is Station No. 4. The main office is so overcrowded that we operate this one for our exclusive members."

At this Miller showed his membership card in a quick flourish, saying we were to enjoy the privileges of the station.

By closing time I had cleaned up three thousand dollars in cash in bills. These I had in my possession. This finished the day's betting.

On the way out, Miller expressed a hope that both Davis and I would return tomorrow and make some real money. It was to be a big day on the exchange and we would have quite an opportunity.

We both said it would be a great favor for us to be able to return and thanked Miller for his generosity.

Davis and I shared night quarters. As he put it:

"We Texans must stick together!"

He surely stuck, for not once did he let me out of his sight all night or the next morning.

The bidding opened just before noon. Davis and I went in together. Miller was already there and ready for a "big day."

We were all sitting around the center table going over the latest stock quotations in the newspapers. Bid slips and other paper paraphernalia littered the table.

I placed a stump of pencil between my fingers so it could not be seen and as I appeared to smooth the paper out and write my bid, I branded the different papers and letters and cards with my own cattle brand. These marks might come in handy later in an identification party, I thought.

Chapter Thirty-Two - The Bear Trap

While we were deep in the mysteries of money making, Zachery entered from his adjoining office and welcomed us into the fold. He had the morning paper in his hand.

"I see, gentlemen, that call money is 3 per cent today." I knew this was intended for me. So I promptly asked in the most humble tone:

"What is this here meanin' of call money bein' three per cent today?"

"Well," explained Zachery, in a school-master way, "I'll just explain to you exactly how it is. Now to illustrate; you earned three thousand dollars here yesterday, well now for that three thousand dollars you could borrow one hundred thousand dollars for thirty days on this Exchange. Do you see?"

"Do you mean to tell me that I could have one hundred thousand dollars to bid on this here Stock Market like I done yesterday?" I questioned, looking as if a miracle had been performed before my eyes.

"That's exactly what I mean!" and he smiled at the great wonder of it.

"Well, give me the hundred thousand dollars' worth of credit. I'm sure willing to take a chance at it," I cried out digging deep into my pocket for my roll.

Zachery passed me a slip entitling me to one hundred thousand dollars credit.

On a tip from Miller, I selected National Lead to bid on.

It was a lucky bid. My, how easy it was to pile up the long green.

At the close of each bidding period Zachery would bring me in my earnings ranging from ten to twenty thousand dollars with the bank markers banding the packets.

Davis and I were racing to see who could win the most by night. Miller was also working just as hard but for his company and not with our selfish motives.

Davis certainly kept up a noble interest. Every time Zachery would appear with more money for us Davis would yell with joy and exclaim that it was too good to be true.

So far I was safe. They evidently considered me the fool I looked.

At night when the bidding closed, we checked up. I had three hundred thousand dollars. I repaid the one hundred thousand dollars credit. This left me in possession of, and actually worth, two hundred thousand dollars in cash.

"One of the rules of our company, Mr. Mulligan," informed Zachery, "is that if you do not use the credit money more than three days, we only charge you half the regular rate of interest. You only used yours one day, so you are entitled to a return of one-half of your three thousand dollars."

He counted out fifteen hundred dollars in loose bills and handed them to me as if it were the pleasure of his life.

I was now worth two hundred and one thousand, five hundred dollars.

I had it stacked on my left arm like an armful of stove wood. It reached so high I had to stick my chin over it to see which was the way out.

This was the psychological moment. More than twenty victimized men had told me that at this exact minute they had been asked to show their membership cards and when they could not produce them the other members would demand the return of the money.

One of them would take the side of the victim and demand that he be allowed to retain his money. The others would defend the rights of the Exchange.

Usually the acting secretary would cry out in alarm that he had made a dreadful mistake in allowing the victim to play the Exchange without a membership card. Two of them would stage a high-powered fight. Revolvers would flash, chairs would be overturned and members knocked down.

In terror, the victim usually dropped his money and fled for his life. Then the friend who took up for him, usually the one who had lured him there, follows after and catches up with him. Together they go, really at the lead of the friend, to some place where the affair can be talked over. The friend declares he will not stand for this outrage. That "they" cannot make a goat of him like that and get away with it. He is for going back and seeing the manager who is always a close friend. So, he supposedly goes to the main office and interviews the manager. Returns with the encouraging news that the manager was very apologetic for the crude action of his employees and has kindly offered to be lenient in the matter and if the victim and his friend can obtain confirmation money they will see that matters are adjusted.

I started for the door with my fortune.

"Just a minute Mr. Mulligan!" Zachery raised a detaining finger. "I would like to see your membership card, if you please!"

"My membership card!" I repeated.

"Yes! Are you not a member of this Exchange?"

"Why, no, I'm not a member of this Exchange!" I backed to the door. "I have no card."

Zachery scowled, "I thought you told me you were a member of this Exchange!"

Miller came to the door and said soothingly:

"Why, Zachery, I told you these gentlemen wanted to make their bids just as I did. I showed you my membership card. That's enough, isn't it?"

"My God, no!" He stepped toward me. "Mulligan, I can't let you have all that money."

"Can't let me have it? Well, I've done got it!"

"Can't have it! Well by God! he can have it!" shouted Miller at Zachery. "He earned it according to the rules of this Exchange and he is entitled to keep it, and furthermore I am going to help him do it!"

At this, Zachery and the others saw I had no intention of dropping the money in favor of flight. This blocked their game.

Instantly Zachery dropped to his knees and began to plead with me to be considerate, to have mercy, that he had committed a grievous error and would probably lose his job.

"Please, Mr. Mulligan, wait until I can call up my Chief and see what he has to say about it. I have violated the most sacred rule of the Exchange."

"Why, yes," I said slowly, not moving an inch, "I'll give you time to call him up."

He went to the telephone and called a number.

I walked over to him thinking, if possible, I would hear whether or not he was using a real telephone or a blank.

They had referred to the "Main Office," but so far I had not been able to locate it. All that I knew was that the office we were in was branch number four. I made a mental memorandum of the telephone number he called.

I heard a voice on the wire ask:

"Is Mulligan a reasonable man?" Zachery answered, "He seems to be very reasonable. I have paid him the money and he now has it in his possession. What will I do about it? He is not a member."

Zachery turned to me as he hung the receiver up.

"Mr. Mulligan," he announced, in his vibrant voice, "my manager says to tell you that under the circumstances we will be very lenient with you."

"That is nice of him," I said, acting reassured.

"He said he would give you, as long as it was our mistake, thirty days time to confirm your bid. You may leave your money in the vaults of this Exchange and at any time within thirty days if you will get one hundred thousand dollars and show us that you have it deposited in any bank in Denver, we will repay it to you. Our sole aim is to be assured that in event you had lost you would have been able to cover your loss."

A very pretty speech and well delivered, Mr. Zachery, I thought.

"That's all right then." I still bore the money on my arm like a waiter with his tray. "Just give me a receipt and due bill for this money as well as a complete statement of this transaction with you and I will leave the money in your keeping until I confirm my bid as suggested by your Chief."

I finished with what I thought the proper shade of deference to their executive.

These little matters were accomplished, and I turned over the money and received in its place the due-bill, the receipt and the statement. Pretty flat pickings after shaking a quarter million from my arm. But what are a few hundred thousand dollars among crooks!

Davis, Miller and I went down to the street and got Davis' car. We sat there for some time discussing latter events.

I observed the team work of the men with interest.

It certainly was difficult to believe that they were simply going through the act. They were "word perfect," as the stage managers say.

I had to watch myself closely for fear of forgetting that I was from the raw country. A few linguistic slips and my game would be up. I hoped I appeared as gullible to them as I did to myself.

We drove around the town as we talked.

"Have you one hundred thousand dollars, Mr. Mulligan?" inquired Miller.

"No I haven't," I answered rather dubiously.

"Well, I'm not going to stand for this business. It's not right and they cannot slip anything like that over me."

"Score one!" I cried inwardly.

"I'll wire my rich old uncle in New York City," he asserted. "Uncle has often wanted to help me and this seems like the time to give him the chance."

This very rich relative had been referred to several times earlier in our acquaintance but the noble nephew had always preferred to make his own way in the battle of life.

I kept saying aloud I wondered if I could ever get the money and appeared to be worried in every way.

"I will only have to keep it long enough to show it here in Denver and that will be long enough to help us all out. Now, Mr. Mulligan, you and Davis don't worry about it a minute. I'll take care of everything."

Davis brought the car to the curb near the big Methodist Church on North Broadway. Still immersed in the problem of raising the confirmation money, we all piled out of the car.

I suppose Davis and Miller simply figured I was pre-occupied with ways and means of getting it, and they could lead me anywhere they chose. They started for the entrance of a building which was directly in line with where Davis had stopped the car.

I followed them, still muttering uncertainties about obtaining funds. I had no opportunity to see into what building I was being lead. The door was ajar.

The interior was like a hotel lobby. No chairs, or persons other than ourselves, were to be seen.

I made a mental picture of the place and from the front door to the steps, which were at the rear, was thirty-one strides.

A poor offering for future identification but better perhaps than none.

The steps at the rear made a turn to the left of a few stairs and ended on a small landing. An elevator ran up from there.

We were lifted to the third floor and went into room No. 310. I wondered that Davis and Miller did not question the ease with which they were able to pull me anywhere and everywhere after them. For this reason I appeared to be worried to death, thinking if they were suspicious, my apparent frenzy might account for it to them.

The upper part of the building seemed to be a regular hotel. The elevator boy was the only human being, connected with the place, I saw from the day I stepped my foot inside until the day I left. It had a mysteriously quiet atmosphere.

The room was large and well furnished. A bath adjoined. The bed that I supposed would be mine, if I was invited to stay, was a little folding affair to the left of the door, which opened from the main hall.

As I passed the foot of the bed, I gave it a quick pressure.

It sprang into the air and closed like a bear trap.

No sleeping on that bed for me, I decided.

When the door had closed on the three of us, Miller exclaimed:

"What's that?"

We came to a listening attitude. From the street below came the raucous cries of "Extra! Extra!"

"Davis go down and get a paper, and let's see what it's all about, will you?" asked Miller.

Davis picked up his hat from the dresser and went down for the paper. As soon as the door was shut Miller launched into a quick synopsis of the disadvantages of Davis being left to roam at will.

"I wanted to get a chance to tell you a few things, Mulligan. Now Davis is all right, he means well, but Lord! how he does talk. Why the whole town will be let in on this stock mistake if he isn't shut up and kept quiet. He is so excited and delighted at the prospect of such a fortune that he can't stop raving out loud. It might not hurt him, but look what it will do to me. Here I am sweating blood to win first honors in the sales . competition of my company and stand to lose my job if he don't seal up that spout of his. Now there is only one way to protect us all and that is for you to watch him. Keep him in this room and keep it locked and make him shut his mouth if you have to gag him."

"That's right, Mr. Miller, we've done gone this far an' we can't afford to spoil this here game now. We can't afford to lose."

I felt this was about what he hoped I would say.

It was getting to be a positive pleasure to see how happy my answers made both of them.

I got the drift of things now. They were coming my way. This was what Furey had said to me when my Dallas swindle took place. "You've got to watch these young fellows (meaning Spencer), they talk too much."

So Miller's crowd thought they were guarding me, while I KNEW I was guarding them.

Davis returned with the extra.

Miller glanced at the headlines.

"Oh! it's only these damned Rangers again. Trouble in the coal fields as usual and the Governor is going to order the Rangers into the fields to quell the riot. Well, that's where those guys ought to be. A lot of able-bodied men lying around the city butting into other people's business, is what they are doing when they're not out showing off."

How unhappy they would have been had they known what this piece of news meant to me — and to them indirectly. While they were rejoicing over the departure of that body of fighters I was sorrowing, as there could be no telling how long they would remain away. It showed me that there was no use counting your Rangers before you had them.

"Now for the business end of this affair," began Miller in an office tone.

He got out some papers and telegraph blanks from the writing table. He thoughtfully drafted the wire to the rich uncle in New York. After he finished he read it to us. It merely stated that nephew had a rare opportunity to double it within the next few days and felt, under the circumstances, that he could accept uncle's oft repeated tenders of loans. Therefore the trifle of one hundred thousand dollars sent at once would fit in nicely with said nephew's plans. He caught up his straw hat, saying he would dash over to the Brown Palace Hotel and send it right off.

When he returned we again went over the pros and cons of getting or not getting the funds.

"Absolutely no reason to be concerned about it," Miller reassured us. "I will undoubtedly have the money by tomorrow or at least word that it is on its way here. My! But it will be good to get it all straightened out!"

With this, he yawned and stretched his handsome form out on the other bed and rested.

At dinner time they went out and ate. They went one at a time. I was never left alone.

Davis invited me to go out with him to dinner, but I thought I had better stick close and see what happened.

When he returned he brought me some sandwiches, but I was afraid of them, so declined, saying I was so tired out with the excitement I was afraid to eat. They accepted this as natural in a man of my age and ate the food themselves.

We all turned in early. As I had expected, the little folding trap was my bed. It headed against the wall near the door from the main hotel corridor. Any one entering the room had to swing the door back against my bed. Before they could see me, they had to look around the door or else shut it.

This made a semi-blind for me and gave me the drop on all who entered. I put the small straight chair on the opposite side of the bed in the corner. I sat on this most of the time. While it put the length of the bed between me and the door, it gave me the advantage of a corner. My right side was against the wall as well as my back.

In this way I could keep my right hand on my right hip gun and be seen by no one in the room.

Not once in the days I was trapped in this den did I undress, get into the bed or close my eyes in sleep. When I felt I must appear to sleep I lay cross-wise on the cot, my hand grasping my revolver shoved under the pillow.

As far as I have ever learned none of the men knew I was armed. It was a mad fight against hunger, sleep and these murderous wolves. The awful fear of falling asleep from nerve strain was the worst battle.

To account for my sleeplessness and abstinence from food, I feigned neuralgia of the face. And I can safely say that had the suggestion produced the genuine malady, it would have been more easily borne than the constant struggle to simulate pain and suffering. Hour after hour I held my unswollen face between my hands. I rocked my head from side to side, stifling moans.

I tried my jaws to see if food could find an entrance, but the stabbing pain locked them in pretended agony. My eyes, from wakefulness, became genuinely bloodshot.

Chapter Thirty-Three - A Letter to My Wife

This scenic effect helped me to simulate sickness with startling reality.

By night, I paced the floor to outwit sleep; by day. I sat in my corner and knocked my head against the wall. When hunger drove me all but insane, I drank water and tightened up my belt another notch.

Davis and Miller were night-hawks. First one, then the other would get up, dress and take a nocturnal prowl.

All night long they would return with newspapers. Each new edition as it came off the press they would scan with quick-moving eyes. Frequently they cut out little notices and made remarks about apparently unimportant happenings.

They lived in a fever all the time. Awake, they acted more like caged wild animals than normal human beings.

Excitement! Ever more excitement! It seemed they were unable to sit quiet and think for any length of time but must have frequent new contacts from the outside to enable them to exist.

It would seem their inner selves were not good company.

They presented that most pitiful spectacle, the human being trying to get away from association with the secrets of its own soul.

In sleep, they turned and tossed as though in the midst of disturbing dreams, then they would start suddenly from their beds, muttering exclamations of cold terror or hot defiance.

Morning. Miller came in early from his last stroll. Davis and I were the only ones in the room. After morning greetings Davis stepped into the bathroom, saying he guessed he'd have to run the lawn mower over his face.

As he shut the door, Miller gave a long sigh and beckoned me to him in the extreme end of the room away from the bath-room door.

"It wouldn't happen again in a thousand years!"

He showed me a telegram from his uncle's wife. It was a model of imitation. Dejectedly he dropped into an armchair, tapping its wooden arm with his long, shapely fingers.

"Hell! Can you beat that?"

I read it in a slow, bungling way, almost spelling out the words in my effort to decipher it. I was thinking to myself that this was just what was needed to force my oil to come to the surface.

"So he ain't there?" I asked, fixing a disappointed gaze on him.

"No! Can you imagine that for luck? Gone down into the interior of Old Mexico to see about his extensive mining interests. You can see what Auntie says. Be gone for several weeks. Well, that's blow number one. It seems to me I have the worst misfortune of anybody in the world. No matter how conscientious and honest I play the game, I always get the worst of it. Now, I don't know what I'll do. Davis is likely to throw a fit when he hears I didn't get the money and ball things up for all of us. My God! I wish I was dead!"

"Well Davis told me as how he was well connected."

"Davis well connected?" he asked in apparent surprise.

"Yes," I said, experimentally. "He tells me that his father owns a big business block including the Moberly Bank and building, in Moberly, Missouri. If he owns all that he sure must be a moneyed man. Seems like to me he had ought to help his own boy out."

Just then the bath-room door opened. Davis emerged, his flesh sparkling with talcum and looking as rosy as a newborn babe. He caught sight of the telegram in my hand.

195

"Oh say! You got the wire from old Unk! When does he say to expect it?"

"When hell freezes over," Miller retorted sourly.

Davis' facial expression changed from pleasure to just the right degree of regret.

("Good work, boys," I felt like shouting.)

He leaned over my hand and read the gloomy message. Then he took it from me and reread it, shaking his head.

"Well, where there's a will there's a way," pronounced Miller, in a voice merging on recovery. "Mulligan here, tells me you are not so badly connected. How about you making an effort to come to the rescue?"

"I'm fairly well fixed, but nothing to brag about. When I got married, my father gave me fifty thousand in Liberty Bonds. I haven't very much money but the bonds are intact in the Moberly National Bank."

"Well, aren't you willing to come through with those and do what you can?" peevishly whined Miller.

"Why sure! I'll do whatever I can. I certainly don't want this proposition to fall down now that we've got it this far. I know I can raise fifty thousand, but I'll have to discount my bonds to do it. I'm so sure of the success of the proposition that I do not mind at all cashing them."

"All of this red-tape will necessarily take time and that's what we haven't!" figured Miller on the comeback.

It will soon be my turn to raise the money, I whispered to my own ear.

And it was!

"I could wire the bank to see if it will be necessary for me to go there to endorse the bonds before cashing them."

Miller indicated the yellow blanks on the table.

"Then get busy," he suggested.

Davis wrote out the wire in a surprisingly short time considering the technical phraseology. In the main it gave the bank authority to use the telegram as an order to transact the deal.

"Of course even if Davis does get the fifty thousand we will still have to raise another fifty."

"Yes, that's so!" I echoed hopelessly. "It appears to me, gentlemen, like we are a'goin' to have a terrible time."

"The few thousand that Auntie mentioned in her wire and offered to lend me will help a little, even if it's only about eight thousand," put in Miller. "What resources have you, Mulligan?"

Ah! now came my turn. I was prepared. The little old letters which I had labored over would have their opportunity to get in on the game. It seemed as if they fluttered nervously in my pocket to spread their pages before the inquiring team.

"Well, now I'll tell you boys, I got a letter from my wife, got it since I been here. Before I left home we leased a hundred acres of our farm down there to an oil company. This here company is a drilling a well at the corner of our field now. An' this letter from my wife tells me as how she has collected fifteen thousand dollars on the lease we signed up before I left home. She has put two thousand dollars in the bank at Ferris, Texas, an' the balance of it in the bank up to Dallas. An' we had some three or four thousand dollars before we got this here cash an' that's all the money we have now, an' we may not have that much now; she might of spent some of it, though she ain't a pertick-lar extravagant woman as they goes. She said as how she was holdin' down a lease on two hundred and thirty-six acres of our land at two hundred dollars an acre. She had signed the lease an' wanted me to come home an' sign it too, and then she said as how I could go back to Denver and stay as long as I seen fit. Besides said as how the company had struck oil in the well at the corner of our field an' was looking to lease all the land they could around this here well."

Their eyes popped almost out of their sockets. Their furtive glances fused into triumphant understanding.

I was now worthy to enter their web which was fast spinning about me.

I droned on in an uninspired way about the discovery of oil on my proper-ty.

"Another good thing, she said, was that it would leave us nineteen acres where the buildings and the big tank of water was an' we could get our own price for that because the drillers would want for to have the water for drillin' purposes. It looks to me, boys, I better go on down home an' sign that trier' lease an' get that money an' then come back here. Then I will have the money to take care of my half of the deal. Davis here can get his fifty an' that will square us with the company."

Of course Davis had read the general outline of the letter over my shoulder three days before when I was in his car. With what I had just given them, backed up with the little Davis had seen, established in their minds that I was a legitimate sucker. I could see that it was mutually settled to press my clean-ing to the limit.

From that minute, the work was co-ordinated and moved forward to the crashing climax like the onrush of a storm.

I let them take the lead in order to side-track any suspicions they might have.

Soon Miller suggested that I send my wife a wire instructing her to close the deal and get the money without my signature.

Davis countered this plan, mildly saying perhaps it would be best for me to return and do it up in proper shape, adding that he would go with me.

After criss-crossing the proposed trip several times it was decided that I telegraph my wife.

I proceeded to do as it was decided for me. In the sluggish awkward man-ner I had adopted to fit my "hayseed" disguise, I wrote out the message.

I wrote in big round style which certainly looked as if I had received any-thing but a diploma in penmanship. This was to plant in their minds my type of scrawling for contrast with my supposed wife's fine, close lettering which I was forced to show later on. The telegram read:

"Mrs, L. A, Mulligan, Ferris, Texas. This telegram will authorise you to sign my name to the oil lease contract, tell the boys I will re-sign it when I come home close up the deal get the money send me a draft by registered letter to general delivery Denver Colorado I want to buy a nice new home here hurry up — Louis Mulligan."

I could only pray that Ferris boasted no citizen by the name of Mrs. L. A. Mulligan.

Miller went over to the Brown Palace with both telegrams. He probably sent mine. Then the waiting began.

My companions counted the hours. They referred to probably what was happening right now. "My wife was just closing the deal," or again, "She ought to be getting the draft in the mail," or else, "Well, if everything went on schedule it will be here in the morning." This went on and on, over and over again.

At times, I felt like telling them what goats they both were, and then again I could scarcely keep my face straight. But what with keeping up the neuralgia farce and watching the door to see who would come in next I had little time for humorous amusement.

It was not long before I realized that this room was known to the gang. One by one, during the waiting hours, different members of the bunco ring dropped in for an informal call. I wondered who had occupied my little folding bed before me.

The pain in my face served as an added disguise, and with my hands clasped over one side of it I felt that unless I were well known to one of the visitors I would not be easily recognized. But when I would hear the entrance signal of two heavy raps followed by two light ones, my heart would leap into my throat.

Those who came in during the morning were of all types and styles in physical composition and criminal classification. None of them had I ever known personally, but several, photographically. I was not introduced to any of them. I kept my painful corner position and apparently few of them more than noticed the humped up figure barricaded by the little unused bed. However, I knew that their sole mission in coming was to give the new prospect "the once over." This was to doubly assure Miller and Davis that I was not a plant.

I lived in dread and hope. Dread that I would be recognized before I had broken into their nest and hope that among the stream of callers, Spencer would float in. Had Spencer come in I would have had him and the others in the room covered before he could have recognized me. My greatest fear was being recognized by some one of them unknown to me.

In the evening Miller went over to the Brown Palace to see if his bank had wired regarding Davis' liberty bonds. He returned jubilant.

"Here you are, old man!" he cried, thrusting the yellow sheet into Davis' outstretched hand.

Davis slit it open.

"What do you bet?" he challenged as his little eyes ran over the contents. Before we had time to place our bets he jumped up and waved it above his head.

"We win!" he exclaimed. He came over to my corner. Miller followed him and together we read the reply.

"It is unnecessary for you to come now to indorse liberty bonds. Draw on us for fifty thousand dollars and we will hold the bonds as security until you come on to settle the deal."

The burden of the remaining fifty thousand now rested on my bent shoulders.

"Well," said Miller with set lips, "now all we have to do is to wait for Mrs. Mulligan to send the draft and then we are set!" And wait we did!

There was a telephone in the room, but it might just as well have been a monkey wrench for all the good it would do me. They telephoned and were in turn called, but no conversations of any direct bearing on the location of the main exchange or of anything pertaining to the problem in hand leaked out. If I had been left alone for even the shortest time I could have called Van Cise and tipped off the general location of my prison, but there was no more chance of putting this into execution than there was of drawing information from the Sphinx.

My brain reeled with fatigue and what plans for getting word to the district attorney's office ran through my mind seemed of the most foolish order. Thus the first day passed.

The next day passed in the same way. Nothing but waiting. All that punctuated this uncertainty was the entrance signal; two heavy raps on the door, followed by two light ones. To my racked nerves, they all sounded like cannon balls thrown against the wooden panel.

Davis and Miller begged me to eat, saying they would bring me any food I desired. I was starved. My stomach gnawed inside me until I could have eaten the bed clothes. I was forced to suffer intensified agony with my face to keep up the waiting game and abstinence from food.

The boys were sympathetic in a kind, watchful way. At night, I cried out with the pain, declaring that I could not stand this agony much longer.

A plan to reach an outside telephone was working in my mind. If I could induce them to take me to a dentist, I could perhaps get to his telephone and let the Van Cise office know that I was still alive and give them some idea of where I was being guarded.

As far as I had been able to find out by way of the newspapers, the Rangers were still in the coal fields. This complicated matters, but still I could not keep this hide-and-seek game going after another day, for my hand would be forced on the telegram sent to my wife.

I knew they would start an investigation to find out why I did not receive the draft. Then the jig would be up.

Between spasms of the worst pains I had had during my incarceration, I told the boys I had been "figgerin'." and that if my wife had received my wire on the dot; and every other thing worked without a hitch, that I could get a reply at the post office tonight.

"A good idea then to go down before it closes." said Miller.

"Yes," agreed Davis with alacrity, "but we'll have to go pretty soon because it closes at 8:30 and neither of us has had any dinner. Mulligan can't you eat a little something tonight? You'll die of starvation!"

"Before you get the draft!" I finished his thought, silently, for him.

"Eat, my God! You ain't got no idea how this thing hurts! I think I'm about to die unless I can get this here molar out or get some relief from this neuralgia." Then I indulged in an orgy of groans moving my head from side to side between my hands. My eyes were bleary enough to help the illusion along.

"He does look pretty well shot up," Davis remarked to Miller.

"I don't think neuralgia is dangerous, but it is painful I know!" answered Miller, which showed he didn't plan on my immediate demise.

"If we're goin' down to the post office I'll just write a little word to my wife an' mail it down to the office," I said.

So I wrote out an absurd letter telling her how sorry I was she had failed to meet me in Denver, but that I had met a lonely widow and was now getting along very well. I cackled in my adopted high cracked voice and passed the letter to the other two to read.

They looked it over with evident amusement.

"What you reckon, boys, the old gal will think when she sees that about the widder?"

They smiled and muttered to each other something about "no fool like an old one."

Chapter Thirty-Four - Visiting the Dentist

In a few minutes I put forth the theory that perhaps a good hot bath would ease my aching face. Before getting into more hot water, I asked the "boys" to hand me some of the several picture postcards that lay on the table.

"I want to send some of these local scenes home," I explained as I slipped several of the "having-a-fine-time-wish-you-were-here" greetings into the letter to the illustrious "Mrs. Mulligan."

Then I borrowed a stamp from Davis. They saw me seal and stamp the epistle. As I put it into my pocket I requested that they remind me to mail it when we went to the post office.

I went into the bathroom and took off my coat and vest; turned my trouser legs up to my knees, and after the tub was filled half way, sat on its edge and splashed as if I were at Atlantic City.

While churning the water with my feet, my hands were busy writing another letter. This one was to Col. Van Cise.

I told him of the happenings since I left the conference in Sansome's house the night of the storm: how I had fallen in with Davis and Miller; of the letters I wrote to myself indicating my oil interests; how they had been read by Miller and Davis supposedly unbeknown to me, and how I had agreed to raise through my fictitious oil interests fifty thousand dollars as my portion of the usual "confirmation money" needed to secure for me the two hundred and one thousand dollars I had won three days before in branch office number four in the Denham Theater Building, Rooms 224-25-26, of their stock exchange.

I also related briefly that I had been forced to leave my earnings in the exchange until the confirmation money was received.

I described my present quarters as well as I could from what I had seen on the way up and from the windows. I mentioned the long lobby of thirty-one strides to the stairway; that I was on the third floor, room 310 and that from my window I could look out on the back of the Brown Palace Hotel. I also gave a list of several advertising signs I could view.

I implored them to come to me at once.

"I have not eaten a mouthful nor have I closed my eyes in sleep since I came into this dungeon two days ago."

My greatest dread, I told him, was of falling asleep from exhaustion. I also told him I had a bad toothache and neuralgia; that it was going to be so bad by morning that I would probably have to be taken to a dentist; there I would try to get him on the telephone, unless I could be rescued and make a clean-up of the joint before morning.

"If I am bumped off before you can get to me this is my true statement."

I addressed the envelope and put a special delivery stamp on it from the supply which I always had with me for such emergencies. This letter I substituted in my pocket for the other one.

The letter to my wife I tore into fine bits under water and let them go down the bath tub drain.

I then bathed my face in cold water to give it a glow; dressed and contorting my face into its neuralgic lines, re-entered the bed room.

Dusk had melted into darkness. The electric signs sprang into brilliance, their glittering colored sparks of light, flashing into relief against the dark sky.

Just before eight o'clock we all went downstairs and got into Davis' Cadillac and drove to the post office. The night was comfortably cool and the keen odors of food which drifted to my nostrils from bakery and restaurant gave me cruel pangs.

They stabbed me with the mad desire for food. I was too faint with hunger to think what would happen if I failed to get the letter to Van Cise into the post box, or what I would do if they should insist on mailing it for me or standing close to me when I did it. I only knew I was "sniffing chuck" as we say on the range and that it pierced me as the smell of fried onions and coffee only can pierce when one's natural nourishment container is a vacuum.

At the post office we all piled out and into the building.

Miller walked on one side of me and Davis on the other.

As I approached the general delivery window I dropped back one step and like lightning pulled the letter bottom side up from my pocket and slid it into the slit in the wall marked "outgoing."

I often think of this in relation to the millions of simple deeds of this sort done every day. The act itself is so unimportant, but the great meaning behind these trifling accomplishments would stagger us if we could know their import. Not much to drop a letter into an opening in a wall, but to me, it might mean rescue; imprisonment for many, while if it were to miscarry or delay perhaps my "bumping off."

"Well," I said, "looks like this ole pain is agoin' to keep up till next Christmas!"

"Come on, Mulligan! See if there is any mail from your wife!" directed Miller, who was standing at the "M" window.

"Anything for Mr. L. A. Mulligan, of Ferris, Texas?" I inquired.

The clerk looked through the pile of letters in the pigeonhole.

"No, nothing today, Mr. Mulligan," he answered.

I turned away and feigned great disappointment.

"Well, it would have to be that things come off on the nick of time if I'd of got it tonight. It's more likely I guess to expect a few delays. Maybe as how it'll come in the morning. „

The men showed their displeasure at a prolonged wait, but tried to cover it by saying some of the usual things about "vile mail service."

They both asked for mail for themselves but, of course, received none.

On the ride back to the room I hailed a passing milk wagon and bought two bottles of buttermilk.

"This will stay me," I said, "and not hurt me to swallow it."

How I would have enjoyed sinking my teeth into a thick, juicy steak, but I dared not have my face improve rapidly enough to accomplish this gastronomic feat.

I couldn't wait until I reached my mysterious hotel to down the milk but snapped the disc from the bottle's neck and poured down the filling fluid. The pangs of emptiness were temporarily satisfied.

I revived enough to make a mental map of the location of the building in which I had spent the past two nights. While I did not find out the name of it, I could have told rescuers how to reach me if I could get word to them.

That night I paced the floor. Up and down, back and forth, over and over again until I expected to trip in the holes in the carpet worn by my ceaseless tread.

The men slept snatches of the same troubled sleep, then went out and brought in the different editions of the morning papers, while in between they talked with me about raising cotton.

We bought the land, planted the seed, cultivated the crop, picked the cotton, ginned it, baled it, sold it and shipped it.

One thing I did during the entire time I spent in this den was to confine my conversation entirely within the limits of my farm. When the conversation reached the boundary of my property I either quit talking or turned it back into the property. In this way I ran no risk of giving myself away.

The night passed in the same endless waiting. It seemed like years between the hour strokes of the clock in the tower.

Dawn came as I was on my ten thousandth lap from bed to window. I could not hope for help to arrive before morning. My letter might have been delivered that night late and then again it might not have reached the district attorney's office until early morning. However I felt that within a half hour after it was in Col. Van Cise's hands, help would be on its way to me.

About eight o'clock I announced I must go to a dentist. I said I could not stand this any longer.

Both Davis and Miller suggested several they knew but, of course, these hardly suited my needs.

I had read in the paper of a big dental office which advertised painless extractions. I thanked them for their offers and said I would be glad to accept, and right away, as my head was cracking with sharp pains.

I intended they should think I was going to one of their practitioners but made up my mind to get into this advertised tooth emporium if possible. The office of the doctor whom Davis recommended was only a few blocks farther down the street than the one I had selected from the paper.

We started. This time we walked; with Miller on one side of me and Davis on the other.

Large bright blue signs lettered in flashy gold told of the superior dental surgery done in the office of my selection.

I looked up at the sign and made for the doorway.

"All dentists look alike to me, boys!" I moaned. "I'm agoin' to take the first one that comes along!"

They followed me, this time. The young lady in the office asked my name.

"L. A. Mulligan," I replied. "Your address, please."

"Ferris, Texas," I ground out, between pretended jerks from the wild tooth.

"But your city address, I mean," she inquired sweetly.

"310 — 310 — Oh! where do we live, boys?" I asked.

They looked at each other for the fraction of an instant.

Then Miller said slowly, "er — er — Hotel Metropole."

Into the appointment book, this bit of valuable information went. The quick scratch of her stub pen tied them to me for future evidence if necessary.

She turned to Davis. "Your name, too, please."

203

"I am just here with my friend," he replied firmly.

A door opened. A white frocked doctor called out, "Next!"

"You are next, Mr. Mulligan," informed the girl.

The doctor came out to me.

"What is the nature of your case, young man?"

It was evident my hands concealed my face effectively.

Taking my facial features into the bowl of my hands I almost bore them to him as on a silver server.

Asserting, without exaggeration, that it was a very "complicated case," I walked past him into his operating room.

He followed me and shut the door with us on the inside.

"I would like to get as far away from the waiting room door as possible," I said, indicating another room which opened off the one in which we were standing.

He waved me into its privacy and closed another door between us and my escorts.

"Doctor, are you acquainted with Col. Van Cise, district attorney of this city?"

"I am!" he answered. "He is a good friend of mine."

"Then please get him on the telephone and talk with him a few minutes to see that his line is clear. If you will do this and then let me speak to him, you'll understand the nature of my case!"

He looked mystified, but the professional mind I have discovered usually works in a straight line. Therefore, he needed no further explanation.

Colonel Van Cise was in. They had a brief conversation, then the doctor gave me the receiver.

"This is Mulligan speaking!"

"How are you and where are you? How are things going?"

I told him in whose dental office I was.

"I'm prostrated from loss of sleep and dying with hunger; otherwise I'm in fine shape!" I said, trying to force a cheerful lie.

"If you received my special delivery letter you will realize I am very anxious to close this deal!"

"It's impossible to close today! The interested parties are in the coal fields. It will be impossible to close until they return to town."

"Something has to be done pretty soon!" I sang out. "Can't you finish the affair without them?"

"It's difficult to finish, it right without these men present."

"Well, do your best! I'm in room 310, Metropole Hotel."

The doctor was standing rooted to the spot with surprise and interest. I nodded in the direction of Van Cise at the other end of the line.

"Will you stand by any agreement I make with Van Cise, doctor?"

"I certainly will!" he exclaimed heartily.

Scenes in the Denver raid — Above, two rangers guarding captives, whose faces are averted from the camera. Below, mountains of money, the bank roll of the fake stock exchange, loaned by local bankers.

"Well," I said into the telephone, "the doctor says he cannot finish my dental work today. But he will stay in his office until after office hours to finish it.

He will call me up when it's ready and I'll talk to you whenI come back here. Be sure to be ready and let me know definitely about this transaction at that time.

When I hung up I asked the doctor to say in the presence of Miller and Davis that he could not finish my work now but would promise to do so today if he had to stay after office hours to do it. He was also to say that he would telephone me when he was ready for me.

When we went back to the waiting room the two men rose seemingly in haste to leave.

They asked me how it felt now.

The doctor replied for me "that he thought he had relieved it a little," and then finished with the speech I had requested him to make. When he asked me where he could telephone me, I again turned to the "boys" and asked:

"Now, where's that we're a livin'?"

"Room 310 — Metropole Hotel," supplied Davis.

This fastened them to me for the second time and in the presence of both the stenographer and the doctor.

"I already have it, doctor!" said the girl.

"Very well then, I'll call you up as soon as I need you, and your friends can bring you down. You seem a little weak from the pain," uttered the dentist with professional solicitude.

"Thank you. I sure do feel like I was about gone in the knees and head," I added, again pressing my hand to my jaw.

When we reached the lobby of the hotel two men went in directly ahead of us. They reached the elevator first. One of them pressed the button and then turned toward me.

I recognized him as one of the men I had seen in Col. Van Cise's office. I knew help was on the way. How much longer this suspense would continue I could have no idea, but I did know that this man and his companion were getting our room located for action.

The arrival of the letter from Mrs. Mulligan was the topic of conversation during the day. Why it had not come, when it would and what *they* would do if it didn't, were all discussed. Evidently I was to have little choice in the matter. They kept asking me how I felt. "Was I better, or wasn't I?" Then in a minute:

"Do you think you could make the trip to Ferris if one of us went with you?"

"Not as I'm a feelin' now, boys," and then my tooth took a sudden turn for the worse.

They trod the floor. Hands in their pockets behind their backs and gesticulating to each other as they cursed their luck and the delayed letter.

I waited with a suppressed excitement for help to arrive. Every footstep I heard approached the door I thought might be the men. My right hand became so used to dropping onto the butt of my gun that it was automatic when the slightest noise occurred outside in the hall.

Along toward dark, the telephone rang. Its ringing was always the signal for rapt attention from all in the room. Whoever answered usually spoke in a slow guarded way and warmed into naturalness as the safety of the situation became assured. Every telephone message was like thrilling news from home; every one eager for it.

"It's someone for you, Mulligan," Miller said.

"Well, tell them please to give the word to you as I'm a feelin' so bad. My head here is crackin' so hard it seems like I can't hear nothin' but thunder!"

"It's your dentist," he informed me, then waited to get the rest of the doctor's message. "He says your work is about ready and if you will come over right away he can fix it for you and give you another treatment. He wants you to hurry as it's after office hours and he is in a rush to get home."

I nodded.

"All right, doctor, we'll bring him over right away!"

This time I was driven to the office. Both Davis and Miller accompanied me. I went directly into the doctor's private office where I had telephoned from in the morning.

The doctor had Van Cise waiting on the line.

"How are things going?" was the first question.

I replied that they had it planned for me to leave on the midnight train for Ferris, Texas, to get the money. They had decided not to wait any longer for the letter.

"But," I said, "I'm going to be too sick to go. If they take me it will be on a stretcher, and I doubt if they'll press it that far."

"Listen, Mulligan, everything is sitting pretty to close this deal tomorrow morning early. We will knock on your door at six A.M. Twice heavy, and twice light. Don't let them kill my men!" he admonished me.

Chapter Thirty-Five - The Longest Night

"Don't worry about what's on the inside. I'll take care of that. But it's going to be fierce if I have to spend another night in that trap. They are determined I'm going to Texas tonight after that money and God knows how I'm going to keep from going. I'll do my best and hope to be alive when your men rap on the door in the morning."

"If you have to go try to wire me before you leave, then take both men off the train at the second station south of here and you'll have help at hand. We might better get these two than lose them all."

This ended our conversation.

Before I left the office the doctor duly squirted one of these highly colored astringents into my mouth and stuffed a wad of cotton between my lip and teeth. I looked and smelled like a walking advertisement for a popular mouth wash.

Again we went back to the hotel room.

I was trying to formulate a plan of action if they started to force me to go to Ferris.

They watched me closer than ever, so I would not dare refuse to go unless I could cook up some very plausible reason.

I had certainly worked my face overtime and it would not look any too good after my dental treatments, to appear unrelieved. All I could do was to sit tight and wait for inspiration.

I urged them to wait another day or two, saying I would then feel well enough to make the trip, but they said there was no use putting it off any longer.

I pleaded that I was always "car-sick," and in my present condition I was certain to be very ill.

They had made up their minds to make me go and said they were sure it would do me good.

I was in a cage, and fighting for my life.

Miller called up the railroad station and found the train left about eleven o'clock.

"Now look here, Mulligan!" he began, as if I were a bad boy, "you just think you cannot stand the trip. Buck up! Don't let a little toothache get your goat!"

I thought to myself, "You better watch your own goat!" I knew if I had to go that I would make it hot for them the second stop out from Denver.

However I hated to run the risk of losing the rest of the gang which I felt sure would begin their afternoon calls on the morrow.

It was my idea that when "Van Cise's army" arrived we would get Miller and Davis out of the way and then lie in wait awhile and get the rest as they came in.

I found I could not hold out against the trip without arousing suspicion.

At ten o'clock they announced we were starting. And start we did.

We paced up and down the station walk. They said it was a little early for the train, but that it was better to be early than late.

I began to feel really ill. I had been pretending for so long that at first I couldn't tell whether I was ill or just thought I was. However I decided in favor of an approaching bilious spell of no unmistakable variety.

I welcomed this internal upheaval as the spring flowers welcome the gentle rains of June.

Thank God! At last I could settle down to feeling like the dickens and not be afraid of forgetting to show suffering.

Large cramps wrapped their arms about my stomach and bent me over. I gloried in being able to act natural for the first time in nearly a week. I helped nature by every now and then smelling of a small phial of medicine the dentist had given me. Its pungent odor sent my empty stomach flip-flopping.

"Boys! Boys! I can't never make a go of this. I'm so sick I'm likely to die!"

"Well when you get into your berth you'll feel better," assured Davis.

"Maybe a bowl of warm soup will help me," I said hopefully, knowing it would either help or finish me.

They accompanied me into the lunchroom. I ordered oyster soup.

Two spoonfuls went down — I made a mad rush for the fresh air. All I remember is that I saw millions of little spinning lights and then everything turned black.

When I came to I was stretched on the running board of our Cadillac, my two little friends ministering to me. How long I had been "out" I didn't know.

I heard the unmistakable choot-choot-choot of a departing train.

"I'm mighty sorry, boys, to have this here sick spell cause you so much trouble. Seems like I ain't got the health I uster have. But I'll try to perk up and, as Miller says, not let it get my goat! When does our train get in?"

"Get in!" sneered Davis. "Hell, it's just gone out!"

They got me back to the room again.

Davis was sullen.

Miller seemed deeply concerned for my physical wellbeing and kept telling me that I was nervous.

This amused me as there was absolutely nothing to be nervous about except two quarts of buttermilk in three nights and three days, eyes that had never closed in that time; confined with two potential murderers in a death-trap and waiting for Rangers who were quelling riots in the coal fields. No, there was nothing to be nervous about.

"I think I'll run across to the drug store, Mulligan, and get you a little dose to settle your stomach."

"No, never mind, Miller," I answered weakly, "I'll be easin' up right soon."

But he would not take "no" for answer and went out after the potion.

Davis was getting a bath, and in the absence of both men I stuck my gun scabbard and all under my pillow. In this way I could lie across the bed with my hand shoved under the pillow and be ready for an instant draw.

Miller returned with a small bottle filled with a dark liquid. He said the directions were on there and that it was to be taken in a little water.

"When Davis gets through his bath I'll sure take a dose of it," I said and thanked him.

Some way or other the fellow's unvarnished kindness sent a sick thrill through me. I looked up at his clean appearing manhood and wondered what blood or combination of circumstances brought such a man to the moral low-lands he had reached.

"The druggist said this would quiet your nerves and make you sleep."

I couldn't help wondering if he had put a time limit on my nap. However I allowed him to mix the nerve steadier and as Davis emerged from his scouring, I took the glass from Miller's hand and went into the bathroom, shut the door and poured it down the drain. Then I shot the hot water into the bowl, gulped loudly, "brrr-r-red" and came out with face awry.

"Taste bad?" inquired Miller.

"Pretty fierce!" I muttered, and flung myself across my bed.

When the clock struck three the boys were still discussing what they expected to do with their money when the deal was cleaned up. They both expected to break the stock market in two places.

Three o'clock! Only three more hours until six!

How could I stand out against drugging sleep another three hours?

Suppose something went wrong and they didn't come then. What would I do?

How could I keep my senses until daybreak?

These thoughts raced, dragged, then twisted through my racked mind. Would I be awake when the signals sounded at the hour of six? It seemed I would go insane!

I got into the bathroom again and buried my face in cold water held in my palms. Then I dipped it into hot water and back again to cold.

This livened the circulation and aroused me for a time. When its stimulating effect began to wane, I could feel a floating, far away drowsiness creeping over me.

The torture was excruciating!

Miller suddenly stood up, hat in hand. "I'm going out for a while. Davis will be here in case you need anything. Do you feel better?"

"Yes, that medicine has begun to take effect, I guess." Now that I was supposed to have doped up I could afford to show improvement.

"Well, I hope you'll be all well in the morning when I come back."

"I may not be entirely well, but I'm a goin' to feel a whole lot better!"

"I hope so!"

"It's a sure thing!"

He unlocked the door and Davis joined him in the hall for a brief executive session. When Davis reentered the room he locked the door and left the key in the lock. This was the first time since my imprisonment that the key had been out of the hands of either one of them for more than a turn in the lock. As Davis went directly to bed, I knew the little metal jailor would remain there until morning.

The sight of that well-nourished, stall-fed Jew crawling in between the inviting cool sheets; rounding his head into the deep, billowy pillows, drove me mad.

Again that horrible, wavy, ethereal, floating sensation began to flood me. I went again through the hot and cold dipping process.

This time my fagged nerves would not respond.

Fright seized me. I scooped up a pinch of tobacco from a cigarette stub lying on the white enamel bowl. I tipped my head back and crumbled the brown flakes into my eyes.

In an instant I thought my head had hit the ceiling! Water gushed from both eyes and daggers pinned my quivering eye-balls to the back of my head.

I was awake!

At five o'clock I got up from my cot and began pacing back and forth.

When one of the boys went to bed he always opened his traveling bag and set it at the head of the bed. I saw they kept a small artillery in their bags, laid out ready for business. All they would have to do would be to stretch out a hand and pull any number of loaded guns from the open case.

This worried me, as the head of Davis' bed was in direct line with the hall door and the opened case between the head of the bed and the door. Therefore Davis could get a shot at anyone entering from the hall before he could get entirely into the room.

Next to the bag was a good-sized rocking chair.

I fussed around the room for a few minutes until the coming dawn made it light enough to see my way without stumbling over the furniture, then tiptoed to the bag beside Davis' bed and with my foot started to push it stealthily under the bed.

This would confuse him when he made a grab for his gun and would give the drop to the other fellow.

As the bag slid on the soft carpet, Davis stirred under the bed clothes and opened one eye.

I deliberately rammed my toe against the sharp end of the rocker and leaped into the air on one foot, yelping with pain. I grabbed the chair and with well-chosen expressions of pain, set it down directly over the open bag. I did it in such a way that when the chair came to rest its back was tipped against the bed, and Davis' hand would collide with it before he could throw it aside and obtain his gun. This would lose him sufficient time to give us command of the situation.

He turned over and faced the other way, saying:

"You've waked me up for sure now, Mulligan."

He did not go to sleep again and every now and then we spoke a few words.

Between the tobacco in my eyes and the pain in my foot I fought off sleep.

I looked at my watch.

It was a quarter of six.

The key was still in the locked door.

I was dressed, by this time and an early summer sun sent slanting rays across the grass green carpet. In a few minutes, seeing that Davis showed no signs of getting up, I walked over to the door and put my hand on the knob.

"I wonder if it rained last night. Seemed to me like I heered it comin' down." I unlocked the door and opened it a wide crack; stuck my head out and looked out on the dry streets through the hall window opposite our door.

Davis quickly sat up in bed.

I closed the door, twisted the key over and back. It sounded like one turn, but was two, which left it unlocked.

Davis slowly lay down again.

I looked at my watch.

One minute of six! The little ticks pounded like steam hammers.

I moved over to the foot of his bed. The footboard covered my body from the waist down. My right hand was on my gun, my left on the top of the board.

"I didn't sleep well last night," Davis said drowsily. "At home, I sleep on down mattresses, with down comforts over me and my head on little down pillows. I certainly wasn't built for anything but comfort!"

One! Two! ...One! Two! The last time lighter.

I swallowed my heart.

Davis' hand crashed against the back of the rocking chair. He spat out a vile oath.

"Lay your black head back on that pillow before I blow it off! Come in!"

The door opened.

The muzzles of two guns preceeded Kenneth W. Robinson and a Ranger. They slid in and closed the door behind them.

We put my own handcuffs on Davis and threw him in the bathroom, locking him in.

"If you hear anyone give the signal on the outside door and you open your mouth I'll puncture this door and you too!" I told him.

Mrs. Robinson had insisted on her husband bringing me two chicken sandwiches. These, I devoured with savagery.

In between bites, and in whispers, I told the men all that had happened in the past few days. When I had given them the history, I said that Miller would probably return any minute. We sat in silence for about an hour; the two officers sitting behind my bed, and I on it.

At seven-thirty the signal sounded on the door. I stepped to the door, unlocked it and turned the knob with my left hand, opening it slowly back against me. My revolver was in my right hand.

"How is the sick man?" were his first words. I wished he had not said just this.

"Better!" I exclaimed, shoving my gun into his stomach and closing the door with my hip. "Stick 'em up, Miller!"

They went up.

"What's all this about?" he inquired, darting a look at Robinson and the Ranger who were coming out from behind the bed.

"There'll be plenty of time to find out!" said Robinson.

The Ranger slipped his handcuffs on Miller and he and Robinson searched him and the traveling bag. In the bag we found evidence that settled their identity.

Davis was Leon Felix, and Miller was Arthur B. Cooper, or "Artful Artie" as his intimates called him. Miller never opened his head.

For two hours he sat on the edge of the bed while we went through all their papers, telegrams and documents.

There were many of the bid slips which bore my brand put on them when I was in their stock exchange — "branch number four."

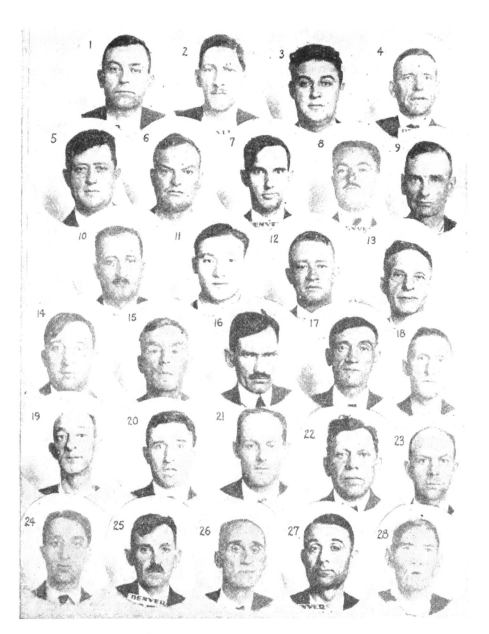

Arrested in Denver raid — Examples of habitual criminal thoughts. 1, Emory King, alias Miller; 2, Leon Felix, alias Davis; 3, Joseph Grady; 4, Byland; 5, Belcher; 6, Olsen; 7 , Reamey; 8, French; 9, Mead; 10, Ferrell; 11, White; 12, Dougherty; 13, Scholtz; 14, Knowles; 15, Smith; 16, Coyne; 17, Williams; 18, Wilson; 19, Sulligan; 20, Brady; 21, Sadler; 22, Beach; 23, Mushnick; 24, Cooper; 25, Potts; 26, Chas. Smith; 27, Kelly; 28, Hardway.

When Miller saw that the brand established the identification of these papers he said nothing but looked volumes.

Toward noon two of Col. Van Cise's Rangers arrived in a car and assisted us to get Davis and Miller into it. While Davis was being allowed to finish his dressing preparatory to being taken away, young Robinson remarked to me:

"Norfleet, you've had a hell of a time, haven't you?"

As he exclaimed "Norfleet," Davis jumped about a foot into the air, let out a yell and keeled over on the bed in a dead faint.

When we got them all into the big car, I never saw a happier crowd of men and a sadder pair in my life.

We drove out into the fashionable residence district on Capitol Hill. The basement of the First Universalist Church, at the corner of Lafayette and Colfax Avenue offered the best "safety deposit vault" for the team and those we hoped to get during the day. When we put our two into the cement corral, there were already more than twenty others there. The basement windows were guarded from the outside and the doors from the inside.

Before taking the men into the place they had been relieved of all weapons or substitutes. They were handcuffed, and as they milled around the big pen they reminded me of rebellious bulls in a small corral.

From the basement the men were taken one by one into the pastor's study and there subjected to a mental search. Two of Van Cise's head detectives and I were seated behind a heavy curtain. This was so that we could identify those who were questioned without being seen. Shortly after we arrived with our prisoners a total of thirty-four had been turned into the religious edifice.

From six o'clock in the morning simultaneous raids had been held in every part of the city of Denver. The Rangers had separated from a central point and spread their net over the city until thirty-four of the world's leading swindlers were brought within the mesh of the law.

At the various fake stock exchanges Col. Van Cise had directed his men to gain an entrance and grab the officers and "members" of the exchange as they put in their appearance for the day's work. With many of the swindling operators victims were also taken. It caused no little flurry separating the goats from the sheep, or the wheat from the chaff. The raids were the best organized I have ever known.

Chapter Thirty-Six - Furey Escapes

Every Ranger stuck to his post and kept absolute faith with his superior. Until the gang was rounded up not a single member of the police department or sheriff's office knew that there was such a thing as a raid thought of.

They certainly stood big-eyed when the news broke.

The prisoners were all tried and convicted with the exception of my old "stock exchange" friend of the deep voice, Mr. A. B. Zachery, the pay-off man. He proved to be J. M. Ross, alias Leonard Rogers.

This man turned State's evidence and got off with his liberty.

The trial was one of the biggest and most sensational that had ever been held in this country. It lasted nine weeks and took fifty-four men to keep the court going. There were none of the usual hitches or delays. It went through from beginning to end like clockwork.

S. Harrison White and Harry C. Riddle were special prosecutors as Col. Van Cise was barred from active practice in this case. But his talents were finding expression in lining up evidence, getting witnesses in shape and doing general directing work.

The defense had thirteen of the best attorneys in Colorado headed by the noted Horace Hawkins. Perhaps they would have fared better if they had employed twelve attorneys instead of thirteen.

The real high-light and big surprise of the trial was the capture of Lou Blonger and A. W. Duff in one of the exchanges. Both men were wealthy business men of Denver and it gave the town a severe jolt to find them not only allied with this gang of thieving crooks but actually directing them.

Duff took it upon himself to make things as disagreeable for me as possible. He knew I was responsible for the raid and therefore blamed me for plunging all of his mates in jail. Duff and Blonger were out on twenty-five thousand dollars bail, each. This gave me the opportunity of my life, for had I not been able to get Duff on the outside of the jail, I probably would never have found out the things I did.

When I saw in the paper he was to be let out on bond, I was waiting on the outside of the jail door for him. As he came down the steps headed by Red Gallagher, his bondsman, I went up to him and we met on the sidewalk. His crowd formed a semicircle in a protecting attitude.

"Good morning, Duff!' I began pleasantly. "How are you?"

"Feeling better. How are you feeling this morning?" he added suavely.

"Lucky! Lucky! Today," I declared, for a purpose. I then took a direct business-like tone with him.

"Duff, are you going to display some sense this morning, or are you going on just as you have been the past few days?"

"What do you mean?" he cried.

"You know what I mean, and I'll ask you just once more. Are you going to use sense this morning? That's plain, isn't it?"

"Yes! Yes! I'm going to use sense if I know how!"

He rubbed his hands together nervously. "I've sent Gerber's money to him! I've sent his money to him!"

This was the first time I knew he was connected with Gerber, who was still in the Huntsville penitentiary, or that he was supposed to send him any money. He evidently was guilty of so many infamous connections and deals that he didn't know which one I had reference to and took a long shot on it

215

being Gerber. This amused me, as well as gave me a definite lead for further information.

"Do you think Spencer is worth all of this tribe we have taken in, and all the others I'll get while I'm hunting for him?"

"My God!" he exclaimed in earnest tones. "Why didn't you come to me, Norfleet, and tell me what you wanted? If you had come to me first you could have had your man and your money back within three days!"

One of his pals nudged him warningly.

"Well, where is Spencer now?" I shot at him.

"Oh — oh, my God! Why, how do you expect me to know just where he is now when I've been in jail? But I know where he was when you put me in there!" He jerked his thumb toward the barred windows.

"One of the boys told me this morning that his suitcase was still there!"

"Still where?" I demanded, and took out my address book and pencil.

"Why up at Mrs. Franklin's. The Empire Hotel!"

I saw Red Gallagher edge closer to Duff and look as if he would like to gag him to shut him up.

Duff appeared unaware of him and kept up the flow of information.

I could not afford to use my hands writing out addresses so I handed my notebook and pencil to Barnhill who stood just behind me.

"Tell the address to him," I said to Duff.

While Barnhill was getting Duff's statement regarding Spencer, I was busy standing off the Duff gang, who looked threatening. There seemed to be no definitely understood plan to annihilate me, but I wasn't taking any chances.

Just as Barnhill was writing the last of Duff's statement a high-powered car raced to the curb and stopped. The driver stepped out onto the sidewalk and I recognized my old friend, Tom Scott, a ranchman of Miles City, Montana. He rushed up to me.

"Frank! what's all this about? I just saw in the papers you were into a mess and I blew right down to see if you needed any help! How about it?"

This was help from heaven instead of Miles City. The right words spoken at the right time!

"Mr. Duff, I want you to meet my friend, Mr. Scott, from Montana, Mr. Barnhill and Mr. Paxton from Texas!"

Duff shook hands with the three stalwart specimens of the western world. I could read on his face the effect their powerful personalities had on him. He showed plainly he was figuring "how much backing has Norfleet anyway?"

I took the book from Barnhill, thanked Duff for his assistance, told my three friends I would be back in a minute, then passed Duff and his mob and ran up the steps into the courthouse.

I showed Kenneth Robinson the information Duff had given me and we all drove in Scott's car to the Empire Hotel.

Here we obtained Spencer's suitcase as Duff said we would and learned that he had left the hotel the morning of the raid.

Above— A. W. Duff, (left) and Lou Blonger, before the Denver Raid, both prominent respected business men of Denver, sentenced to long penitentiary terms for complicity in operations of Denver fake stock exchange.

Below — Andy Anderson (left) and Walter Lips, deputy-sheriffs at Los Angeles, California, highly respected officers and idols of the silver screen before "double-crossing" Norfleet. The $20,000 obtained by "shaking down" Joe Furey, alias J. Harrison (part of which came from Furey's little child's savings account), has earned them fourteen year sentences in San Quentin penitentiary.

Mrs. Franklin said he had written a note enclosing a portion of his room rent and instructing her to forward his suitcase to Salina, Kansas. The note was sent by a messenger.

In the suitcase were enough fake credentials to convince an army of men. There were contracts, bid-slips, fake exchange membership cards, and every kind of fictitious document known to the swindling fraternity.

Robinson took charge of the case and contents, preserving them for future evidence.

I was sorely disappointed about missing Spencer by such a close margin, but in a way thankful to get such a hot tip on him.

Van Cise understood that I was determined to keep after Spencer and that I could not afford to let this new lead get cold, so he excused me from all duties connected with the coming trial of the thirty-four men and generously offered to assist me in any way needed.

I left Denver that night for Salina, Kansas.

There was no trace of Spencer there and I satisfied myself that he had not gone there. Probably it was a mislead and he had gone in exactly the opposite direction. This method of procedure is the usual thing with fugitives when sudden flight is necessary. I back-tracked to Denver and from there to Ogden, Utah.

In Utah the railroad police said a man answering Spencer's description had boarded a train from there a few days before for Helena, Montana. This hopping from town to town and state to state indicated that he was a scared "hombre."

From Montana I followed him into Canada again. He had crossed the line at Nelson, but I was just too late to nab him. From there he struck into Eastern Canada headed for his old home at Kingston, Ontario.

I communicated with the authorities at Montreal, Canada, and through the finger-print comparison they found they had just freed him before they received my letter. He had been arrested on suspicion and gave the name of "William Percy Hurd," under which classification he had been "mugged," finger-printed and turned loose. Too late again.

I ordered dozens of these new photographs, as the ones I had were eleven years old, and he had changed a great deal. Armed with these late pictures I felt I would soon have him.

Before leaving Denver, Frances Wayne, a newspaper reporter on the Denver Post, wrote a feature story of my activities in rounding up the notorious gang. In the article, she compared me to the Northwest Mounted Police, "who never miss their men."

This story I sent to a number of the Royal Mounted Police headquarters throughout the Dominion of Canada. In almost every case I received replies congratulating me and pledging their support in my behalf. That they kept their word was proved, as when Spencer was finally arrested he told me that when he found out he couldn't stay in Canada, he wondered if there was any place on earth where he could stop to take his breath.

One of Spencer's new pictures I sent to little Lucille Carson asking her to help me again. I suggested she watch Helen Harrison, who was supposed to be living at the Cliff Hotel, in San Francisco, and see if Spencer ever showed up around her.

In the meantime I worked the trail back as far as Denver where a telegram was waiting me from Lucille . It said that Spencer had been in San Francisco within the last few days and was supposed to be headed northeast in the direction of Salt Lake, Utah.

He was making the trip in an automobile with a Nevada license.

With this information I hastened to Cheyenne, hoping to head him off somewhere along the Lincoln Highway. But success did not crown my efforts, as I saw nothing of him.

I did meet, however, two detectives in Cheyenne who told me they were watching for a man and woman who had swindled the Boulder National Bank, of Boulder, Colorado, out of eighteen hundred dollars.

Thinking Spencer and his traveling companion might have done the job, I showed his picture to them. They studied it carefully and expressed the opinion that it suited in many respects the description of the bank robber.

I forwarded one of the photographs on to the Boulder Bank, asking them to let me know if that was the man who had robbed the bank. They replied it was not.

I knew that some of Spencer's wife's kinfolks lived at Ward, Colorado, so I made this my next destination. I hung around there for a few days, but learned still less than in Cheyenne. Then I went to Denver again.

Overland Park had recovered from the flood and was again the tenting ground for thousands of tourists.

I tacked up two of Spencer's pictures in the registry office of the camp grounds. The registrar was informed that I would pay a reward for his capture and promised to watch all who passed through the camp gates.

I talked with Van Cise, but he had heard nothing of my man.

I continued on down the State in an automobile with a man who was traveling in that direction. We went as far as Colorado Springs. Nothing developed here.

When I reached Raton Pass, which is due south from the Springs and in New Mexico, a night watchman told me he felt sure he had seen the original of the picture in company with a woman pass through the town on the way south.

I decided Spencer was now making for El Paso, on the Mexican border. On this hunch I went as far south as Roswell, New Mexico, and scattered his pictures throughout that section of the country.

Finding that an automobile was the best means of tracking Spencer, I went back to Hale Center and got my own car. Ruth, my fifteen year old daughter, drove me on the trip. We went first to Mineral Wells, a health resort, which is sixty miles west of Fort Worth.

When I put the car in the garage, I showed my picture of Spencer. The garage man looked at it a minute, then he called to another man in the shop and showed it to him.

"Looks like the car belonging to that fellow is in the garage here now!" said the first mechanic.

"It sure does look like him all right," replied his helper.

"I hope so!" I put in.

"Why yes, I'm doing some repair work for him and he ought to be in now any minute."

I stepped into a little oil-house and waited. In a few minutes I saw him enter the garage. He was Spencer all over. I walked quickly up behind him and tapped him on the shoulder saying: "Howdy!"

He turned and looked me full in the face.

"I beg your pardon!" I apologized, "I thought you were a friend of mine."

I was certain he was not Spencer. From the back he was the image of him and though his nose was not broken and crooked like Spencer's, yet in the face he resembled him strikingly.

"That's all right, Mr. Norfleet!" he answered laughingly. "I know you and I'll bet I know who you thought I was. You thought I was your man Spencer! I have been told by several men who have seen his picture that we might be twin brothers."

"You're right!" I admitted.

I could not place the man, but I did not want to embarrass him by inquiring his name.

"Only a few minutes ago when I was getting some mineral water at the bar, the bartender remarked that he had seen my brother a few days before and thought it was I."

Without waiting for another word I made a beeline for the bar-room. After talking with the salesman a minute or two I flashed Spencer's picture on him and asked if he had seen this man before.

"Yes!" he replied, wiping his dispensing hand on his white apron. "Yes, I seen that feller. He's been here 'bout a week. I ain't seen him for a day or two, but his woman was sittin' round the lobby of the hotel night before last. They got a cottage up on that hill there an' I been sending mineral water up to them regular."

I bade him good-bye and went to the police station where the Chief and I circled the outlying districts with telephone calls, sending out word and trying to get a lead on him.

Getting no results by morning Ruth and I left for Fort Worth, working the towns all the way. From Fort Worth we went on to Dallas.

I told the police department that Spencer had just left Mineral Wells; that I had not been able to pick up his course and wanted them to help me.

Captain Gunning summoned his detectives and gave orders for a look out.

Awaiting possible results from all of my lines thrown out, we took two days rest at my Ellis County farm. When we returned to Dallas I received a wire from home stating they had received information that a man answering Spencer's description was in Salt Lake City.

I had suffered so many disappointments I didn't get excited or throw my hat very high in the air. The remarkable likeness to the stranger in Mineral Wells dampened my enthusiasm. Perhaps this very man was the one in Salt Lake.

I telegraphed to George Chase, the Bertillion man in the Salt Lake City Police Department, and from whom the information had come, to arrest him and I would be there as quick as I could make it.

My daughter and I then drove home and I left the next morning to see if it was Spencer.

The train being late, I accepted a ride with a young "honey-moon" couple from Fort Worth, by the name of Tomlinson. I rode with them to the New Mexico line, then hastened on my journey.

By the time I arrived in Salt Lake City, George Chase had him in jail.

They walked him out into, the office where I was waiting.

"How are you, Spencer?" I asked.

"Don't you call me Spencer!" he replied defiantly. "I am Mr. A. P. Hunt!"

"Well, you'll do me for Spencer!"

At this point his mousy little wife pattered across the floor to me and looking up into my face said in a tiny, thin voice:

"Spencer isn't our name. Our name is Harris! That's Charlie and I'm Mildred!"

"Well, Mildred, he'll do me for Spencer!"

"We've had a hard race these last few years, haven't we, Spencer?"

No answer from "Charlie."

"You know, Spencer, I never owned but one good overcoat in my life, and while I think of it I want to ask you what did you do with it?"

"My God, Frank!" he blurted out as if we were long-lost friends reunited. "What did you do with my coat I left in your room that night in the Westbrook Hotel at Fort Worth? I saw you wearing it once in Florida, but I didn't have time to get it from you."

He turned to Chase.

"That man," indicating me, "can be in the way more than any damned man in the world. He always comes along at the right minute for himself and the wrong minute for me."

"You remember the Scotchman," he said addressing me. "The Scotchman who was arm in arm with me in Dominion Square in front of the Windsor Hotel the night you used my coat tails for a sled? Well, that bird had eight thousand dollars in cash in his pocket. He was going to take the boat the next morning for Liverpool. We had him drinking and on our hips, and if it hadn't been for you separating us I would have had the money. He thought my name was Spencewood."

221

I remembered just before being slugged in the jaw that a bristling little Scotchman had snatched a card from Spencer's pocket and held it before my eyes exclaiming "Spencer is not his name."

That was once a Scotchman made eight thousand dollars and didn't know it.

Spencer laughed a hard, hollow laugh.

"We beat you the first time, but you have beaten us all the other times! Well, what's the use?"

Mildred burst into tears. She went up to him and buried her scraggly little head on his shoulder.

"Don't cry, Mildred! For God's sake, don't!" he patted her absently. "I'd rather die and go to hell tonight than live as I have since I met Norfleet. Every knock on the door, every telephone bell, every stranger in the night has raised hell with my nerves.

"I'm glad! glad! It's over at last. Don't cry for me. I'm through now, but I can draw a free breath at last!" He bent down and kissed her.

She walked into the adjoining room and shut the door but the sound of her sobs came to us.

The Federal authorities claimed him on a narcotic charge in Salt Lake City and refused to turn him over to me, so for the time being I was forced to content myself with the knowledge that he was confined in jail.

A few days later he was tried on the narcotic charge and sentenced to the Leavenworth Penitentiary for two years.

I have filed my warrants, and when his term is up he will be brought back to Fort Worth, Texas, to be tried on my swindling charge, to which he has already confessed.

At Denver, I went up to see Van Cise and get whatever mail had accumulated for me in my absence.

In the West Side Court I was handed a package of mail. A telegram lay on top. One of the clerks said to me:

"Well, have you heard the latest about Joe Furey?"

"No!" I cried out.

The years swept past my mind. What could it be now?

I took a long breath and got ready for the shock.

"Has he escaped?" I asked, ripping open the telegram.

"Yes!"

My eyes ran over the words in the message. I looked understandingly at the clerk.

"That's right!" I replied. "Joe has escaped this time for good!"

J. F. Norfleet,
Care of District Attorney's Office,
Denver, Colorado.

    Joe Furey died in the Huntsville Penitentiary and his body is to be shipped to San Francisco for burial. — Coleman.

J. Frank Norfleet

Conclusion

Spencer's trial at Fort Worth has just been completed, too late for the account to be incorporated in the main story.

Upon learning that a parole was about to be granted Spencer, releasing him from the federal penitentiary at Leavenworth, Kansas, District Attorney Robert K. Hanger sued out a writ of habeas corpus and had Spencer returned to Fort Worth for trial on indictment charging him with swindling Norfleet.

The jury promptly returned a verdict of "guilty" and Judge George E. Hosey sentenced Spencer to serve eight years in Huntsville penitentiary after he is released from Leavenworth.

John Baskin and Henry Bishop were Spencer's attorneys, while District Attorney Hanger was ably assisted by Hon. W. H. Tolbert.

Thousands of Norfleet's friends had hoped Spencer would take the stand in his own defense as it would enable the State's attorneys to get into the court records any possible corroboration of the evidence contained in the affidavit of Joe Furey, on file with the District Attorney for the last three years.

After spending a total of $75,000, (including the original $45,000), Norfleet has again emphasized the significance of the "Creed of the West":

"Treat the other fellow *right;* then *make* him treat you right."

The curtain goes down on the last act. The old "Trail Hound" at the end of his "long, long trail," has "treed" his last quarry and delivered him to the keepers of "human wild game."

The law of Man and of Nature is fulfilled.

Man's law says: "An eye for an eye; a tooth for a tooth."

Nature says: "Obey my LAW of Cause and Effect, or PAY."

Spencer for years has disobeyed the law both of Man and God; now he must PAY.

How far must we search in Spencer's life to find the birth of his idea of inferiority? Was it when only a little boy he accepted the thought that he was so feeble-minded he could not compete with others of his own generation according to the rules of fairness?

Arriving at manhood did Spencer continue to "fudge" and "cheat"?

The thought of spending several years in prison is punishment for this man, yet prison, in itself, is not the worst thing that can happen.

It all depends upon the prisoner's reaction. If he spends his time hating every person connected with his apprehension and planning new crimes to be committed after his release, then his opportunity to make a new start has gone.

His old debt paid, he can now break the chain if he has spent his time in constructive thought.

A shock is sometimes a blessing in disguise. Certainly anything which awakens the consciousness to the relative values is well worth while.

Today the book is balanced.

Norfleet "invested" a total of $75,000 of his own private funds but in return has the satisfaction that he not only succeeded in capturing all five of his men but has done his country many million dollars' worth of good.

On the crooks' side their account with Norfleet shows disaster from the very first.

Taking from him $45,000 compelled them to pay out $82,900 in "protection" to peace-officers, lawyer fees and cash bonds forfeited; to say nothing of the indirect loss from his warning other "prospects" before the bunco-men could "close."

Financially there was no profit in robbing Norfleet.

Further disasters brought about as a result of getting the old "Trail Hound" after them include the death of their leader, Joe Furey; the suicide of Ward; the incarceration in prison of Gerber, Spencer and Reno Hamlin, besides some 75 other members of associated confidence rings.

If this book served only to arouse the public to the insidious danger lurking for the unwary from this cooperative organization of criminals, peace-officers and bankers, it would fail in its purpose.

This danger is so far-reaching that a remedy must be found.

Many crises in the past have been met and overcome by educating the people in the methods of prevention.

Since hygiene and physical culture have been taught in our public schools, America has produced a more intelligent, healthful and vigorous youth.

In these public schools the lessons in prevention of crime may be taught easily and constructively.

As hygiene and physical culture develop the body, so knowledge of the "Power of Thought" will build up the mind and soul.

Throughout the ages some few in every generation have known these laws as evidenced by the sacred writings of all religions, from the ancient Bhagavad Gita Hebrew Qabalah and Hermetic Philosophy down through the Christian Bible. A thread of these truths runs through the Ten Commandments, the Beatitudes, and each and every religious creed and cult of all time.

Modern psychologists are now re-discovering the great power of these laws.

Intelligent business men have found they are scientifically and practicably correct.

That man is punished BY his sins as well as FOR them, is accepted by all thinking people. That punishment begins when the intent to do wrong is formed in the brain and continues until the desire ceases, is also self-evident to the mature investigator.

The Lowly Nazerene when healing the sick man, to the utter consternation of his disciples, said: "Son, thy sins are forgiven thee."

The Master recognized the disease of the body was but the result of the sinful mind. By relieving the tension and congestion caused by wrong-thinking and wrong-doing, the sickness was overcome.

Now it is time to teach these truths in our public schools!

Let us help our children to think only good, constructive, clean thoughts as they make mental pictures of their future.

Every day is "planting-day" in the public school. It is now time for all people everywhere to learn these truths instead of only the few in each generation.

Let us plant the pure wheat in the fertile soil of the child mind and reap a harvest of golden grain instead of the abundant crops of tares that now fill our "prison-barns" to over-flowing.

The man who can control his thought may have anything in reason in this life.

Wm Franklin White

"I hold it true, that thoughts are things,
  Endowed with bodies, breath and wings;
And that we send them forth to fill
  The earth with good results, or ill.
That which we think our secret thought
  Speeds forth to earth's remotest spot;
Leaving its blessings or its woes,
  Like tracks behind it as it goes.

"We build our future, thought by thought;
  For good or ill, we know it not:
Yet, so the universe was wrought.
  Thought's but another name for Fate.
Choose then thy destiny and wait!
  For love brings love and hate brings hate,
"You never know what thought will do,
  In bringing you hate or love:
"For thoughts are things and their airy wings
  Are swifter than the carrier-dove.

They follow the law of the universe;
  Bach thing creates its kind.
They speed o'er the track, to bring you back
  Whatever went out from your mind."

(Anon.)

I certify that the experiences related in this book arc true and are not exaggerated. I have endeavored to be just and fair to all. Some names I would like to have included were expunged on advice from my attorney. The facts in this book are written with malice toward none and charity toward all but with a sincere wish that these truths may be of service to my countrymen.

Sincerely yours,

(Signed)

J. Frank Norfleet

Printed in the USA
CPSIA information can be obtained
at www.ICGtesting.com
LVHW090925290724
786663LV00002B/195